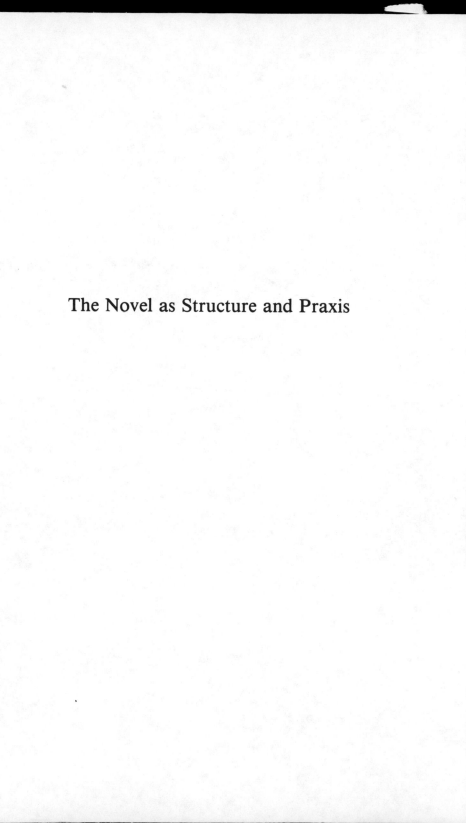

The Novel as Structure and Praxis

THE NOVEL AS STRUCTURE AND PRAXIS

From Cervantes to Malraux

Everett W. Knight

HUMANITIES PRESS
Atlantic Highlands, N.J.

Library of Congress Cataloging in Publication Data

Knight, Everett W.
　The novel as structure and praxis.

　Includes bibliographical references.
　1. Fiction—History and criticism. I. Title.
PN3491.K6　　809.3　　　　　　　　　80-15024
ISBN　0-391-00938-9

Manufactured in the United States of America

TO

Christine

Paul,   Peter   and   Julian

You can hold yourself back from the
sufferings of the world, that is
something you are free to do and it
accords with your nature, but perhaps
this very holding back is the one
suffering that you could avoid.

Kafka

TABLE OF CONTENTS

INTRODUCTION

One still hears such phrases as "the secrets of the universe," "the exploration of reality," and "the nature of the exterior world," and yet these expressions betray a metaphysics which has already passed into history. We can see why a Leonardo or a Descartes should have been fascinated by the problems involved in "understanding reality"; it is easy to see as well why a great contemporary—Jean-Paul Sartre—should have remarked that he is passionately attached to understanding man.[1] The early scientists helped provide us with the means of dominating the natural environment, and acts of God have progressively diminished to the point where even earthquakes, severe ones at least, have become acts of men in the sense that it will shortly be possible to predict them and so minimize loss of life. If man has always been a wolf for man, it is because he has never possessed the means of placing himself permanently beyond the reach of want.[2] Now that those means are in hand, the obstacles are social and political structures, in other words, other men. The natural milieu is no longer inhospitable. Man's only enemy is himself.

Renaissance scientists slowly elaborated a new method which Descartes, in a famous essay, set out in clear form. But along with their work in methodology these men had unconsciously created a new object which had not existed in medieval culture and which we call nature. The new method was inseparable from the new object. Change the object from nature to man, and the method must change as well. Consequently, Sartre, like Descartes, is the author of an essay on method.

It is not too difficult to understand that man cannot be *both* the interrogated (a part of nature) and the interrogator. He must choose. Maurice Merleau-Ponty compared our predicament to what happens when we touch one of our hands with the other. A sort of contact is made, and something may even be learned. But this all occurs within the same bodily system; there is no "outside." Exactly this situation obtains when one person carries out an experiment upon another. What is learned is learned as a function of the particular initiative taken. This initiative prepares the subject to yield information of the kind being sought. Where is man to be located then? Is he the "prepared subject" or is he the "initiative?" He is the latter, obviously, since no one would argue any longer that he had contrived to occupy a position "outside" (outside class and history, like the 19th century novelist and the present-day 19th century academic) such that his vision would fall from no particular angle and be affected by no particular light, the result being the revelation of something as it "really is," the discovery of something given once and for all. Any position, consequently, is an initiative, a complex of questions to which only certain replies will make sense.

An indispensable preliminary therefore to any research is the examination of its inherent complex of questions; there has to be an attempt to fix the coordinates of our own position. These coordinates will give rise to certain problems only. But why should one particular matter constitute a problem rather than any other? What are we trying to accomplish, consciously or otherwise, by such an initiative? For example, I have just been invited to write about Maurice Maeterlinck and to send the result to a new literary journal which is to appear in India. The scholars responsible for this venture have therefore borrowed from the barbarian horde which overran their country in the 18th century not only a language but also a tendency to hold that an inquiry into Maeterlinck might be of more enduring interest than one into, say, the prevalence of starvation among present-day Indian citizens. But then starvation, it may be said, is the special province of certain specialists, economists, sociologists, agronomists and the like, who have received special training permitting them to eschew those impassioned value judgments which becloud the vision of the uneducated, of the nonspecialists. And yet it was a group of impassioned nonspecialists—the Chinese communists—who did away with starvation in a country where it had been endemic. If we grant that people should eat and that we dispose of a technology which makes it feasible for them to do so, then the obstacle, as we saw a moment ago, must be the way in which our capitalist-imperialist nations are structured; and an element of that structure must be the existence of a nonposition which the educated may occupy and thanks to which the essential becomes invisible or is transformed into a statistic.

If, then, the researcher, be he interested in the economy or the history of the novel, wishes to dissociate himself from starvation, ecological catastrophe, nuclear war and other benefits of an advanced capitalist society, he will be looking desperately for a new method which, given the proportions of the disaster which threatens, will have to constitute an entire new rationality.[3]

The immediate objection to all the foregoing is of course that it condemns us to an historical subjectivity, or relativism, so complete that philosophy in any real sense of the term becomes impossible. There has to be a point "outside," something trans-historical for thought to aspire to; otherwise philosophy deteriorates into a series of more or less well-organized but nonetheless strictly personal, subjective views of man and his condition. But what if there is no choice?[4] What if we have reached the point where children would no longer believe in Santa Claus if only adults would let them alone, the point where no intellectual can honestly see how a transcendent could be discovered from *no* particular historical and cultural situation, so that what is presumed to have been discovered was in reality placed there (as far as its fundamental significance is concerned) by the exigencies of that situation? Furthermore, what if one of the exigencies of our contemporary situation (in view, principally, of our technological omnipotence) were precisely the suppression of all forms of thought having recourse to anything beyond and above man and his works? That this is actually what has happened is established surely beyond any doubt by the existence of modern art, the best examples of which (as we shall see in the case of the contemporary novel) lose all intelligibility if we assume them to be in any way concerned with a fixed reality or an eternal verity. Is it conceivable, in other words, that a philosophy which in the last analysis makes of man a "produced thing" (as do positivism, the neo-positivism of some structuralists, the Stalinists' "dialectics of nature," etc.) rather than the "producer" is contrary to the whole revolutionary drift of our times, be it in art or in the struggles for liberation all over the third world? Scientific rationalism is in full decomposition; so that thinking, which presupposes the existence of something concealed and a-temporal, along with the "mineralization" (Sartre) of man which results, is structurally associated with that rationalism and therefore can be of no use to us.

These arguments are all *de facto,* to be sure; but to insist they be *de jure* is to demand what can no longer be provided.[5] It is to hold that classical rationalism, far from being well advanced in its decline, looks forward to a fruition which will startle the world and stop history, goggle-eyed, in its tracks. It is to be a 17th century theologian saying to Newton this is not what we want, this is not enough, and refusing to be interested in the very best his age could produce.

Historical parallels, however, are easily broken down. Classical rationalism represented not merely new ideas but a whole new culture with its own religion, philosophy and way of life which over several centuries, had supplanted feudalism and produced a different human type. There is nothing of that sort today. Even if revolutions in other parts of the world result in "new men", we shall nonetheless have to invent our own revolution, but without benefit of an alternative culture standing ready made and clearly adapted to our needs. This is what gives an appearance of justification to the conservative's reluctance to quit what he considers a secure mooring only to find himself adrift with nowhere to go and no idea of how to get there.

The system that emerged from the debris of medieval culture had no sooner become politically as well as economically responsible for the destinies of the West than its thinkers and writers discovered that criticism of their own class and its activities was a matter of plain integrity. Science and the enlightenment had established the fundamental "sameness," or equality, of all men in the interest of undermining the feudal caste system; but then the requirements of capitalism and of private property were such as to render any genuine equality, any real social justice, unthinkable. Because so flagrant a contradiction could not easily be overlooked (Balzac, for example, insists upon it in all his best novels) there came into existence a social group whose very function was to be critical; the liberal or academic intellectual is there to cast a sceptical eye upon whatever exists or may be asserted. However, he was not simply invented to answer one of the needs of a society compelled to recognize in everyone of its members a human being. Rather he is a slightly modified version of the 18th century writer and *philosophe* who (as will emerge from our study of the picaresque form) criticized traditional institutions and values, but only on the basis of an immutable, universal order.

This did not make the work of the rationalists any less revolutionary, since economic pressures provided an irresistible complement to their efforts. But after the French revolution that same assumption of an order transcending human praxis would appear to be the only way one can account for the staggering aplomb (referred to as "objectivity") with which the liberal intellectual "criticizes" the ruthless exploitation to which his class and "civilization" has submitted this planet and its peoples. We are confronted by the paradox of a criticism which is a functional part of the system; it exists to give the impression that abuses which cannot be overlooked are being remedied. So that the 18th century rationalist, who represented a genuine alternative and who was genuinely outside what was left of feudal society, became, a century later, an employee whose work it is to take for granted there is still a position outside, an objective viewpoint (which was that of the 19th century novelist) from which one can arrive at unbiased, impersonal decisions based upon facts, upon a reality unaffected by anything foreign to it.

The liberal intellectual (who is identical with the conservative or reactionary intellectual, since the form of government they all represent resorts periodically to fascism of one kind or another) therefore holds that not only should we not resign ourselves to the historical subjectivity dialectical reason involves, since that would deprive us of a sense of direction, but that there is no need for this at all because the present system is self-adjusting. It invites us all to a constant critical vigilance supplemented by rational discussion as a result of which any contingency may be met successfully.

We will leave aside the hypocritical "unconsciousness" of the liberal contemplating, since the turn of the century, the planetary history of the white man's civilization and instead try to understand why it is that although there certainly exists no alternative culture in the sense that bourgeois rationalism offered a fundamental new choice to the 18th century noble, we nevertheless know that the system itself must generate a revolutionary option. All the great revolutionary figures from Marx to Guevara were middle class in origin, and Marx explains that the goal of revolution is simply to put into practice the political and social ideals that which inspired the French and American revolutionaries toward the end the 18th century. It is inconceivable that men seeking genuinely revolultion is simply to put into practise the political and social ideals that inspired the French and American revolutionaries toward the end of that order a structural disequilibrium, an organic contradiction which can only be resolved by the system's complete reorganization. Built into the mentality of every well-educated and informed citizen of Western countries there have to be two mutually exclusive options. The first—that of the great majority—consists in the more or less implicit assumption that men exist as individual entities and that these entities are ordered and explained by a transcendent, be it religious or scientific. The second is the refusal to use the first option as a means of obscuring the self-evident: the fact that we have created an economic and political system which, to survive, is obliged to give money precedence over men. This is self-evident in the sense that no metaphysical proposition concerning the "nature of man" or of the universe need be put forward; it is simply a question of being properly informed, although, admittedly, it is not always easy to be properly informed, since the very function of orthodox economics is to confuse all the issues.

To be sure, the statement that the *essential* (the self-evident) has nothing whatever to do with the ultimate nature of man and the universe is in itself a metaphysical pronouncement involving such notions as praxis and structure.[6] The only way we will escape this recurring difficulty is by making the liberal position untenable by describing it. The 18th century scholastic was not wrong because the *philosophe* "proved" him to be wrong but because for historical, *de facto* reasons he had become grotesque.

Western countries have not only entered into another period of economic crisis. It is now far more common than it was even in the thirties to talk of an ideological crisis as well, of a general breakdown in confidence, especially among the young. But what if it could be demonstrated, as I am sure it can, that a "crisis" has existed since Balzac, in the sense that the one art form no responsible critic can fail to associate with the rise and decline of the middle classes—the novel—gave expression during the 19th century, during the period of its highest achievement, to precisely that organic contradiction just mentioned? What if the basic structure of the classical novel involves two distinct levels of discourse existing in absolute contradiction to each other?[7] This would establish that for almost two centuries increasingly large numbers of people have been faced with a choice: either remain within the purview of scientific rationalism to pursue a truth universal and timeless, or, what is today at least far more rational, acknowledge that we have created a culture which is, in the literal sense, schizophrenic. Each of us is divided against himself because we are the products of a system which, to survive, is obliged to systematically violate its own ethic. (The Americans did all in their power to destroy Vietnam so that it might be free.) This latter choice is not so popular since it transforms all our problems into immediate, concrete economic and political ones, while abstract or "non-positional" speculation and research appear in their true light as the praxes of a tiny, privileged minority.

In our investigation of the novel from Cervantes to Malraux we shall therefore assume a methodological principle which follows from the eclipse of scientific rationalism as a metaphysics postulating a concealed absolute on the one hand and, on the other, man as a being who is both determined by that absolute (hence a thing) and capable of striving, or not, to know it (he is consequently also—and incomprehensibly—initiative). That principle involves the attempt to fix two positions: the investigator's within his own society, his social class; and his society's as a whole compared to others.

If in his essence man is, initiative or praxis (rather than as we shall see, in the classical novel, essentially substantive) then he occupies a given position with a view to achieving this or that. The orthodox scholar who attempts anachronistically to cleave to a point of reference outside history or for whom literature is fundamentally esthetic enjoyment is, in reality, helping to perpetuate a system which exists not for men but for profit. Our position on the contrary will be an *avowed one,* a Marxist one, but also one which has been indispensably complemented by the work of Sartre. This perspective has been chosen in preference to a number of others—all *necessarily subjective*—first, because if the intellectual recognizes in his "objective" work a more or less selfish and serene class allegiance,[8] he will then be able to replace a conception of man and his world which, outside the universities and counting houses is everywhere recognized and condemned as a praxis of oppression, with a series of immediate and long-range tasks all tending toward man's gradual liberation from other men, that is, the abolition of class societies. The impulse for such an undertaking comes not from whimsically subjective moral values, but from the impossibility—apart from recourse to hypocrisy or a refusal to be informed—of living in a society for which the right to "life, liberty and the pursuit of happiness" is self-evident, and whose economic structure at the same time compels it to practice racism, famine, war. Secondly, the perspective chosen *must* permit a fuller "visibility" of the subject under study. We must be able to make more sense of the novel from this position than from any other, with no reasonably important aspect of the form left unaccounted for.

To express all this a little differently, the inevitable subjectivity of the observer's position can be mitigated if he places himself *ahead in time,* in the kind of society everyone wants. From that vantage he will see more clearly what exists now. Though he may not admit it, the "objective," "uncommitted" observer, also places himself ahead, since the only conceivable practical effect of his work, however "critical," will be to enable the system, by its own momentum, to pursue its destructive course. We must replace the imaginary perspective of scientific rationalism with a genuine perspective which can be defined as the act of looking back upon a reality from goals understood to be constitutive of that reality and not determined by it.

However, it would also be useful to try to see our culture as a whole—to the admittedly very limited degree that this is practical—from the vantage point of other cultures, the primitive culture from which ours evolved and those still in existence today. This is what I should like to attempt very briefly now.

CHAPTER I

Primitive technologies, however complex, are over-specialized, having been dictated by sometimes extremely specific geographic and climatic conditions. The people using them are tragically vulnerable to perturbations of those conditions; drought or excessive rain can easily mean starvation. There is no going elsewhere except within homogeneous regions, such as the desert, the frozen North, perhaps the South Pacific. When migrations do occur, the migrants either disappear into the local populations (the Vikings in Normandy), or they return before long to their homeland (the Huns), or there is a period of chaos out of which a new system evolves (the fall of Rome and the rise of feudalism). The Romans did not colonize in our sense of the word; they dispatched soldiers and administrators to guarantee the payment of tribute. But there could have been no tribute to pay had not *local* systems of production and government been respected.

Primitive peoples' vulnerability is due not only to the overly successful adaptation of their technologies to often exceedingly specific natural conditions, but to the fact that their cosmologies, that is, in reality, their mentalities, their outlook, are also inseparable from these conditions. To occupy the land of a primitive people is to defile sacred places without which accounts of the origin of the earth and of men begin to lose conviction.

In sharp contrast to this firm rooting of primitive cultures in small areas there is the white man's permanent occupation of such vast territories as North America, South Africa, and Australia, and the extermination or confinement to reserves of the native populations. The original settlements could not have survived had their people been forced to adjust their needs to the new environment. By the 17th century Western Europe had developed a "universal technology;" tools sufficiently versatile to enable the white man to adapt a new environment to his needs. The rifle, for example, is a universal tool in the sense that it can be used to kill any game, whereas primitive peoples usually have a great variety of techniques depending upon the habits of the animals hunted. Another such tool of the white man was a sailing ship able to find its way to any part of the globe and of sufficient size to enable emigrants to carry with them, in the form of goods, enough of their habitual "environment" to see them through the crucial first months.

It was during what we call the neolithic revolution that men developed technology (pottery, weaving, domestication of animals, agriculture) enabling them, in the best circumstances, to arrive at a kind of equilibrium between their needs and what could be wrested from a given environment. If we look now for the origin of the second revolution, the industrial, which was to permit men to adapt their environment to themselves, we come upon the Western city of the early Renaissance.

The city was—and in the minds of many country people remains to the present day—a scandal; a gathering place for brigands, drifters and moneylenders; a permanent bohemia where people make a profession of disputing ancient values; the home, in brief, of free men. This is what distinguished the medieval Western cities from those of Asia and of antiquity; the former existed in defiance of rather than an extension of the established order. As a preliminary to altering nature men had for the first time created a "nature" of their own, and this was perhaps the fundamental scandal. There is no empty, unused, indifferent space (as was required by Galileo's eternally straight-moving projectile) in primitive cosmologies. One could consider that the medieval Western city was the first such space in that it was man-made, non-sacred and therefore, to the mentality of the time, non-existent. It was the first "negation" of the Aristotelian-Christian plenum, an opening which introduced play into the system, the first genuine alternative in that it was "unnatural." During the Middle Ages all land was sacred. Each occupier held his portion in trust from a superior situated at some point in a hierarchy culminating in God. The burgher, however, was attached to no land; he could exist only in so far as he could own goods (since land was, originally, always already allotted, always, in a sense, common land) which, in turn, he could keep only if, in concert with other free individuals, he surrounded his property with a defensive wall, the walls of the city.

The basic unit of primitive societies is not the individual or family, but the entire group closely knit by often extremely complex structures of kinship. Thus, one of the most effective tools for all primitive groups is the *group itself*.[1] The sparser and simpler the goods and equipment of which a society disposes to protect itself against the vagaries of natural conditions, the more vital it is that these conditions make sense, so that correct propitiatory measures can be taken in times of crisis. But also, the more local the climate and environment that a primitive system makes intelligible the more important it is that the group exist as a single, self-contained individual so that its "faith" will not be weakened by contact with the inevitable scepticism of foreign mentalities. Hence primitive peoples' laws of hospitality in accord with which a stranger is either completely integrated or kept sternly at a distance; he must either be converted or destroyed.

Absolute unanimity is necessary to the primitive group not so much that tasks may be carried out more efficiently but so that when the group's technology is unequal to the emergency, when it is unable to alter the environment, there remains the possibility of altering men. Medical science, although it has allowed us to reduce enormously the vulnerability of human life, leaves us perhaps no better off than those primitives who deal with death by explaining it, by adapting themselves to it. In some cultures, for instance, the woman who loses most of her children in their infancy loses only one child who, with each pregnancy, makes another attempt to enter life. The dead continue to reside with the community. The more effective our medical tools, the more inexplicable, absurd and therefore outrageous death becomes. Those dances of primitive peoples which end with the collapse of the dancer relieve tensions far more effectively and healthfully than do the various drugs we use for the same purpose; and one could cite innumerable cases of quasi-miraculous psychosomatic feats common in historical and primitive societies.

The condition of this self—as opposed to environmental—transformation is a singleness of vision (which we like to call gullibility or superstition, but which is simply the absence of that abstract intellectual curiosity characteristic of the Westerner) without which the group cannot function as an implement and bring the enormous weight of its conviction to bear upon whatever individual may require it. The cures at Lourdes are usually temporary because the group of pilgrims is temporary. The primitive group, however, never disperses; so its cures can be re-effected whenever necessary. In her book, *Search for Security,* M. J. Field marvels repeatedly at how quickly Africans recover from what in our part of the world would be considered downright insanity.[2] The difference, surely, is that the African is the victim of a visitation; he is possessed. The cure can be rapid because it is a simple matter of expelling the intruder. In other words, the African is not an individual in our sense and consequently does not have to be either readjusted to his group through the long complex process of psychoanalysis or kept from it in an asylum on grounds that a hypothetical mental apparatus—a crucial component of the Westerner's "individualism"—is defective.[3]

Today the primitive group disintegrates more and more rapidly not because of the seduction of Western ideas, but because the accumulation of private wealth (the original basis of those ideas) is made practicable for a tiny number of the group's members who, finding themselves transformed into individualists, are obliged to adopt Western ways, since the primitive group is antipathetic to personal wealth, insisting that it either be shared or that it exist, as in aristocratic societies, to mark preordained divisions of humanity. Medieval society also was scandalized by the notion of secular goods, goods existing in and for themselves or, in other words, private goods.

The function of the medieval Western city as a "universal tool" was to assure the security of a wealth which was neither sacred nor held in common. Cities of other times and places had existed in symbiosis with the environment, whereas the medieval city initially lived parasitically upon it. Consequently people who had shaken loose from the land could go there without posing a threat to what we have seen to be the primitive group's necessary "narrowness." In fact, the urban group might actually be reinforced by displaced persons bringing skills or wealth in exchange for which outlandish attitudes and dialects might be tolerated. The city was concerned neither with production for survival (manorial economy being completely self-sufficient), nor with the region's defense (the work of the warrior caste) nor with any administrative or sacred function (the rôle of the clergy).

What had come into being was a secular group existing exclusively for the sake of the individuals who comprised it. A merchant could best serve his fellow citizens by bringing more wealth to the town, that is, by serving himself. Any other, more directly civic activity (defense of the town against attack being self-defense) was entered into by agreement between contracting individuals. The result was a contradiction which with time was to become more ineluctable than any other in our society: how could one reconcile a moral, contractual obligation to the community with the necessity of augmenting that private wealth which informed the burgher's entire function and existence? Each had a clear duty to his fellow citizens since the new universal tool could only be operated collectively; yet the whole purpose of the city was to make practicable the flourishing of the individual as such. There existed on the one hand an abstract moral obligation, which bourgeois rationalism has never been

able to render compelling, and, on the other, a concrete obligation to the self to which that same rationalism has given very little explicit attention. This contradiction—in Marx's language, that between the public and the that public service in the highest sense of the term, service of the kind provided by the Voltaire of the Calas affair, by Dreyfus's defenders, and by those Americans who organized to end the war in Vietnam, is always obviously necessary or desirable; yet for our philosophy and science, which have always had the greatest difficulty in making room for value, it is irrational. What is not irrational, but perfectly natural (hence the "realistic" appraisal of human beings so common among "intelligent" people) is the reshaping of public responsibility to private ends.
ing to air and water pollution to private ends.

Until recently, men were not guaranteed the essentials of life. Thus warfare for the purpose of protecting or acquiring indispensable supplies had to be taken for granted as an inevitable aspect of human existence. But if man has always of necessity been a predator for his fellows, he has also been obliged to maintain *within the group* a reciprocity without which working and fighting efficiency would be impaired. If, further-more, the prohibition of incest is the one common characteristic of prac-tically all human societies, and if we hold that the purpose of sexual self-discipline (the point when, for Claude Lévi-Strauss, nature becomes culture) is to make possible the equal exchange between groups of each one's most precious possession, its women (who will be "equal" in respect to their sexual integrity), then we can consider that the universali-ty of the prohibition of incest is tantamount to the universality of man's wish to recognize the humanity of his fellows by granting their right to receive exactly what they give. The exchange of goods (which, among primitive peoples, may well be identical in nature) is an attempt to com-municate as a substitute for destroying, and encounters between Eu-ropeans and primitive peoples the world over were, at first, almost always friendly. These early contacts quickly ceased to be peaceful because the white man had come not to enter into communication through equal exchange nor for simple practical reasons (to barter) but to engage in trade. That is, he had come for a reason inscrutable to those savage or childlike minds: personal profit.[4]

The medieval merchant is our forbear, and we have been taught to ad-mire the quiet persistence with which, in the teeth of churchly scorn and robber baron rapacity, he sought to move his ships or caravans from one city-oasis to another. The free circulation of goods and the opening of new markets required or made possible the development of virtues we are perhaps rightly pleased to regard as a great contribution to the history of man. As in the case of life in the cities, it involved a new form of association among men, a contractual one which could be freely entered into regardless of race, creed or color, in contrast to the preordained and immutable *liens de dépendance* of feudal society. There can be little doubt but what the requirements of an ever expanding commerce had much to do with the slow development in European peoples of two qualities very much their own: personal initiative and intellectual curiosity. (Among primitive peoples, distinguishing oneself in any notable or unaccustomed way often leads to feelings of guilt and the anthropologist will only rarely be questioned about his society by the people he is living among.) If Christianity has been one of the most intolerant and vigorously proselytizing of religions it is because it has always been so exposed to the universalizing influence of travel and commerce, because its defense against the threat of perspective has had to be so unrelenting.

The Mediterranean is the meeting place of three continents, and its peoples have been offered through the centuries a greater number of cultural choices than would have been possible at any other point on the globe. It has been argued that the origin of philosophy in ancient Greece was the need to create a universal language of abstract rationality which would force agreement upon city-states bent upon each other's destruction.[5] Something comparable may have happened in medieval Europe where, above the thousands of manorial establishments attached like primitive tribes to tiny areas there gradually came into being detached, individual observers, wary of Bacon's idols, who made it their business to compare, to interrogate, to doubt, and in so doing helped create the scientific method and the novel, in each of which there is a seeking after knowledge (it is by no means as simple as that, however, in some forms of the novel) on the part of an individual who, in theory, works without preconception; who, in other words, belongs to no particular group. And insofar as an ethic is involved, it is that no final conviction be arrived at until the Great Scheme itself is eventually revealed through the labors of those men strong enough to substitute hypothesis for belief.

We saw that the medieval city marks the coming of an entirely new kind of association among men, one to which the individual contributes, more or less reluctantly, for his own good, while in all primitive forms of association the individual derives from the group his individuality which, consequently, barely exists in our sense of the word. The conduct of the burghers of Calais was heroic because it was not required of them. They sacrificed themselves. One does not, in contrast, talk of heroism or sacrifice when a feudal lord is killed defending the manor because he has no choice; he is simply the momentary incarnation of the dynasty apart from which he has no individuality.[6]

For primitive societies the Great Scheme is always already there, palpable and complete, and there is nothing for the individual to do except occupy with honor a place which far exceeds in importance the people who successively occupy it. Any form of wealth, for example, is held in trust; it belongs to the place and not to the individual; so an avaricious nobleman is no more imaginable than a cowardly one because prestige is associated not with the wealth itself, but with the number of dependants it can be made to support. Outside our society, therefore, begging is not usually considered disgraceful since the beggar is offering more than he receives: the opportunity for the donor to acquire, however briefly, an additional dependant. An African will not ordinarily return money he has borrowed from a European (that is, from a man who is always wealthy by African standards) since doing so would be a kind of discourtesy on his part, implying the white man might not be able to extend his family or retinue beyond its present limits.

No place awaited the burgher, so he had to make one for himself (success being the result of his having what would eventually be called merit). And the greater his wealth, the more secure his place. Yet after centuries of bourgeois influence and rule it is difficult for anyone to accept unquestioningly the notion of a wealth entirely and therefore irresponsibly private. To make it appear natural the bourgeoisie had to create a new religion (Protestantism) and a new philosophy (science). Even then the Enlightenment represented in large part an attempt to construct new forms of reciprocity (liberty, equality, fraternity) upon the ruins of the old. If hypocrisy subsequently became a way of life in our culture it is because the 19th century bourgeoisie was obliged to declare that private wealth and public well-being were one and the same although it knew perfectly well that it was talking nonsense. In between Protestant attempts to sanctify wealth and the advent of the proletariat there stretches the serene and confident Age of Reason which can be so described because men as *individuals*, were able to perform a *social* function. Men in isolation cannot bring about a new and better social order unless, as in the 18th century, they assume such an order to exist already, but concealed. In this latter case the individual pursuit of free trade or free thought could hasten the removal of institutions and attitudes which had for centuries overlain and beclouded the pre-established harmony.

To talk of free individuals and of private wealth in connection with the medieval city is, to be sure, an absurd oversimplification since the individual remained for centuries very much a Christian, and his wealth, especially during the construction of the great cathedrals, was often turned to public uses. Yet in societies where everyone's subsistence could not be assured there was a perverseness in self-enrichment which caused it to be left, especially in earlier times, very much to the Jews, that is, to a group sufficiently outside the prevailing culture for a "natural" perverseness to be attributed to it. The medieval merchant or moneylender was a marginal person; but before moving to the center, which the new philosophy and religion were preparing for him, he managed, especially in Italy, to transform his city into those city-states where there took place what we call the Renaissance.

We have seen that life is so precarious in primitive societies that the group has to exist as a kind of tool; only the group can generate the degree of conviction necessary to provoke intervention of the right kind at the right moment, to enable individuals, for example, to deal "psychosomatically" with troubles we now try to meet with drugs and surgical instruments. But of course we have no means of knowing exactly to what extent modern science, with the living conditions it has helped to produce, creates the afflictions it then tries to cure, nor the extent to which the patient's faith in science is indispensable to the success of efforts to help him. In other words, one's cultural group may be made invisible, but it is certainly never suppressed since it both produces the tools of which the individual will make use (Robinson Crusoe could not have survived without the tools and supplies he managed to salvage from the wreck) *and* a reality (nature as raw material) which can be made to sustain life through the use of tools and techniques alone—with possibly a prayer for good measure. The Renaissance, therefore, marks not the group's slow disappearance, which is unthinkable, but of reciprocity, that is, of the group as the smallest practicable unit. Only the group as a whole was of sufficient consequence to confront the sacred face to face; it constituted a permanent delegation to solicit a sacred which spoke its language and was always accessible, the individual being simply a point of entry for an otherworldly which was not otherworldly at all, but a permanent and often visible part of the community. That visibility of the sacred we have come to call mysticism; and the protestants grew increasingly chary of it because, for one reason, there is something grotesque in the notion of the sacred communicating with a private individual rather than with a hierarchical figure or with someone so totally anonymous (like Joan of Arc, originally) as to be the group itself assembled at a single point. In Renaissance tragedy, only royalty or near royalty could conceivably enter into contact with the Divine; but by the 16th century royalty itself had become so private (that is, solicited by passions incompatible with its public rôle) that God had, correspondingly, withdrawn to that vanishing point of the new pictorial art where, as Pascal's Deus Abscondus, he illogically exacted faith in his *indubitable* existence.

The Renaissance city-state formed a precarious and unique "collectivity of individuals" in Italy, where it was able to be itself the lord of the manor; a situation reflected in an art which remained sacred in content (collective) whilst becoming profane in execution (the notion of beauty, appropriate only to qualified, individual appreciation) until the point was reached (first in Giorgione, according to Pierre Francastel) where this contradiction could be partially suppressed by the creation of a new object—nature—at once sacred (God's handiwork) and profane (man's dwelling place) so that the artist could create an edifying thing of beauty simply by copying. In the North, conditions were more "dramatic"; however powerful the city might become it had an equally powerful hierarchical feudal superior to deal with. I believe tragedy reflects precisely this crisis of allegiance, the tragic hero being a man for whom fate had so arranged things as to make it rigorously impossible for him to choose either the collectivity (his honour, his *gloire*—the dynasty) or himself (love, unscrupulous ambition and so on) without being destroyed. Tragedy came about because the private aspect of human existence had attained sufficient importance to interfere with a man's *automatic* execution of his public, feudal obligations. It is as though the bourgeoisie were formulating through tragedy, a scruple which even later on, when it had fully elaborated a new culture, it was never able to put aside, once and for all. Is it possible that what a man desperately wants and needs for himself should be incompatible with what he owes everyone else? Tragedy answered yes; but tragedy was a moment's equipoise after which the private dimension of men's lives was able to expand in a world gradually being divested of the dictatorial, self-evident presence of the Divine.

The tragic hero as the representative of the collectivity expected, in ageless fashion, a sign; but it either was not granted or came in so debased a form (the various ghosts in Shakespeare) that it could serve only to increase the hero's perplexity. The sign (like the goal of the revolutionary) shames individual preoccupations out of existence, and the bourgeois obviously could not prosper in such a world; nor, on the other hand, could he purely and simply enrich himself without a cynicism which was to come only much later. It was unthinkable that an entire social class continue to engage in daily activities which were their livelihood, and yet which made no sense in terms of the nature of God and man, which were directed, in other words, exclusively toward private accumulation. The bourgeois could not protest against the sale of indulgences on grounds he wanted to keep his money. In the 16th century it could still be held that money given for indulgences was money given to the community; so the wealthy had to argue that what a man did with his money was a matter to be settled between him and his God. Even more generally, whatever a man did (and Luther showed a surprising latitude in this respect) he could do safely provided his faith was unshakeable. Furthermore, predestination played a vital rôle in many Protestant theologies. Thus, the practical activities of the merchant or moneylender were of no consequence whatever; they were mere appearances, the outward working of an inner destiny. What was exacted was not, as in the case of the primitive, the fulfilling of some sacred and therefore public responsibility, but rather an attitude, a show of belief. (The bourgeois' obligations to the city were contractual; so his failure to observe them could involve only secular penalties and not the tragic annihilation a feudal lord could incur by, for example, a failure to defend the manor.)

It is proper to hold that over several centuries, the Middle Ages shaded insensibly into the Renaissance, but only on condition we see as well that in the first half of the 15th century a qualitative change took place; namely, the invention of a perspective for which there had been no precedent and which, until Cubism, was to remain peculiar to Western art.

Since the work of men like Pierre Francastel and Rudolf Arnheim in art and Alexander Koyré on Galileo, there is little excuse for our attributing to the Renaissance the discovery of the "true nature" of the "exterior world." What in fact took place was the slow elaboration of concepts which made possible a total and coherent restructuring of the real. If, then, the real as we have come to know it was not discovered but, to a great extent, brought into being, we can reasonably assume that the material and psychological requirements of the new men—the urban-merchant-individuals who, by the 15th century, and especially in Italy, had restructured the economy—were not foreign to the kind of universe emerging from the work of the early artists and scientists.

The new art not only opened the wall behind medieval painting, it opened it to infinity and so brought into being space as a separate, independent component. Previously, the relationship among figures or the requirements of whatever sacred tale was being told generated the necessary space; but once space achieved an existence of its own figures had to be distributed within it, and since the new space (unlike that of Roman murals in which the background is at a distance) was thought of as homogeneous it could be organized coherently in its entirety. In other words, figures and objects could be placed in perspective, and this "rational" distribution came in time to be looked upon as the true subject of art (especially in 19th century estheticism) for it is what we call beauty and, as such, is quite foreign to primitive art. Such art (which is not art in our sense of the word at all) is incantatory; it strives to create forms that the sacred will consent to inhabit, to possess as, from time to time (or even permanently as in the case of insanity in some cultures), it possessed animals or human beings. The cathedral was literally the house of God and, as such, a sort of instrument utilized by the collectivity in its struggle against an environment it had not yet sufficiently mastered to be able to think of it as a spectacle one could conceivably represent with "scientific" or "beautiful" accuracy. Primitive art, being that of a real presence, could not, without absurdity, concern private individuals. The enormous bulk of the cathedrals had to be animated by the ardor of entire populations without which they are like colossal sea shells; not the work of barbarians, as the 18th century thought, but of men for whom the idea of the cathedral as a work of art would have been unintelligible because the work of art excludes the group. The work of art is an object of contemplation, and the group does not have to settle for contemplation since, depending upon whether it is primitive or revolutionary, it can bring pressure to bear upon the sacred, or it can liberate praxis by abolishing an obsolete social order.

Great art, to be sure, is always the product of exceptional individuals whether or not their names have been preserved. But where art—as in primitive cultures—is essentially a device enabling the supra-human to remain in more or less constant communication with men, that art is necessarily a matter of public concern.

Renaissance painting invites the distinction between form and content that dominated art criticism for so long and at the same time makes it clear that such a distinction should never be drawn. For while painting continued to make use of medieval subjects, its manner of doing so drained away all urgency and transformed them into traditional themes. In a perspective drawing the necessary relationship, that without which the composition could not exist, is that of each individual to infinity, to that vanishing point which is the "eye of God" freezing all that exists into a beautiful, perfectly ordered, small-scale model of the universe. The medieval world, being hierarchical, could be presented in two dimensions; the eye moved from heaven to hell or the reverse, and in so doing it might encounter groups of people existing as groups, identifiable by a position which was necessarily higher or lower and therefore, also, significant. But when, with the Renaissance, the hierarchy was "flattened out" and the eye enticed into the distance, then the group could no longer easily exist. It broke down into individuals each with his own position fixed in perspective; and that position, furthermore, could be, and usually was, totally without religious significance.[7]

Where the artist tried to retain religious significance he fell into the anecdotal, into an art which the Protestants very properly saw to be scandalous and which they suppressed. It was deeply contradictory for a painter to relate a sacred episode involving (as they all did in one form or another) the free passage between realms (as, in the mystery plays, beings rose from below or descended from above) while making use of a technique (perspective) appropriate to a world ordered with such all-embracing, geometrical precision that the increasingly improbable intervention of the sacred had to be placed at the confines of infinity. Such an art was scandalous in the sense that for a discerning viewer the true subject was not, for example, the raising of Lazarus, but the expertness and taste with which the painter used the new technique for representing reality as it "really was"; and in the best instances the result was "beautiful." Eventually art fell to the point where it became the meeting place of two individuals: the artist, for whom the subject matter of his work became merely a pretext for the exercise of his individual gifts, and the viewer, possessing sufficient refinement (sufficiently removed from the indiscriminate masses) to look beyond what was represented to how it had been represented.

Insofar as Tolstoy, in his crotchety *What is Art,* laments the passing of medieval reciprocity (the existence of a group self) it is easy to sympathize with him, but on condition he grant that Renaissance art was, in its own way, as fine as any, that for every possibility lost another was created and that, above all, reciprocity can be restored only in an historically appropriate form—as praxis and certainly not in the form of that primitive anonymity of the individual which results where the sacred or the otherworldly can be implored or can take it upon itself to interrupt the ordinary course of men's lives. Tolstoy rightly felt that great art necessarily concerns the entire population; what he forgot was that, for the aristocratic culture which existed between the end of medieval civilization and the Enlightenment, the entire population was purely and simply the courtly elite. Renaissance tragedy is that art form in which, for the last time in Western culture, the individual enjoys the prerogative (which, however, he is unable to exercise) of a more or less direct communication with the divine, a communication which would have been impossibly trivialized had the person concerned not been regarded as representing mankind as a whole.[8]

In the vertical universe of the Middle Ages the serfs occupied a relatively low position, but they could also be regarded as sustaining what rose above them; so that the serf as well as the nobleman existed, so to speak, by divine right, since the whole structure would have collapsed without him. With the Renaissance, it is as though the hierarchy had softened in places to produce at the bottom an anarchical, barbarous sub-humanity and, at the top, that strange short-lived hybrid, the sacred individual, sacred because there remained a public responsibility (and therefore Renaissance art could, in good conscience be universal) which, however, since it was no longer self-evident, left room for personal yearnings or ambitions destructive of a sacred rôle and yet imperious. This is the inner intensity or conflict we look for in the later, more consummate work of Renaissance painting and sculpture as well as in its theatre.

There was a period in the evolution of Renaissance painting when figures in the foreground seemed in danger of falling into a chasm which had opened between them and the landscape. The progress of art consisted in bringing forward the world in the distance until it swallowed up the people in the foreground who then became a part of nature. Saints might continue to look adoringly upward; they were none the less "boxed in," the only way out being in the direction of an ever receding vanishing point. The whole paradox of the Renaissance is that while it extended the closed world of Aristotelian thought to infinity, it also, since infinity cannot be sensuously approached, confined man to a private realm of faith or speculation, thus incidentally creating the two great options of bourgeois culture, hypocrisy or scepticism. Great Renaissance artists and thinkers passionately resisted that confinement for they were men who, though modern in intellect, were medieval in their affectivity. Scientists, even as late as Pascal and Newton, were theologians, and their lives were marked by inner stresses comparable to those we have seen to be the stuff of tragedy. Renaissance painters were not artists in the contemporary sense but craftsmen; in their own eyes, they were not "self-expressive," but rather were accountable to their fellows. If places we would today think of as small country towns, like

15th century Florence, produced great artists in such astonishing numbers it was partly because, although large fortunes had been accumulated by private individuals, the prestige of wealth was a civic affair; so the display of wealth in Renaissance city-states was as close to the potlatch as to the walled estates and art collections of the present-day millionaire.

We have seen that the medieval city was a "tool" serving to augment and protect private wealth. But also no peculiarly urban or bourgeois culture could exist until the city was strong enough to become itself the lord of the manor; and if this happened earlier and more extensively in Italy than anywhere else in Europe it was thanks not only to geographical conditions particularly favorable to commerce but to the existence in Italy of an aristocracy which, since antiquity, had been more urban than rural. If we look upon the early city-states as representing a kind of plural lord of the manor we can appreciate that the Renaissance artist, though subsidized by private wealth, worked nevertheless for the community at large. Here, direct, sensuous access to the sacred was still practicable, and there persisted, therefore, that primitive reciprocity which represents the "singleness" of mankind still able to engage in a dialogue with the beings or forces that determine its existence; a dialogue which ends tragically with the heroes of Shakespeare and Racine. The supreme achievement of Renaissance art would not have been possible if the artist had not encountered in the depths of his own subjectivity eschatological obsessions which were common to the great majority of his fellows and which science pushed into limbo for two centuries. If great art requires above all that the artist find within himself the voice of the entire community expounding upon the nature of man and the universe, then primitive art will be consistently of a high order, and I see no objection to this.[9] One is tempted to argue that the difference between primitive art and our own (before cubism) is that, by and large, theirs is nonrepresentational. But if the real is an aspect of praxis, if, in other words, it can no longer be regarded either as given (as for the empiricist) or as having been in one way or another projected from a mental source (as for idealism, positivism and some forms of structuralism), then all art is representational or none is, whichever one prefers. Art then becomes what Sartre calls an *analogon*, that is, material traces or devices with the help of which a civilization will stabilize and preserve the real by filling in its interstices with imaginary quantities peculiarly its own. It is possible that primitive groups "add" more to indications provided by their artists, but we cannot be sure of this since we can no more know how much we add to, for example, a still life, than we can judge our own appearance.[10]

Nevertheless renaissance art differs in kind from the primitive, and, as I have been suggesting, perspective as we have known it in our culture may be the simplest way to understand the change that came about. In the ladder-like, qualitative conception of the world and its beings of the Middle Ages there was no place for an individual divorced from the group from which he derived all his essential characteristics. Therefore, the problem of communication that besets the modern artist could not exist. The romantics, with their notion of inspiration, tried to reopen direct access to the beyond, to reestablish the "singleness" of the collectivity in its negotiations with the otherworldly. But it was far too late. The artist could be neither anonymous (that is, a craftsman) nor the occupier of a preordained place; he had become a particular kind of *individual,* a genius. He was no longer simply a person recognized by the group as being especially proficient in the manufacture of cult objects but, on the contrary, a man so *different* from his fellows as to be in danger of going unremarked or unappreciated by them. Conversely, the development during the 19th and early 20th centuries of what purported to be revolutionary thought and activity appeared to revive, as an antidote to the lonely, ineffectual grandeur of the bourgeois artist, the possibility of a responsible art, one practiced by men content to efface themselves so as to serve. If the result—socialist realism—has been so dismal an experiment it is because art cannot flourish where, as in Stalinist Russia, it is not allowed to be one of culture's great constitutive functions. Stalinism is the philosophy of Homais which, having imbecilized Marx, came to power in a country where most of the population was still illiterate. It was not necessary, however, for scientific rationalism to find a directly political expression in Stalinism to exclude art from any "consultative" capacity in the elaboration or discovery of the truth since, between Racine and Kafka approximately, the artist became increasingly an exceptional individual working, sometimes despite himself, for a tiny elite of connoisseurs. Or, at the other extreme, he became a man providing entertainment, especially in the lower reaches of fiction, for the unrefined, for the masses.

We are going to assume that the various cultural phenomena we associate with bourgeois rationalism—linear perspective, scientific law, individualism and so forth—are objective structures of the world but that they are also the result of a selection, of a "deliberate limiting of possible interpretations"[11] and, furthermore, that this selecting takes

place on the basis of what André Martinet calls "functional
pertinence"[12] (or praxis) the declared purpose of which may serve to conceal from men what is really happening as opposed to what is supposed
to be happening. In addition, we will assume that what really happens
men want to happen at least insofar as they do not actively seek to prevent it.

Marxist materialism is simply the assertion that men are obliged to
guarantee themselves against cold and hunger and that any society's
super-structure (religion, mythology, science), while it may at times itself
become a decisive factor, can be understood only by relating it structurally with the particular manner in which the culture in question conducts its struggle against scarcity. Monastic communities existed in the
Middle Ages for religious reasons to be sure; but, more fundamentally,
they existed because feudal society (unlike that of ancient Egypt) was
unable to produce agricultural surpluses with sufficient regularity to support a priestly caste that did no work. This does not mean that religion
was an illusion; a world view cannot be an illusion since there is nothing
"outside" it. Thomism reflected feudal society's hierarchical structure,
but what else was there for it to reflect (or, better, to "complete") before
the city-states began to evolve their new culture? In attempting therefore
to understand this new culture which is still our own, I shall assume that
it was a praxis and that, nevertheless—before the introduction of the factory system at least—there was no alternative to it. It would clearly be a
mistake to dissociate the voyages of discovery (praxis) and the new
physics (superstructure). This has almost always been done in the past
because it was taken for granted that Aristotelian-Christian thought was
mere metaphysics, while science is humbly and sceptically experimental.

But what if science were simply the metaphysics of the first primitive
culture capable of envisaging the earth as a whole? This cannot be so it
will be answered because science verifies its hypotheses: the examination
of moon soil justifies the Renaissance scientists who argued against the
Aristotelians that the heavenly bodies were composed of substances not
essentially different from those on earth. But, of course, every cultural
system obtains the answers it requires. For as long as that system—given
the unique point at which it is situated in time and place—produces the
greatest benefits for the greatest number, its hypotheses will continue to
be verified. The Ptolemaic system remained satisfactorily verifiable for
as long as navigators stayed within the Mediterranean. We have no means
of knowing how much of what constitutes science now will eventually
become error or even superstition as a consequence of being placed dif-

ferently in some broader organizational scheme. Renaissance science did not, as was supposed, disprove Aristotelian principles; rather, it showed their irrelevance to the needs of a new society. It did so not out of pragmatism, but from the supreme vantage point of a new, all-embracing world view. In the same way today, while it is true that the moon is made up of substances similar to those on earth, if we bear in mind the present needs of mankind there is nothing whatever we can do with such a "truth." But there is not much we can do without it either unless we adopt a wider rationality, that of dialectical reason (thought as praxis) encompassing analytical reason rather as the new astronomy took up that of Ptolemy as a particular instance.

Until the end of the 18th century the wealthy bourgeois in Western literature was more often than not a figure of fun, a bizarre soul who had devoted a harrassed, conscientious life to building up a fortune which any nobleman, usually "haughty, gallant and gay," had a moral and perhaps even legal right to plunder or confiscate, thus leaving us with the feeling that the monied old fool had been taught a lesson. How did individual, secular property eventually become "sacred"? How could merchants and moneylenders persuade their fellows that a life devoted to transferring wealth from the community to their own coffers was somehow a life well spent? How, later on, could tradesmen and entrepreneurs convince themselves it was fitting and proper for the manufacture and distribution of goods to have as a primary purpose their own enrichment and that of their families; in other words, how could they convince themselves that an article is an exchange value and only incidentally a use value, that use value is exchange value, that the purpose of life is money, and that money precedes men? In a society plagued by severe shortages of goods and foodstuffs, enormous private fortunes were accumulated not by using the new tools, the city and the ship, to facilitate a more equal distribution of much needed products but, on the contrary, by impeding that distribution through hoarding and trade monopolies which worked to depress prices at supply points and to raise them at places of delivery. The most pressing cultural task for the bourgeoisie, consequently, was to evolve a superstructure which would enable it to transform a praxis operating self-evidently to the detriment of the great majority (including sections of the aristocracy, in some instances) into the mysterious operation of concealed universal laws. Yet, at the same time, there can be no question before the 18th century of hypocrisy or deliberate mystification for the simple reason that feudalism and the medieval church were not viable alternatives. What André Malraux said of revolution is applicable here: whatever was not bourgeois rationalism was worse than bourgeois rationalism. There was therefore a sense in which the unscrupulous pursuit of private gain did not work to the "detriment of the great majority." But, then, this fact certainly could not have been appreciated in the immediate except by an infinitesimal number of men in a position to suspect science's potential.

The history of the bourgeoisie is, purely and simply, the history of the manner in which exchange value has supplanted use value; or, in language more appropriate to our particular inquiry, the replacing of the public by the private realm and the consequent necessity of assuming the existence of a universal order without which a society of autonomous individuals each pursuing his own goals for his own benefit falls into chaos. That order, nevertheless, was not entirely invented, it had been revealed by the global ventures of ships from Western Europe and by the concommitant development of astronomy (that is, of universal physics). The "order" of botany, for example, was "discovered" because all plants were finally becoming available for classification. Science was the possibility of a definitive organization since *all* the facts could now be assembled. An encyclopedia is an inventory of what we have; once it is complete, everything will find its place, like tinned food in a shop. Descartes considered number and extension to be primary qualities and therefore independent of the perceiving subject. From a purely philosophical point of view Berkeley was right to point out that there is no reason to declare quantity any less subjective than color. Yet if we look at the problem in terms of cultural praxis Descartes was right because whatever the world might be discovered to contain would have to have dimensions, and thus it could be dealt with mathematically. On the other hand, the voyages of discovery were undertaken for the purpose of opening trade routes. They came about not through the "restless curiosity" of Western man but through the money-lust of merchants, of men who lived in admirable harmony in cosmopolitan communities (it appears there may have been a small Chinese colony in Siena in the 13th century) offering the first image of what may eventually become one world, but also living there so as to augment an often already colossal personal wealth.

In between the breakdown of the primitive group and the rise of Marx's revolutionary proletariat there existed (and, of course, still does) an "abstract humanity," humanity as a "reservoir" or mass from which there could emerge individuals complete in themselves (because in communication with the concealed order); which could, with no harm, be temporarily suppressed, as in *Robinson Crusoe*; and which, when it attempted to recall itself to the attention of the well-to-do 19th century individual, had to be ruthlessly put down lest it submerge civilization. If humanity could exist in this way as a "spectacle," as a negative quantity, "abstractly," it was because the wealthy Renaissance bourgeoisie found itself taking no part in the directly productive and indispensable activities of a society within which nevertheless it was able to exercise an occasionally decisive influence since the realm's solvency sometimes depended upon it. But of course, later on, in the early days of the factory system, the bourgeoisie was forced to discover the virtues of labor. If value, rather than being a property of the precious metals, derives ultimately from labor (as Adam Smith argued), then one could establish the viciousness of leisure whether in the aristocrat or the agricultural worker who might pass the winter months simply keeping warm, waiting for the spring to soften the earth. We owe to the moneymen the full utilization of the year for labor or, where it is necessary to crush rivals or secure markets, for war. We may, consequently, forget that the wealthy bourgeoisie has always constituted a leisure class in the sense that the "labor" of the merchant or entrepreneur consisted in expropriating surplus value, never in contributing to the quantity of surplus value being realized.

As in the case of an "abstract humanity," therefore, autonomous individuals could at one time reasonably exist since the rich bourgeois wielded very real power derived neither from occupancy of a preordained place in society nor from having demonstrated some personal worth or skill in a common endeavor. The merchant was neither a shipbuilder, nor a seaman, nor a navigator, and yet the whole enterprise was his doing. He controlled it from a distance (as would a spectator), perhaps even anonymously, and for his own benefit; so that while all-powerful the merchant was also vulnerable, not only because of the uncertainties and irregularities of trade but because the unshakeable loyalties of feudal or revolutionary relationships cannot exist between private individuals. The dealers in money knew nothing of the skills with which men shaped wood or iron, confronted the elements or grew food. For them, the adversity of matter took the form of acts of God against which there was no recourse except in prayer. Consequently, for the bourgeois, a man's worth was less a function of his practical abilities than of his probity, that is, of his determination to fulfill contractual obligations which could in some instances interfere with his self-seeking. But of course that self-seeking is the very essence of bourgeois existence. The means by which one amassed a fortune could easily involve denying the use of a product (including food) to one's own fellows so as to increase its exchange value (this being the whole purpose of trade monopolies). At the same time, though, these men, who derived their wealth from usury and plunder,[13] were compelled to have confidence in each other's readiness to honor bits of paper, compelled to rely absolutely upon representatives perhaps many months away from direct supervision.

Thus there came into being a class ethic which was a praxis, that is, which answered the practical requirements of the bourgeoisie and yet, at the same time, did so honestly in that it would have been impracticable, before Hegel and Marx, for anyone to doubt the universal order of science. If wealth often accrued by unsavory means and to the detriment of the community at large, it was no doing of the merchant, moneylender or entrepreneur, whose sober, austere, self-disciplined and virtuous life was proof enough that, like everyone else, he was simply the long-suffering executor of Another's will. Since the bourgeois was prepared to act against himself (his word was his bond; he had duties to fulfill whatever the consequences to himself; he despised self-indulgence in all its forms) he could not be accused of selfishness and greed. Rather, what might to the careless observer appear to be greed was in reality the means by which a rational and/or religious order wrought public good out of private opulence.

But, as we know, the same culture that produced this class ethic also created universal tools, universal trade, a universal philosophy (science) and appealed—in order to bring about its revolution—to the notion of a universal man, that is, value comes from labor, and labor is an attribute of *all* men who are therefore equal. Nevertheless, this universalism has always and everywhere been subordinated to the requirements of private, individual wealth. A particular economic praxis involving the insane substitution of money for men (of exchange value for use value) complemented itself with a philosophy of the universal—science and humanism; so that advances in science, invariably and necessarily accomplished "for mankind" are invariably absorbed into the profit-taking process, with the result that nature—the outer garment of God—has become the raw material of industry, its very air and water being used, and destroyed, with criminal and idiotic complacency.

If this contradiction is indeed structural, if, as suggested at the beginning, it should long since have drawn us from our nostalgic, "objective" quest for, or contemplation of, the Timeless, then it must constitute the basic structure of the 19th century novel since it is through that novel that the bourgeois vision of things attains its fullest and most perfect form.

CHAPTER II

The advent of nature as a new object, as spectacle, involves a contradiction so damaging and insuperable that its clear formulation marked the end of scientific rationalism. A spectacle can exist only for a spectator, that is, for someone divorced from the spectacle, and such an observer could not possibly be that predestined or determined *object* which was man for Protestantism and for science. To be sure the spectator's initiative is minimal, a mere orientation, a turning toward, but even that is infinitely beyond the capacity of an object, inert by definition. Philosophy labored to eliminate one of the two, but in vain. Without a spectator the existence of many "foreign additions" such as causality cannot be accounted for, and without the spectacle the genuine discoveries which men have made throughout the history of science become inexplicable.

However, what is a problem for philosophy may be an aspect of the praxis of a social class, that is, in reality, a solution. So it is with the mind-body problem, which became almost the whole of philosophy for two centuries. Men were related to nature in two ways simultaneously: they were part of the spectacle in the eye of God (body), and they occupied a vantage point close to that of God himself in order to understand the laws regulating Divine perspectives (mind). This astonishing conception of man as being at one and the same time a thing and omniscient is implicit in the art of linear perspective and in that of the novel.

The infinity of God consists in his being not only at the vanishing point from which he views his world as through a peep-hole, seizing upon the spectator to fix him motionless in place as an additional object in the landscape (the space of the painting being, theoretically, that of the spectator as well), he is also at the back of the viewer who, consequently, although fixed into place like a rock or tree finds himself in the axis of Divine vision so that the whole wondrous harmony is accessible to him. We are, at one and the same time, both a part of nature and, miraculously, outside it; a part of nature in the landscape and also the quasi-divine viewing individual sometimes represented in the art of portraiture which strives to suggest that invisible inner world with which we apprehend and appreciate the invisible order of the outer.

It is generally felt that anecdotal art (like programme music) is somehow inferior, and this attitude is perhaps justified inasmuch as it is the artist's prerogative to show forth the great harmony through *any* subject matter. It consequently seems otiose to draw the viewer's attention too strongly to whatever may be happening in the picture. But if the artist can and perhaps should resist the temptation to recount, the novelist obviously cannot. Both, to be sure, begin with the assumption that there exists a universal rational order which it is the privilege of man to contemplate (as opposed to the sign of primitive cultures, which is a summons or an answer), but that order—in the form of linear perspective—is the condition of the artist's work; whereas it is what the novelist hopes to be able to conclude with; it is the conclusion we are compelled to draw from what has been related.

The Renaissance is that period during which the primitive sign was slowly replaced by a principle of organization of the whole of the real made practicable by the coming into being of the terrestrial globe as an entity and by the conviction that matter was homogeneous throughout the universe.[1] Art therefore came to deal with what "really exists," and it was supposed that artists of preceding centuries had shown merely what they wished or imagined to exist. In the case of painting we can see that the artist has copied objects familiar to all of us. But how was the novelist to assure the authenticity of what his readers could never actually see? How could he reasonably expect the reader to accept the reality of a narrative he had necessarily invented? Necessarily, since an account of **public events is history and of private, autobiography, and if such accounts are honestly conducted, that is, if no previously elaborated thesis** is being insinuated, then there can be no conclusion; or, more accurately, each reader will be free to draw his own or, where a conclusion exists, it will be relatively trivial. But art must conclude, however negatively, however implicitly, and that concluding "statement," as we have seen, must concern the nature of the universe and of man.

It was the good fortune of the artist to be obliged to discover a universal principle of order since only then, it was assumed, could he be "true to nature"; he could not otherwise copy reality with sufficient accuracy. The novelist, however, was concerned not with the visual but with **the moral order corresponding to it; an order which, reflecting back from** the final pages of the book, would enable the reader to see that an apparently haphazard series of events had, after all, contained a meaning.

But where a meaning was adopted, as in the case of a novelist like Samuel Richardson, far from enabling the writer, like the artist, to organize and clarify the real, it caused him to so narrow and impoverish it that the meaning he discovered there was inevitably, for many readers, partial and inconsequential. Obtrusive moralizing in fiction made for a novelist who was a poor spectator, for one who was seeing too little. The picaresque hero, on the contrary, was a traveller, sometimes even, as in *Candide* and *Gulliver's Travels*, going beyond the seas; so though the novelist was obliged to "copy" events of his own imagining, he could at least cause them to happen in many different places and to involve people from many different walks of life. But precisely because the novelist sees more clearly and looks more honestly he is not able to conclude with the discovery of that Order which, in the world of Newtonian science, had to be there. The picaresque hero puts established wisdom, opinion or custom to the test of his personal experience with negative results. But since he was a spectator, that is, unable to alter reality (at least intentionally, as do members of revolutionary groups today), and equally unable to "alter himself" as can the primitive—since he was a spectator, and hence unable to intervene, the world had to be rational. Picaresque fiction, consequently, is in a light vein; things turn out quite well in the long run and there is always time for some hearty fun. It was the literature of an ascending class confident it had something better to offer than Church and Throne; yet what was being offered was necessarily already there (overlain by historical error and human folly) since the bourgeois has no access to the public realm which he is not obliged to conceal, his goal being a self-enrichment incompatible with his recognition of the humanity in all of us. If the picaresque novel is bourgeois in its "obligatory" assumption there exists a universal rational order so that man as a solitary spectator can orient himself, it is true as well that the hero is never fully satisfied he has managed to achieve this; and his unrelenting, often "immoral" scepticism could not have found much sympathy with some elements of the bourgeoisie of the day closer in outlook to Richardson than to Fielding or Voltaire. Because the bourgeoisie had in the field against it nothing more formidable than feudal and churchly irrelevance, it could afford a corrosive negativeness against which the classical novel, however, developed a supremely effective defense.[2]

It is important to distinguish two radically different kinds of individualism in Western culture: the individual as "part of the spectacle," as "foreign to himself," motivated "from elsewhere" and individualism as the demand that the truth be transparent to each of us, that it exist for each of us, that each of us be able to embrace it as his own. But truth in this sense is not truth as ordinarily understood at all; it is praxis. It is what, for self-evident reasons having to do with hunger and cold, we are striving to achieve; the pronoun is necessarily we so that a truth which does not have to be taken on faith, one which can be experienced, is the privilege of the revolutionary group. What happened from Balzac onward was this. Individualism as definable *entity*[3] became the subject matter of the novel, while individualism as inquiring or protesting *activity* (where it continued to exist at all) became a trait of the author himself or, possibly, of one of his characters, in which case it ceased to be the autonomous inquiry of picaresque fiction and became the simple emanation of a person of a certain "kind." To put this differently, 19th century fiction marks an attempt to place the novelist in a viewing position so favorable that all he need do is copy the spectacle as accurately as he is able. Ideally, the novelist will be so completely divorced from the phenomena he observes as to be able to observe even man himself with no risk of subjective distortion. This is something the picaresque novelist had not presumed to do, for the reader is *with* Don Quixote, Wilhelm Meister or Tom Jones, whereas he observes and "understands" Rastignac, Emma Bovary or Micawber.

The classical novel is the product of the separation between the protagonist and the author so that the first may be "seen" by the second. This development had been long anticipated in art; but while art could suggest an inner intensity, it could not enlarge upon its moral quality, and where it attempts to do so—as in Hogarth—we are left with a series of illustrations for a novel. Painting can effectively convey a situation or event, but if we are to be sure of a person's identity—his moral quality—it must be tested through time; only the novel could spread itself out sufficiently to accomplish this. If, furthermore, man is to be regarded as assembled within himself at some given point not constituted by what he can be seen to do, then his words or deeds may be deceptive; they may be an appearance serving to conceal rather than reveal what he "really is." So that, once again, identity is best treated in the novel since, exactly as in science, we may have to pierce the veil of appearances to reach an essence we are obliged to describe, it being impracticable simply to show it. For example, Balzac says of Rastignac: "He experienced that fine and noble secret remorse the merit of which is seldom appreciated by men when they judge their fellows and which causes the criminal, condemned by earthly magistrates, to be absolved by the angels in heaven."[4]

Balzac takes it quite for granted that when we consider our fellows it is, ultimately, for the purpose of forming a judgement; and this all but unnoticed implicit assumption is what we will discover the classical novel to be really about. But this assumption involves an extraordinary contradiction: the identification of objects inevitably takes place with a view to . . . . ; that is, it is accomplished by particular men pursuing particular goals, and this, as we have seen, is as true of scientific pursuits as of any other, the difference being that scientific "identification" had to hold universally. The identification of men is what we call a judgement, and the criteria used are not quantitative but moral. They are, consequently, far more deeply and unmistakably rooted in a particular culture or even group within that culture than is science. How then is the novelist to assume that God's view of reality which is necessarily his in a culture dominated by Newtonian science? How is he to pronounce upon man as such (as he must, since he belongs to a global culture and since great art is concerned with the whole of reality) making use of values like sexual morality restricted not only to his own society but to his own class? How could the novelist deal with the problem of the relativity of moral value (and of the religion upon which it was based) which the Age of Reason had forcefully drawn to the attention of educated people?

What the observer sees depends upon the position he chooses to occupy. When, as in scientific rationalism, that position is assumed not to exist, then what is seen is dictated in its entirety by the culture to which the observer belongs; he is blind. We accept readily enough that this blindness (the happy condition of the value-less) be the natural state of the orthodox economist or sociologist, but it is impossible to suppose it compatible with greatness in art, even in the case of Balzac and Zola, who imagined their novels might make a contribution to science. This blindness, or ethnocentrism, is no impediment to great art in primitive societies, to be sure, but only because primitive art and "science" are *ethno*-centered and not *class*-centered as in our society. It would not have been possible for any of the great classical novelists (with the possible exception of Tolstoy, who came sufficiently late) to see in scientific rationalism a praxis and consequently a class phenomenon. But they would have had to suspect that the criteria they were using to effect what we shall see to be their structurally indispensable characterizations we unhesitatingly call middle class morality. How then did they avoid a crippling narrowness? How did they, at least in the best instances, achieve a perspective upon their own class?

The 19th century novelist was granted omniscience so that he might delve into the secrets of the human soul. But if he sought to make a further use of his absolute viewpoint so as to inquire into the social, economic and historical conditions that would tend to produce a "soul" of this or that kind, then simple honesty would compel him to admit that the order which should have begun to reign with the passing of feudal obscurantism did not really exist after all as picaresque novelists had—jokingly of course—suggested might be the case. The classical novelist could choose to investigate his society as a whole (that is, all the "causes" that produced this particular character) unfragmented into the areas of study which were gradually marked out and assigned to the various academic disciplines; but where he did make such a choice he was forced to admit that insofar as one could see and experience, insofar as one prolonged the picaresque tradition of confronting the self-evident with the traditionally alleged, then the new order was in reality a chaos, the war of each against all carried on with all the old ferocity, the only difference being that what could formerly, in more "primitive" times, be given a meaning thanks to religion (and therefore, in a sense, dealt with) had become for some people perfectly natural, perhaps even one of the famous iron laws of the economy.

But if being an honest and competent spectator required that the novelist condemn the society his own class had brought into being, he was nevertheless unmistakably (with, in the 19th century, the single exception of Stendhal) a spokesman for that class since the reader would fail to see what the novel was about unless he interpreted correctly the author's condemnation of his society, that is, unless he saw in it a manifestation of identity. In fact, the more eloquent the condemnation (Balzac's Vautrin, for example) the more memorable the character.

I suggest, therefore, that in the masterpieces of 19th century fiction there can be found two levels of discourse, the explicit and the implicit. These are in contradiction to each other and represent the expression, in that art form we associate most closely with the bourgeoisie, of what we have seen to be the fundamental contradiction of that class: its universal aspirations (explicit level) in irreconcilable conflict with its particularist demands (implicit level). Let us take the example of Balzac's *Les Illusions perdues*.

The subject of this novel is a very common one in 19th century fiction; writers as different in almost every respect as were Flaubert and Tolstoy often treat, in one form or another, of great expectations and of their disappointment. Perhaps the Western notion of progress has given rise to expectations of happiness so ingrained we need to be continually reminded that after all, we are not, as someone put it, promised anything. And yet as social beings if not as individuals we were promised something; we were promised a society that would make sense, that would be rational. Otherwise Balzac would have found it perfectly natural that everything (including, in *Les Illusions perdues*, literature) should have become a commodity, that everything, including men's minds, should be up for sale. But, instead, where the picaresque novelist merely wonders, Balzac denounces in the strongest terms. If he is able to do this and yet remain, for many, the greatest of those who have worked with this most important of bourgeois art forms, it is because, on another level of discourse, the implicit, Balzac is saying that we are not primarily social beings but individuals with an identity; so that what happens to us in the course of our lives will depend not upon the nature of our society but upon the kind of person we are. What destroys the hero of *Les Illusions perdues*, consequently, is not a vicious society but a defective identity; for the reader learns at the novel's very outset that Lucien de Rubempré is weak; reading the novel is simply the process of having that weakness confirmed (or "tested") in a variety of circumstances until finally it brings about Lucien's suicide.

In Western art since the Renaissance, the landscape is offered as a sort of microcosm of the universe, and in his own way, the novelist is also concerned with "everything"; either by going to see and trying to draw conclusions, as in the picaresque, or by a vision encompassing the entire *comédie humaine*. But while the artist, as we have seen, is able to show order, the novelist has to speak it. When Balzac incorporated the hero into the spectacle he appeared to be granting himself the means of doing this; for the picaresque novelist had stood at his hero's elbow and had therefore been insufficiently removed from vanity fair to see it whole. However, Balzac's apparently trivial innovation—that of setting his hero or heroes at a distance where we could see them—meant in reality that he had taken up a position which was that of his whole class; for one cannot "see," that is, judge a person except on the basis of a moral order which, after 1789 (and already in *Les Liaisons dangereuses* and later on in all of "aristocratic" Romantic literature as well) could only be bourgeois. In other words, *Balzac implicitly made use of what, explicitly, he was looking for*. He was, consequently, free to condemn the whole social order for not being an order at all and to advocate a return to Church and Throne; free to do so since in order to understand the novel the reader had to share that very mentality which is part and parcel of the mad scramble for money and respectability. *Les Illusions perdues* is about the career of Lucien de Rubempré whose "weakness" would be invisible to anyone

not sharing the Protestant-capitalistic ethic; for it consists in Lucien's in-
capacity for sustained hard work, his inability to be frugal and to resist
temptation. Lucien, in other words, was a true feudal aristocrat. But if
we take that view, the novel's whole moral import escapes us; we do not
understand it. Inversely, Balzac's contemporaries could easily fail to be
impressed by his attacks upon middle class civilization since none of the
true substance of the novel would be lost without them. The reader could
still follow with interest the various tests to which Lucien's identity is
submitted to determine whether it had been correctly stated at the beginning, for we shall see in a moment that "errors" often occur.

Renaissance tragedy marks the end of the sign as a guide to conduct.
Henceforth men would have to make up their minds as individuals; they
would have to look inward to conscience rather than outward as they had
always done in the past for indications the precise meaning of which
would be determined by the collectivity or by a caste appointed for that
purpose. The novel, consequently, has always been much concerned with
the problems of personal morality. But where this was obsessive, as in
Richardson and Rousseau, the wholeness of the spectacle, which
becomes a segment rather than a microcosm, suffered. Balzac seemed to
find the solution by demonstrating that it was unnecessary to exhort to a
stricter or higher morality; one could simply show a chaste or dissolute
person and the account of what happened to him would constitute in
itself a moral lesson all the more effective for having been simply
"copied" from life. If people are of various kinds, then the novelist can
take a cross-section and Wessex, Middlemarch, Yonville l'Abbaye or
even the Pequod become the universe, and the novelist scoops up the
whole of humanity.

Balzac perfected an art form which is profoundly bourgeois because
man as inquiring subjectivity, as response to the evident, becomes absorbed by man regarded as a moral object. It is then possible in the best
liberal tradition to see everything, to be the perfect spectator, and still be
blind. Vautrin, for example, in his famous conversation with Rastignac
in *Le Père Goriot,* sees bourgeois society and sees it whole. He sees the
total relativity of moral values, he even sees the death of God well before
Nietzsche. Yet all that the reader can, if he wishes (following certain immediate indications from Balzac himself concerning Vautrin's
"cynicism"), take to be a revelation of character and not of the world he
lives in; in fact he is eventually almost obliged to do this when he
discovers Vautrin to be "evil," since from an evil self there can issue only
evil sentiments or ideas. There is, of course, no point to the novelist

speaking as himself rather than through one of the characters since then he simply reveals his own character, his own "subjective view." If he goes too far in his wish to instruct or inform his reader, if, in other words, the explicit level of discourse entirely usurps the implicit, the novel is destroyed. It then becomes a thesis novel, the consequence of the author's having forgotten he is a spectator and therefore able to "tell" only insofar as he can do so through "showing." What he shows is necessarily identity since only character, it was implicitly supposed, can be regarded as both thing (and therefore "visible") and as value (hence the novelist can, in appearance at least, convey a message without intervening).

In *La Comédie humaine* people appear occasionally who, while "good," express sentiments indistinguishable from those of Vautrin in *Le Père Goriot,* Gobseck being the most striking of these. Nevertheless, whether good or evil, whatever a character says must be taken primarily as an indication of identity, otherwise we are dealing not with the classical novel but with the picaresque (in which case the character is, although unsuccessfully, putting questions to the natural Order) or the contemporary, that is, from Kafka onward (in which case, as we shall see, identity is eliminated as a matter of principle).

Only the novel has the space in which an identity can be convincingly tested through time. But even in the novel only a very few characters can be looked into with the desirable thoroughness, so that the reader may find himself at a loss in attempting to judge many of the lesser figures. They are not intended, however, to be judged, for they represent society at large, and they do so in one (or both) of two ways: merely as supernumeraries, a living fund upon which the novelist draws as may be necessary in demonstrating or revealing an identity, or (especially in Balzac) in the interests of the explicit level of discourse; for example, the various people through whom Lucien de Rubempré learns that literature is bought and sold like any other commodity or the two daughters of old Goriot who make it clear that even "filial instincts" can be undone by money.

Lucien de Rubempré is destroyed not by society but by himself. Similarly, old Goriot is brought low not by society working through his daughters, but by his "nature"; he is the "Christ of paternity," as Balzac puts it. But while we can understand the moral of *Les Illusions perdues* (one is not weak with impunity) what are we to make of those novels in which the hero is good, like old Goriot, but comes to grief nonetheless. In this case even where the reader has chosen to ignore the explicit he is still left with an implicit which appears to be saying much the same thing: namely, we have created a society in which not only may the good be persecuted but where this may happen because of their moral superiority and not despite it.

Of course we meet the classical novelist here on his own ground by assuming, with him, that there can exist people who are by definition "good" (Dostoevsky's Myshkin, Flaubert's Félicité, Zola's Gervaise in *l'Assommoir* and Florent in *Le Ventre de Paris,* all of whom come to harm because of their fine qualities). But even so the question is a delicate one since the novelist is forced to deal with that contradiction we have seen to be inseparable from bourgeois civilization, the conflict between universal possibilities (at least since the agricultural and industrial revolutions) and individual necessity (that of arriving at a satisfactory self-definition unthinkable apart from personal wealth). Balzac insists upon the implacable logic with which Vautrin demonstrates to Rastignac that worldly success is utterly incompatible with almost any conception of what constitutes human worth. Ours is that incredible culture which exacts a form of comportment of which it is obliged to disapprove. One succeeds always at the expense of others (and, in fact, for reasons Marx would eventually explain, the greater the number of the others—as in capitalism and colonialism—the greater the success); and yet without that success one remains part of mere human raw material from which we must struggle to emerge into an individual existence. Wealth signifies far more than comfort, it is the verification of an inner "superiority"; while being without money (as everyone on the dole is still given to understand in one way or another) is the revelation of one's mediocrity or even, possibly, of some ingrained evil. If the spectacle being presented by the classical novelist is to be thoroughly convincing he cannot throw a veil over the obscenity of money; but unless he does so he will be led on to explain the relationship between money and a character—preferably the hero—of whom we are being invited to approve, who is "good," "superior" or both.

In the vast majority of cases the issue is, of course, simply evaded. This is the solution of the English novel in its entirety, a solution often referred to as its rural tradition, that is, in plainer language, its refusal to notice such developments as the industrial revolution and the very rapid growth of the cities which accompanied it. To express this differently, the English novel reduces social and economic problems to questions of individual quality so successfully that the explicit level disappears almost completely (Jane Austen); it is trivialized by ironic detachment offered as an apology for abject conformism (Thackeray); it is brought to bear with great indignation upon abuses which the system itself was slowly correcting or which were derivative in nature (Dickens); or, finally, identity is expanded into a generalized moral discourse (George Eliot). One of the problems of the 19th century novelist was to be universal without looking too closely into what was really going on in the factories, the mines and on the farms; to be a competent spectator without really seeing. And yet if the essential subject matter of the novel is identity, if it is held that social conditions are created by kinds of people rather than the reverse,[5] and if we take it that "human nature never changes," then why should not definitive observations upon humanity and society be practicable simply through a sufficiently careful examination of a single country town? The novelist can then do without Balzac's often embarrassingly wide-ranging inquiry or Zola's tasteless curiosity about conditions of life among the poor.

But then why is greatness in 19th century fiction (Balzac, Dostoevsky, Tolstoy, Zola) in direct proportion to the depth and sincerity of its social criticism, of its explicit statement? Character may be dwelt upon with great subtlety and insight, but when that is very nearly the full register of a novelist the result is an art too conspicuously serving the needs of a single class. Artistic work of a very high order and yet absolutely impenetrable to all but a tiny courtly group existed in the past. But these were "sacred" arts, products of cultures for which there could not exist that notion of human equality to which one is led if, as for the bourgeoisie, political legitimacy is to be founded, in the last analysis, upon productive labor, a capacity for which must be attributed to every man. And yet if we read 19th century fiction carefully we will find remarks of this sort: "Good Luke felt, after the manner of contented hard-working men whose lives have been spent in servitude, that sense of natural fitness in rank which made his master's downfall a tragedy to him."[6] In the course of some idle prattle which was characteristic of her, one of the Bennett girls in *Pride and Prejudice* remarks to her indifferent listeners that a soldier had been flogged; where there exists a "natural fitness in rank" there can easily be a natural fitness in flogging, especially where we can persuade ourselves that it is precisely people in the lower ranks (after the manner of good Luke) who are the most sensible of natural fitness. To the bourgeois mind men are "equal" in the sense that they can always be seen to be men and not some other form of life, just as we can always identify wood as such. And as wood is of different quality and value, so are men, the vast majority of whom, it so happens, find themselves best accommodated in "contented servitude."

Why is it usually so difficult for the contemporary reader to detect the "class racism" endemic in the classical novel? To see in Dickens the sadistic strain that George Orwell detected there? To see that Jane Austen's whole work is an elaborate system for the grading of human beings, the hero often being the person most expert at this task, the first to recognize that A lacks sufficient refinement to associate appropriately with B? Beneath the leaden nobility of sentiment and demeanor one finds in the Victorian novel is the hysterical vituperation of all the best known French writers of the day confronted by the Commune,[7] the horrified disbelief of the American Southerner learning that blacks, like their masters, are beginning to carry guns. Racism, whether of social class or physical appearance, is based upon a more or less deliberate refusal of a possible awareness; possible because such awareness existed not only in men like Stendhal and Marx, but also no doubt in the population at large in the sense that it needed simply to be mentioned to carry conviction. How else could Balzac remark, "Virtue, socially speaking, is the companion of well-being and begins with education."[8] Whatever one's interpretation of that rather mysterious "socially speaking," the meaning of the whole sentence is clear enough: virtue (that is, the identity of most heroines of the classical novel) is not innate but purchased, like everything else in our society. Although the remark just quoted is not spoken by any character (and therefore cannot be ignored on grounds it is intended primarily as an indication of identity) but by Balzac himself, it is still merely an expression of "subjective opinion" and may therefore be discounted, while identity can be "shown," since the reader can be informed of the appearance, words and deeds of a person who is good or evil, generous or miserly, and so forth.

Such, then, are the two absolutely indispensable and yet absolutely contradictory constituents of the finest novels left to us by classical fiction. On the one hand, the explicit content, a matter simply of looking honestly at middle class society making full use of the critical lucidity and humanitarianism which is part of the education of every child born into Western culture; on the other hand, the implicit content, another aspect of that education, its class aspect, the tendency to regard lucidity, rationalism, humanitarianism and the like not as a cultural orientation primarily, but as a question of personal merit, a form of "success," a matter of individual quality, a possibility of self-definition.

If the explicit level of discourse is not to be trivialized (as in the English novel) if—as we must—we take seriously the talk of Vautrin and

Gobseck (and a host of lesser characters as well), if we are obliged to heed Dostoevsky when he dwells upon the hunger of children, or Tolstoy upon the selfish stupidity of high society, then is there any way for the novelist to prevent the reader from debasing the explicit content into an indication of identity or into a "merely personal" opinion of the author? Balzac sometimes attempts a solution by causing the goodness of the character to consist not only in middle class morality (i.e., chastity, honesty, truthfulness) but in his revulsion from a society in which money alone matters. In *Colonel Chabert,* for instance, Chabert discovers that genuine goodness (in the sense of an active concern for one's fellow man) will be at a disadvantage or even persecuted in a world which tolerates, in the way of goodness, only the observances. Where this theme is fully developed, however, the protagonists tend to be women or old men, that is, people who are not confronting life but withdrawing from it. The reader is able to interpret that withdrawal not as a denunciation of his society but as a character deficiency (notably in the case of women who, for bourgeois society, are deficient by nature), as a manifestation of senility perhaps in Chabert and Goriot who, in any case, had already been "successful" each in his own way in their earlier years. What is required is that the novelist show in detail a young man possessed of those qualities to which our culture, hypocritically or not, attaches the highest value, and confronted by the necessity of being successful (since the alternative is the life in death of the Vauquer boarding-house in *Le Père Goriot*) in a society which grants success only to the callous and the corrupt.

Let me put the problem in a somewhat different way: The novel is able to make a statement simply by copying (because what it copies, identity, is an already moralized reality), but how can that statement advocate renunciation and asceticism in a secular society? It was already practicable for at least some men to be atheistic in the contemporary sense (consisting not in denying the existence of God but in finding the whole debate anachronistic to the point of silliness); furthermore a man's very self-respect depended upon success (this being the story of Julien Sorel in Stendhal's *Le Rouge et le noir*), just as the American black cannot live without the esteem of a white majority which he nevertheless, and very properly, despises.

We have seen that there is no genuine greatness in 19th century fiction where the novelist fails to denounce his society for hypocritically or cynically betraying all its own ideals; but (as we shall see when we reach Zola) where this process compromises identity, the novel is diminished.

The classical novel can live with a weak or nonexistent explicit level of discourse but not without the implicit. We may therefore be certain that this latter will not be sacrificed (Stendhal alone suppresses identity but only by anticipating the contemporary novel and being vastly underrated for several generations) in the novelist's attempts to resolve the conflict we have been discussing. On the other hand, of course, where the implicit alone survives the result is the degradingly stupid and sentimental world of popular entertainment (rewarding the good, punishing the evil) or, at the other extreme, the intelligent gossip of famous old maids, like Jane Austen, George Eliot and Henry James, concerned not with what their neighbors do, which would be vulgar, but with their "quality" as human beings. In each case the novelists are poor spectators because the real escapes; in the former instance because it is made to serve the good and obstruct the evil, and in the latter because it is ignored in the interests of good taste or one's dedication to fiction as a craft or both.

Since the implicit level of discourse—identity, the strictly class content of the classical novel—could not be dispensed with, why not attempt to universalize it, to raise it above class? Rather than simply taking it for granted, as does the English novel, why not attempt to demonstrate its necessity, with the demonstration providing the essential explicit level of discourse? In practise this meant retaining the inquiry, the interrogation, the reason, of the picaresque novel and applying it to bourgeois society (or, in the case of the Russian novel, to a feudalism *embourgeoisé*) so as to reveal a social and moral corruption so unrelieved that if society nonetheless continues to function it could only be because there exists, after all, an order, *but an order religious rather than rational in nature.*

This, then, is the way in which the "good" character confronts, rather than simply withdrawing from, an evil society. Goodness consists not merely in middle class morality, but in a sort of sixth sense (conscience usually, as with Rastignac and Raskolnikov; but also whatever it was that enabled Prince Andrey, in *War and Peace,* looking up at the sky from the field of Austerlitz to sense a Meaning to which we others are inattentive) of which the Divine—necessarily invisible in a culture dominated by scientific rationalism—makes use to enter the stream of daily life. Thus, the three greatest 19th century novelists (excepting, as always, Stendhal since, from the point of view of the novel's basic structure, he is a contemporary)—Balzac, Dostoevsky and Tolstoy—are saying that individual goodness might have, paradoxically, a supreme social function since reason (contrary to what the 18th century had supposed) is not only inadequate to the needs of our times (Tolstoy) but can actually lead to crime (Dostoevsky, Balzac).

This is why readers have always, instinctively, attached the highest importance to *Le Père Goriot* in the work of Balzac. Vautrin proposed to Rastignac the most perfect of crimes since not only was detection extremely unlikely, but being a fully rational crime there was no need for feelings of guilt, and Vautrin himself was quite without them. The essence of Vautrin's demonstration to Rastignac is extremely simple. Our society operates to the benefit of a very few who are therefore obliged to rule by force. But since that force is exercised through the legal and financial system it can be successfully concealed, like the machinations of the banker Nucingen which are nonetheless criminal for being legal. The assassination Vautrin proposes to Rastignac is innocence itself in a social system which makes the starving of women and children a profitable and therefore honorable undertaking. Rastignac, unable to answer Vautrin, has no alternative but to be guided by his conscience which, as it turns out, serves him well. All that stands between us and complete chaos—that is, generalized crime, since there is no way we can refute Vautrin—are therefore religious values and those people (the "good") who maintain them even against reason and logic.

In *Le Père Goriot* Balzac remarks, " . . . there is a God and he has prepared a better world for us or this earth is utterly without meaning."[9] It is as though Dostoevsky and Tolstoy, with the barbarous enthusiasm of men living far from what had been the centers of the European Enlightenment (much of which was carried over into 19th century scientism) were saying that the novelist ought to stop being ashamed of concentrating his art upon what, for the scientific mind, was necessarily a monstrosity—identity being simultaneously fact and value—and insist that since identity rests in the last analysis upon religion the novelist should see to it that religious sentiment be authentic rather than (as in the English and sometimes the French novel) a flagrant expression of class interest in the form of middle class morality. Why should this not be done (in a manner reminiscent of what Pascal and Kierkegaard had attempted) by using reason, ironically, to subvert reason? In this way the novelist can afford to be a spectator who misses nothing, and the explicit level of discourse can be developed in full. But then reason overreaches itself; the more irrefutably it is demonstrated that life in our society is impossible for a man of any worth, the more inadmissible such a conclusion becomes. Reason is discredited, and in the resulting uncluttered space of the mind God can appear as a sort of evidence,[10] and identity (individual private existence) is given that metaphysical foundation without which it must disappear, without which, for the bourgeoisie, this earth is "utterly without meaning."

Apart from *Le Père Goriot* Balzac does not go very far in this direction; ordinarily he uses reason in the orthodox manner—in his case, to prove the necessity of a return to the uncontested authority of monarchy and church. In Dostoevsky's novels, however, reason induces men not only to murder, as in *Crime and Punishment* and *The Brothers Karamazov*, but to a kind of hysteria of rationality (*The Possessed*) which, we are made to feel, could bring about the collapse of the whole social order. In *War and Peace* Tolstoy illustrates the dangerous or criminal consequences of the use of reason alone by taking an historical example, the Napoleonic invasion of Russia. If by "reason" we mean the analyses of these events left to us by historians on the one hand and, on the other, the presumably rational decisions arrived at by Napoleon and the Russian generals, then Tolstoy is able to show that the work of the historians is superficial to the point of absurdity while Napoleon and his adversaries were accomplishing exactly the reverse of what they supposed: Napoleon, imagining he was engaged in the conquest of Russia was in reality destroying himself, while the Russians, supposing their retreat beyond Moscow to be a defeat, were in reality taking the one course of action which could have saved Russia.

The critics usually deplore Tolstoy's disquisitions, in *War and Peace,* upon the French invasion of Russia and upon the general question of the meaning of history. They have done this because, lacking a theory which would integrate the novel structurally with bourgeois culture, they place a vastly exaggerated emphasis upon formal values. What Tolstoy has to say about the Napoleonic period is of exceptional interest for it marks the only attempt upon such a scale by a 19th century novelist to demonstrate that the basic categories of the novel can be used successfully to deal with historical figures and events.

The explicit level of discourse in fiction quickly becomes self-defeating where a thesis is being propounded. But where it remains simply critical, not only can it be successfully absorbed into the narrative it is, as we have seen, an indispensable element of the best classical fiction. In *War and Peace* Tolstoy does exactly what Balzac had done in those novels (and especially in *Le Père Goriot*) where he speaks without restraint or illusion about the kind of society the middle classes had brought into being. Balzac talks of the omnipotence of money, and Tolstoy of war, but it is shortsighted to treat one apart from the other. Napoleon was, to a considerable extent, the way in which Balzac's Nucingen and his kind manifested themselves outside the borders of their own country. War is banking carried on by other means. The Bonaparte family was the most incredibly "successful" of the century; it became so rich as to be able to confer upon itself the supreme legitimacy—that of royalty—and so realized to the fullest degree the ambition of the bourgeoisie: public recognition for private gain. For the bourgeois, aristocratic wealth was illegitimate because it had not been acquired, that is, it was not "merited." The underlying structural rôle of wealth in our society is to make it possible for "all" men (who, in bourgeois society, are consequently equal) to demonstrate a "merit" which would otherwise remain hidden or which might not exist at all. If, therefore, money is primarily the visible portion of some inner superiority the means of acquiring it are of little importance, since those means will have proceeded from a source by definition "good." It is one of the functions of the explicit level in the novel to denounce nonsense of this sort, but where this happens we are not much further advanced since the novelist is simply advocating that we show more discernment in determining which persons are "good" and which "evil."

In Dickens, for example, where the explicit level is weak or irrelevant the reader learns nothing of what goes on in Bounderby's factory (*Hard Times*); his "evil" consists not in his conduct as a typical entrepreneur of the period but in the fact that his wealth had not been entirely acquired. He was not the self-made man he claimed to be. If Tolstoy, even though he too deals with identity, is so much greater a novelist than Dickens, it is in large part, because the "evil" of the earth are not always to be found among thieves, prostitutes and union organizers but, equally, among the important or even the mighty. Where Tolstoy looks for the source of Napoleon's wealth, he finds it not in merit (in military genius, in Napoleon's being the "hero of the revolution") but in wholesale murder. Tolstoy shows how absurd it is to attribute the events of the Napoleonic era to the genius of a single man, so that we are reminded somewhat of Marx for whom our society is not the work of particularly gifted individual entrepreneurs; rather, such men were the consequence of what our society as a structured whole had made possible at a given moment. But while Marx's purpose was to elaborate a wider rationality, Tolstoy sought to undermine reason as such,[11] to exacerbate the scepticism which legitimately accompanies any system (19th century scientism, for example) proposing a total rationality with no reference whatever to praxis, to the point where such scepticism, given the increasing urgency of contemporary problems, can be made to topple into the "self-evidence" of Divine providence or, in our own day, into the absurd.

What Tolstoy is saying explicitly in *War and Peace* is that Napoleon is to be judged as being this or that kind of man on the basis of what he actually did (or, more accurately, what the historical conjuncture made it possible for him to do) rather than on the basis of the pseudo-science of history under cover of which a value judgement is being made, that of Napoleon as a great man, a benefactor. What Napoleon did was to commit the crime of war justified by a rhetoric which—since he was the hero of the bourgeois revolution—concealed ambitions which were almost entirely personal.[12] All this is undeniable—as are the views of Vautrin and of Ivan Karamazov—but for that very reason cannot be endured. If the science and philosophy of the historians (which Tolstoy mistakenly assumes to represent the full range of human thought, whereas, of course, it is merely that of a given class within a given culture) are so fallible as to present crime as the work of genius, then we clearly need something more. In the classical novel that something more is, in one form or another, Divine providence.

Once one has rejected the possibility of understanding history in Marxist terms, in terms of human purpose, we are left (apart from the fatuities of scientism) with God's purpose. But then how can we be sure that some evil, say, the Napoleonic campaigns, is not in reality the mysterious working of God's will and therefore a good? The classical novel in conformance with class interests (and consequently on the implicit level) answers that there are good and bad people, the former being those most sensitive to the full viciousness of the world's ways (explicit level) and who find a solution in (to borrow the title of one of Tolstoy's novels) a "resurrection" to a visceral, primitive belief, the latter being the exact opposite—those least inclined to question a social order in which they are often very "successful" and least accessible to a revelation of the Divine. Bad people are the vehicles of the world's evil, while the good, since there exists a providence, need do nothing in particular except abide in faith.

One can appreciate the importance of diverting the student's attention to formal values if the "world's greatest novel" rests upon such a foundation. And yet it must, since *War and Peace* would remain totally incomprehensible to the reader who failed to make the identifications that Tolstoy clearly indicates. We see at once that Pierre Bezuhov and Prince Andrey are apart from the others and that Tolstoy approves of them; in fact, the goodness we immediately suspect in them is confirmed throughout the novel. Similarly, we conceive a dislike for Prince Vassily, for his son and daughter, for Dolohov and for Mademoiselle Bourienne which proves fully justified since most of the misfortune that befalls the two heroes is brought about by this group of "evil" people.

The question arose a moment ago as to how we could combat evil and be sure we were not setting ourselves against some great, inscrutable, providential scheme. The answer was that we can see good and evil embodied in people. But with such an answer we have granted ourselves too much since all we need to do now to solve political and social problems is eliminate evil people.[13] If, unhappily, it is not as simple as that it is because *identity can be concealed.*

So it is that Pierre Bezuhov discovers with horror that he had married a "dissolute woman" but one who, nevertheless, makes a "favorable impression . . . on young and old, on men and women.[14] In the same way the universally popular but nonetheless evil Anatole Kuragin causes Natasha to suppose she is in love with him. Prince Vassily and Dolohov, each in his own way, are consumate worldlings so not only can evil conceal itself, it does so very commonly. In fact, according to Tolstoy, that is exactly what happened in the case of Napoleon and the Russian general Kutuzov. Napoleon, regarded even by his enemies as one of history's great men was a brigand; Kutuzov, in appearance a bungling old fool, was in reality an essentially "good" man who, refusing to engage the French after Borodino, spared the lives of thousands of men and became the instrument of providence for the deliverance of Russia.

In *War and Peace* Tolstoy had the temerity to try to demonstrate what other novelists had taken—or pretended to take—for granted, that the world of fiction and reality are one and the same, that men who actually existed can encounter imaginary characters on the same ground.[15] There are two parallel but interconnected novels in *War and Peace,* each with its own explicit and implicit levels in contradiction with each other. In the novel proper there are many passages where Prince Andrey or Pierre Bezuhov reflect upon the stupid, futile and vicious nature of society (this representing the explicit discourse), and the reader easily overlooks the fact that these reflections must be taken primarily as confirmation of the two characters' identities. A contradiction then arises very like the one to be found in Balzac. Since a highly developed explicit level is indispensable to genuine greatness in the classical novel we are obliged to take it seriously, and yet we cannot. Just as Lucien de Rubempré and old Goriot are destroyed not by their society but by themselves (their identity), so Prince Andrey and Pierre Bezuhov are confronted not by an evil society but by a certain number of evil people. So if in response to the explicit level we ask indignantly what is to be done, the answer is, of course, nothing at all since we, along with the novelist himself, are spectators and not participants. All we can do is try to be accurate in identifying the people presented to us (the detective novel exploits the fact that disastrous errors are always possible) since in that way alone can we appreciate the designs of providence which, once known, we can at least avoid working against.

The main difficulty in extending this scheme to the public realm lies in the fact that, since there is a providence, the only way to be absolutely sure we do not obstruct its work is to do nothing. And although in the case of men with public responsibilities this would hardly seem practicable, Tolstoy suggests that it is for the simple reason that the good receive guidance; since guidance can take the form neither of reason nor of a sign, it consists in a "feeling" indicating infallibly the course of action to be followed. Thus Kutusov often would have been hard pressed to explain his decisions (where he could be said to have taken a deliberate decision), which, nevertheless, as it turned out, were all for the best.[16] Once Tolstoy had settled the problem of extending private morality to the public realm he was free to utilize the structure of the novel proper for history as well. The explicit level becomes his contention that historical processes determine events by making use of individuals whose personal contribution is minimal (just as, in the novel proper, it would appear that bourgeois civilization as an impersonal whole was determining the lives of the characters) while in reality all the reader knows for sure is the "evil" of Napoleon and the "goodness" of Kutuzov which, consequently, become implicitly the determining factor exactly as in the private lives of fictional characters.

The whole design of providence is certainly beyond the compass of men's small minds; what the good are bidden to do they will not themselves understand, and all that matters therefore is their state of being. Hence Pierre Bezuhov can propose, as a practical political measure, the formation of a "society of gentlemen," a grouping of the good to withstand the "catastrophe" of revolution.[17]

The classical novelists are adamant and unanimous (and in this they are the supreme spokesmen of Western liberalism) in holding that no persistent and conscientious attempt to combat the social ills denounced on the explicit level can possibly be compatible with goodness. But, of course, given the implicit level of discourse the very idea of combating social ills is absurd since those ills are in reality the existence of evil people who are disposed of by providence (Napoleon is driven out of Russia, Pierre Bezuhov's evil wife Ellen is carried off by a sudden and mysterious illness) or by human justice, while cases of less virulent evil (Prince Vassily) are dealt with most effectively by the contempt or pity of the good. It is strange, at first glance, that the good must on no account take it upon themselves to rid the earth of its evil even though it has been conveniently concentrated in a small number of individuals.[18] Melville in particular made it his business to warn us on this score. One might suppose that Billy Budd's shipmates would have congratulated him for cleansing the ship of the monster Claggart, but instead there is general if reluctant understanding of the natural fitness of Billy Budd's execution, even though he had not intended to kill Claggart! Captain Ahab is one of Dostoevsky's possessed; his half-crazed determination to destroy evil results instead in the destruction of his ship and crew.

I have been trying to demonstrate that there is nothing in the classical novel that may be construed as opposition, in any real sense of the word, to the bourgeois vision of things. But art can, nevertheless, like children, be indiscreet. What is maddening about the liberal intellectual today as in the 19th century is his refusal to discuss exactly what metaphysics and what politics he might be a party to whilst pretending to be uncommitted; whereas the novel, as it should have, insisted that if we are to be spectators, if we are to look at the crimes of which our society is guilty and if we are to continue to abstain (as a spectator by definition must) then we are all criminals unless the spectacle is preordained by a beneficient God (as for Balzac, Dostoevsky and Tolstoy) or unless it constitutes a reality we can at least know, even though we cannot change it, as in most 19th century realism after Balzac. But if the almost complete abstention of the good character makes more sense than does that of the liberal, the fact remains (as Sartre shows in his book on Jean Genêt) that it is the existence of the "good" that calls into being that of the "evil." Unless passivity is made an indispensable trait of the good, why should they not organize themselves for the purpose of exterminating the evil and inferior? This of course is the solution Western culture has found for its political and economic problems during the past century and a half; it has simply pronounced—though not always in so many words—certain groups or races to be expendable.

All of this amounts to a further contradiction in the classical novel (reflecting, as always, a contradiction in bourgeois culture). The rational examination of middle class society[19] (the explicit level) reveals a state of affairs so appalling—the universal substitution of things for men—that religious values reassert themselves in a kind of self-evidence. The noblest elements of the Christian tradition, universal brotherhood and the like, become a matter of *salut public*, but if we take the refusal to judge our fellows as a particularly precious aspect of that tradition we enter into direct conflict with the novel's implicit content. Identity, since it is a given, can never be changed but only, as we have just seen, concealed; once the evil has been identified the reader forms a judgement of which there can be no remission. Otherwise identity is not a given, and we are dealing not with the classical but the contemporary novel the purpose of which is often and in many different ways (Camus' *L'Etranger* being one of the best examples) to denounce the vile and arbitrary assumption that men are susceptible to being judged definitively, that they are, in other words, fundamentally substance rather than praxis.

In addition to extolling passivity and Christian charity in the good, novelists tried in various other ways to circumvent the contradiction that although the novel is about identity, that is, it invites the reader to sit in judgement, it is proven on the explicit level that, without a general reinforcement of Christian sentiment totally incompatible with the self-righteousness of a moral judgement, our society with the aid of its value-free reason could sink, as it in fact did, to unimaginable barbarism. One possibility might be to encourage the reader to look upon the "evil" more in sorrow than in anger, and after *War and Peace* unmitigated villains like Dolohov and Pierre Bezuhov's wife Ellen disappear from Tolstoy's novels. Evil at first appears to have been transformed from a "natural force" into a motivated behavior. In *Anna Karenina,* Anna and Vronsky commit adultery, but out of the passion they have for one another. Yet the reader knows there is a factor he must take into account which has nothing to do with any moral decision Anna and Vronsky might arrive at as free individuals; in the last analysis he is to judge Anna and Vronsky on the basis of what they are and not what they do.

In the article on Tolstoy in the Encyclopedia Britannica we read: "There is an inevitability about the tragic fate that hangs over the adulterous love of Anna and Vronsky. 'Vengeance is mine, I will repay' is the epigraph of the novel and the leitmotiv of the whole story." But then the article continues in this way: "Anna pays not so much because she transgresses the moral code, but because she refuses to observe the proprieties customarily exacted in such liaisons by the hypocritical high society to which she belongs." What are we to believe? That Anna is destroyed inevitably by a beyond which announces the form its vengeance is to take in the identical dreams of Anna and Vronsky or that she is destroyed by her hypocritical (and hence bourgeois as well as aristocratic) society. This is, of course, exactly the contradiction between explicit and implicit levels we have seen to be peculiar to the classical novel as an art form. Just as Lucien de Reubempré is brought to suicide not by the social order but by that weakness which is his identity, so Anna also is driven to suicide not by her society but because she is evil, however much indulgence we may be allowed to have for her. It cannot be otherwise. If Anna is being punished for what she did (her adultery) rather than for what she is, there is no reason for the awful inevitability which haunts the novel since she could have repented (mercy as well as vengeance being the Lord's). Or the implicit level could have been suppressed, that is to say, the explicit made genuine, in which case Anna would not have been punished "inevitably" by her own "nature," but by society for committing what Dostoevsky's Alyosha would have called, in a hushed voice, an act of rebellion. But in the 19th century this latter possibility was open only to a man capable of restructuring the novel, only to Stendhal whose adulterers—Julien Sorel and Madame de Rênal in *Le Rouge et le noir*—perish not through the vengeance of the Lord but through that of a bourgeoisie frightened silly by a freedom not only of word—this being the extreme but occasionally attainable limit of the liberal's courage—but of deed.

We saw that social problems do not lend themselves to rapid solution simply because evil embodies itself in certain individuals; not only must the good refuse to take Divine vengeance upon themselves, but evil may disguise itself in a fair form. So it is with Anna and Vronsky. But we have also seen that a classical novelist is great as a function not only of the effectiveness of his explicit attack upon bourgeois society but also as a function of his ability to give an appearance of universality to middle class morality; in practice, his ability to render the Divine as tangible as was compatible with an irremediably scientific view of the universe (which meant, in turn, not falling into the mysticism-for-the-man-in-the-street of Balzac's Swedenborgian novels). Hence the vague but "self-evident" revelations vouchsafed the good in Tolstoy, but also the doom which stalks Anna.

The expression "a change of identity" is a contradiction in terms. One does not speak of a table changing into a chair; the table is dismantled (destroyed), and the wood used to make a chair. People are not tables, but for classical bourgeois thinking they are—implicitly—objects. They can, of course, undergo innumerable more or less superficial changes, but it is not possible in the classical novel for us to be allowed to approve of a character at one point and disapprove of him at another (unless, obviously, identity has not yet been finally established). What then of characters like Dickens' Scrooge and Tolstoy's Ivan Ilyitch? Scrooge does not change from a bad to a good man; he reverts to an original goodness which had become masked by a sort of caricature of heartlessness, a consequence of the unhappy love affair of his youth. Ivan Ilyitch, until the time of his death, was the quintessential bourgeois and hence he represented everything contemptible. Nevertheless, throughout his life there are fleeting moments of painful lucidity during which he is at least aware that something is wrong and which betray a hidden goodness brought completely to light by the imminence of death. The only difference therefore between Ivan Ilyitch and characters like Prince Andrey and Pierre Bezuhov is that his awareness of the Divine is longer delayed.

In Balzac and Dickens probity, evil or any other trait (avarice, weakness) important enough to constitute an identity is so indwelling that it is almost always reflected in physiognomy. The signs are there, although they may of course be misread in cases of concealed identity. Why should it not be said that Tolstoy avoids this naivety by placing good and evil "outside" his characters, who are the largely innocent tools or vehicles of one or the other?[20] This may be a "logical" possibility, but it is certainly not a structural one; for where a classical novel is not essentially the discerning of kinds of people, it will be of lesser importance. (Before the structure collapses, however, it twists itself into some fascinating new shapes as we shall see when we reach Proust and Joyce). In his preface to a *Critique of Political Economy* Marx explains that there exist 'categories' (use and exchange value, labor and the like) to be found in all societies but which, nevertheless, are meaningless (not "concrete," in Marx's language) until we have discovered what rôle they play in a given social and economic structure. In bourgeois thinking, on the contrary, these categories are independent elements which enter into rational combinations as determined by natural law. Man himself is one such element. He is possessed of a nature independent of the social structure into which it enters.[21] Since these elements carry their own intelligibility (whereas, for Marx, they receive that intelligibility after their position within the whole has been ascertained) the progress of knowledge is that of the further analysis of what has been timelessly given. So it is with the nature of Anna Karenina whose conduct (her adultery) emanates from (that is, it is the "proving of," the "demonstrating of," this being "freedom" in the bourgeois system, that which distinguishes man-objects from other objects) a nature we are obliged to consider evil since the notion that evil could "inhabit" her is a primitive one, unthinkable after the firm establishment of bourgeois individualism and the rationalism which accompanies it.

We have seen that with *Anna Karenina* it is as though Tolstoy had grown reluctant to attribute absolute evil to a fellow creature.[22] Nevertheless, since we are dealing with a major character in a classical novel Tolstoy was obliged to make clear exactly what Anna was, and this he does at that point in the novel where she falls so seriously ill that her life is in danger. The reader is prepared for the solution to the enigma of Anna's identity by mention, on two occasions, of her feeling a "duality" within herself (see pp. 265, 268), one which frightened her and which is confirmed finally when she says to her husband, "I am still the same. . . . But there is another in me as well, and I am afraid of her. She fell in love with that other one, and I wished to hate you but could not forget her who was before. That other is not I. Now I am the real one." (pp. 375-76). But as it turns out it is the "evil" in her which gains the upper hand while the "good" subsists in the form of a shame so intense that it makes her life impossible, and the Lord's vengeance is carried out.

It is only by entirely eliminating the implicit (that is, what the novel is really about) in *Anna Karenina* that one can suppose Anna to be a sincere and courageous woman brought low by a hypocritical society. The critics, of course, reluctant to admit that our greatest novelist can be at times a bearded old crank straight out of the Old Testament[23] will tend to take this view, but it requires careless reading. For example, when Levin eventually pays Anna a visit he is quite "vanquished" by her, and describes her as "an extraordinary woman. Not on account of her intellect, but her wonderful sincerity . . . " (p. 635). Tolstoy's heroes, however, enjoy the assistance of an "inner voice" or a "feeling" which, in the present case, reveals to Levin that "there was something not quite right about his tender pity for Anna" (p. 635), and very quickly afterward he realizes ". . . he should not have gone there" (to see Anna) (p. 636). The reason he should not have gone is given at once. "Though she [Anna] had involuntarily done all in her power to awaken love in Levin (as at that time she always did to all the young men she met) . . . " (p. 637). Any change in Anna which may seem to take place toward the end of the novel is in reality the more clear emerging of her "evil" until the point is reached where her shame is no longer able to protect her from herself. "If I were immoral I could make her husband [i.e. Kitty's husband Levin] fall in love with me . . . if I wanted to. And I did want to." (p. 688). Given Tolstoy's scale of values only a thoroughly "bad" woman could want to do such a thing; so there is no justification for not seeing in Kitty's attitude that of Tolstoy himself: "Kitty was confused by the struggle within her between hostility toward this bad woman and a desire to be tolerant to her; but as soon as she saw Anna's lovely and attractive face, all the hostility vanished at once." (p. 686-87). Such is Anna Karenina, a "bad woman" but one whose true identity is perhaps more successfully hidden, partly by a "lovely and attractive face," than that of any other character of great classical fiction. She is a pendant to Levin whose appearance and manner—that of a country bumpkin—misleads almost everyone since he is not only absolutely good but, against a considerable part of the philosophical genius of the West (p. 713), absolutely right!

At one point or another in *Anna Karenina* Tolstoy discusses most of the great social and political problems of the Russia of the time. Yet those problems weigh very lightly or not at all in the lives of the principal characters. For example, Levin's existence, which would appear to be almost entirely taken up with the difficulties of introducing into Russia more rational methods in agriculture—a matter to which he is devoting a book[24]—is, in reality, determined by his relationship with Kitty who nearly brings them both to grief by committing an error of identity: she was temporarily blinded to Levin's inner goodness by Vronsky's exterior glitter. Vronsky comes close to destroying Kitty and Levin because he is the man Kitty's father sees him to be, "a little Petersburg fop. They are machine made by the dozen, all to one pattern, and all mere rubbish." (p. 51). Anna wreaks havoc on the lives of her husband, Vronsky, and possibly her son because of the kind of person she is. There is no room for chance occurrences, and the nature of her society (its hypocrisy) has very little to do with it; public opinion would have been satisfied by a divorce, which Anna refuses when her husband offers it, presumably because his extraordinary generosity causes Anna to feel all the more painfully the burden of her guilt and her "evil."

According to the implicit content of the classical novel life's difficulties are essentially those which arise in determining accurately the kind of person with whom we have to deal. In effecting a judgement the moral criteria used must not be too blatantly bourgeois, otherwise the novelist's pretention to being an objective spectator of the real loses credibility.[25] *Anna Karenina,* therefore, is interesting in that Tolstoy places two "evil" characters at the center of attention and invites the reader to forgo one of his liveliest pleasures, righteous indignation, so as to be able to consider Anna and Vronsky with sympathy and understanding, "objectively," so to speak.[26] But of course very few readers would have consented, with Stendhal, to see in adultery not a moral issue at all but simply a comportment, appropriate or not, depending upon circumstances, and Tolstoy would have been the last to encourage such a view.

Anna Karenina is consequently an invaluable document for the study of bourgeois hypocrisy in its noblest and artistically most perfect form, For in a system in which good and evil are qualities of people (rather than forces exterior to man in competition for his soul as in, for example, the Faust legend) one is obliged as a good Christian simultaneously, and hence hypocritically, to plead for indulgence for the sinner and also see to it that he is, where possible, eliminated from society.

In judging the quality of his characters the classical novelist has recourse, implicitly, to a scale of values peculiar to his society or class. If the explicit level of discourse is simply a refinement and elaboration of that scale of values (to the point of founding it ontologically, as does Tolstoy, in a proof of the existence of God) it follows that the novelist will be able to keep the two levels more tightly interwoven than would otherwise have been the case. This is Tolstoy's esthetic superiority over Balzac. It would be practicable with some of Balzac's novels to remove the explicit level, leaving the "novel proper," a much diminished work, but undoubtedly still a novel.

Not so with Tolstoy who gives the impression of placing himself at a greater distance from reality so that the explicit as well as the implicit seems more to have been copied from than contributed to the real. This is perhaps what is most peculiar to Tolstoy's genius: the degree of moral fervor he brings to bear upon a reality of which, paradoxically, he is a detached spectator. However, the more successfully he persuades the reader that his (Tolstoy's) moral fervor is an aspect of reality itself, the more the explicit level will become the mere appearance of opposition to the system as it exists. We have seen that Balzac's readers disposed of various devices enabling them not to notice the extraordinary attack upon their society to be found in the observations of characters like Vautrin and Gobseck; nevertheless there is in Balzac at least the suggestion that the system as a whole—including its economics—might need changing. There is nothing of the sort in Tolstoy. *Anna Karenina,* consequently, is an astonishingly contradictory piece of work: Tolstoy asks understanding for Anna, condemns society for its hypocrisy toward her, and at the same time it is he alone who persecutes Anna by making it impossible for her to be right (as Stendhal's Madame de Rênal is right against the whole of her society) by pronouncing her a bad woman. In a sense Tolstoy is even worse than the society he despises since his moral indignation is real while society's is merely feigned. Tolstoy places

himself in the preposterous position (which he keeps well concealed) of
having to approve the ostracism an allegedly corrupt society imposes
upon his heroine. We saw that Levin strikes many of the other characters
in *Anna Karenina* as a man of little account; his thinking is muddled and
his manners ungraceful. Yet he more than anyone else in the novel embodies the good and the true. Levin's refusal or inability to adhere to the
standards of society gives the appearance of an opposition, of a noncon-
formism, which is in reality the supreme conformism, for it derives from
what we have seen to be the very foundation of bourgeois civilization:
the preeminence of the private realm. Levin differs from others not by
advocating that a different direction be followed but, on the contrary, by
going further in the direction which is already theirs: toward the
autonomy—whether economic or cultural or both—of private existence.
Levin saves *himself*. The revelation which comes to him finally (p. 724),
as to all the good in Tolstoy (except to the women who either do not need
it or are not worthy of it, one does not know which) is of such a nature
that it cannot even be shared with his beloved wife Kitty (p. 740).[27]

The same analysis can be applied to *The Death of Ivan Ilyitch* which is
a magnificent attack upon bourgeois values. But no sooner have we over-
run the enemy's positions than they have to be handed back since the
novel is implicitly, and therefore principally, an inquiry into the identity
of Ivan who proves himself, against all appearances, to have been good,
which is to say, as always in Tolstoy, open to the Divine. Two possibilities have to be ruled out. First, *The Death of Ivan Ilyitch* cannot
be simply the account of a man's conversion, otherwise why should
Tolstoy have *invented* the man, the circumstances and the events? It
would have made better sense to have anticipated the work of someone
like Oscar Lewis by interviewing a man whose life had been comparable
to that of Ivan. But then of course we would not have had a work of art,
that is, a work which both copies and constitutes the real in one and the
same movement. We know what the classical novel as a work of art
"adds to" the real (be it an adultery or a conversion); it adds the identity
of the people involved. So the second possibility to be eliminated is that
The Death of Ivan Ilyitch is the record of how one man became another,
this being inconceivable except in a work of fantasy like *Doctor Jekyll
and Mr. Hyde*.

The Death of Ivan Ilyitch, however, does mark a progress (the
mellowness of age, in part, no doubt) comparable to that which carries
Tolstoy from *War and Peace* to *Anna Karenina*. As in this latter novel he
attempts—thus bogging himself down in a hopeless contradiction—to

curry sympathy for evil. So in the case of Ivan Ilyitch Tolstoy may be suggesting that Ivan is everyman, that each of us has within himself Anna's "duality;" so until the last moment there is hope the good will emerge in all its splendor making possible a final judgement that is favorable. But Ivan could not have proven the existence of what was not already there "inside" him. *The Death of Ivan Ilyitch* is a superb character study, but it is also utterly pointless if we assume that Ivan becomes a different person. The reader is expected to detect in Ivan, thanks to hints that Tolstoy drops inconspicuously here and there, the presence of something which is in a sense foreign, and yet more truly Ivan himself than anything manifested on the surface. This is clearer still in the case of Anna Karenina. Her plight is very like that of the Bolsheviks brought to trial by Stalin during the thirties. The tragedy of those men was that they shared with their persecutors the same Marxist scientism which enabled the Stalinists to accuse them of having "objectively" betrayed the revolution whatever they may have thought "subjectively" they were doing. The accused, therefore, were foreign to themselves; they were, despite themselves, counter-revolutionary, as Anna was, despite herself, "evil"; so that the Bolsheviks wrote their confessions in the spirit in which Anna committed suicide. Both Anna and the accused of the great trials killed themselves *as others;* they looked upon themselves either from the point of view of God or from that of the "laws of history" incarnated in the Stalinists. They were destroyed not for what they did but for what they were, necessarily, for where the existence of God (at least as a being with which one associates an absolute moral code) or of the "laws of history" is ruled out as a matter of principle, there is no possibility of condemning one's fellows since however great the majority that adopts a particular course of action the decision taken remains "subjective" and as such involves an element of risk, a very real possibility of error. It may be necessary to compel the minority to obey, but this can be done without removing its right to oppose again on *other* issues, that is, without imposing upon it a definition (a process which Sartre calls the mineralization of man) which would exclude, *a priori,* the possibility of its being right about *any* issue.

The essence of the Christian view of men, presumably that of Tolstoy, is "judge not"; and yet the whole purpose of the classical novel is to grant the reader the privilege of judging infallibly, like God. The greatness of Dostoevsky is that he partially withdrew that privilege. The absolutely good remain (Alyosha, Myshkin), but their goodness consists primarily in their *refusal to judge.* This apparently insignificant change is the beginning of the end for the classical novel. For that novel came into existence, as we have seen, when Balzac discovered its subject matter to be men themselves as individuals[28] rather than, as in picaresque fiction, the universe and the condition of man in general within it. When one calls into question the possibility of passing judgement as to what kind of person this may be, then of course the inquiry loses its raison d'être, and some other art form begins to develop. To put this differently, Dostoevsky relinquishes part of the omniscience of the classical novelist (*The Brothers Karamazov* is in the first person) to achieve a more ambiguous experience of people and a less indubitable, "unsituated," observation of them.

Balzac and Tolstoy we found to be unremittingly critical of bourgeois society; and yet since they take for granted the practicability of identifying human beings they must also take for granted those moral criteria we use in judging our fellows. With few exceptions, the criteria of both novelists is simply middle class morality, despite Tolstoy's attempts (especially at the end of *Anna Karenina*) to give the deity a sort of phenomenological evidence. Dostoevsky's achievement as a novelist and his greater appeal for most present-day readers may be accounted for by the fact that, while the two levels of discourse remain clearly discernable in his work, the explicit is not as readily put aside by the implicit as is the case with Balzac and Tolstoy. In *War and Peace* Pierre Bezuhov is obliged during the French occupation of Moscow to witness the execution of a group of almost certainly innocent men accused of being incendiaries. A few hours after this horrifying experience Bezuhov, being "good," has his faith reinforced. There is nothing as crass as this in Dostoevsky. In *The Brothers Karamazov,* explicit protest reaches such a pitch (in the chapter entitled The Rebellion) that the ordinary position of the reader, that of a spectator, becomes almost untenable. Ivan's anguish is contagious not only because through him Dostoevsky reminds us that suffering—particularly that of children who can see no end to it because their time scale is not ours—cannot be annihilated in retrospect even if an after-life exists but also because we may not be entirely innocent of that suffering; in other words, it may be too convenient to attribute it to the existence of people evil in themselves.

In the cases of Balzac and Tolstoy, if the reader, as a natural reaction to the explicit discourse, asks what ought we to do, the answer has to be: discover which people have a nature such that they can only do evil. Tolstoy adds that people may well be the victims of their own evil so we must not be too hard on them. But evil remains, nevertheless, "within" them, a part of them; whereas with Dostoevsky it becomes possible to envisage evil as something people *do,* sporadically, for excellent reasons, rather than as a "natural entity" either clearly visible or carefully concealed. Dostoevsky is saying that people do evil out of an obsession with the good. If we number him nevertheless among the classical novelists it is because, although evil in his work is essentially comportment rather than substance, the good remains something trans-cultural to which all men aspire, the self-evident in Dostoevsky being less the existence of God than the necessity for Christian love.

Nevertheless, by granting a kind of innocence to all men (Smerdyakov, in *The Brothers Karamazov,* is a murderer, but Ivan Karamazov bears a heavy share of responsibility for the crime) Dostoevsky reduces the area in which vital identifications can be carried out, and one need look no further for the preference critics have usually accorded Tolstoy (at least until the existentialists began to seek out their predecessors), for to tamper with identity muddles the spectacle. We no longer know exactly what is out there, what we are being invited to view; it becomes difficult to judge, even though it is more important than ever to be able to do so since the explicit has been intensified. Someone has to be made responsible for these horrors before we are obliged to feel that we ourselves may be in some way involved. For if everyone is innocent, everyone is also guilty. ("Who doesn't desire his father's death?" as Ivan asks at his brother's trial).

All of this takes the form of a certain monotony of characterization. For Dostoevsky people differ (and this applies to some extent even to the saintly characters like Myshkin and Alyosha) only in the form taken by their attempts to deal with a self-contempt from which they suffer through falling short of an ideal of goodness which haunts everyone. Old Karamazov, for example, conducts himself very badly, but his evil is not the natural emanation of a "substance"; it is his means of dealing with the contempt in which he is held by almost everyone who knows him. Old Karamazov struggles to become the man he already is in the eyes of other people; so to some extent Dostoevsky anticipates Sartre's analysis of interpersonal relationships. Most readers are surely puzzled to have Dostoevsky suggest, as he does on two or three occasions, that, of Karamazov's children, it is Ivan who resembles him most closely. What likeness can there be between the degenerate old clown and the refined and intellectually brilliant Ivan? Presumably Dostoevsky means that, of all the characters in this novel it is these two who suffer most severely from that humiliation which, for Dostoevsky, is man's estate; and the remedy in each case is so desperate as to be, in reality, a despairing acknowledgement of defeat. Ivan himself is appalled by the conclusion to which reason leads him ("all is lawful"), and old Karamazov's defiant buffoonery (like Ivan's reason, eventually) simply makes matters worse. The difference is that Ivan's humiliation is the consequence of his helplessness in the face of man's inhumanity to man while that of his father results from a life of brutal self-indulgence for which he must reproach himself.

In Dostoevsky then evil is, so to speak, simply a "mistake" which men make either because they have had recourse to reason alone (which, twice in Dostoevsky's work leads to murder, as it does in *Le Père Goriot*) or to the cruelty people have for each other when they are unable to maintain a minimum of self-respect. By restricting in this way the field in which identities could be established Dostoevsky was forced to other structural modifications. How, for example, could he, on the explicit level, denounce with even more feeling than other novelists the barbarity of his society and, at the same time, deprive himself, at least partially, of the implicit level—the elimination of evil individuals—which provides the only remedy? If evil is an act rather than an identity then anyone can fall into it at any time, and there is no hope whatsoever since revolution (that is, "collective reason") for Dostoevsky as for Tolstoy is the supreme evil. The answer is that no one, according to Dostoevsky, can do wrong without being immediately and painfully aware of it. Wrong doing is against nature; so the difference between Dostoevsky and other classical novelists is the difference between Raskolnikov in *Crime and Punishment* and Anna Karenina. Evil is a part of Anna's very being; her falling in love was gratuitous since Vronsky was just another Petersburg fop. With Raskolnikov, on the other hand, evil was a momentary lapse, a momentary corruption of the heart by reason; so while Raskolnikov was happy to spend a good part of his life in expiation, for Anna there was only suicide. The hero of Tolstoy's *Resurrection,* it is true, is able to expiate his crime. But, as with Ivan Ilyitch, this is an instance of the emerging of a concealed good identity. The ability to distinguish infallibly between right and wrong even in the most trivial affairs which in Tolstoy is a privilege of the good (at least after the revelation has taken place) is, for Dostoevsky, an attribute of man as such. Hence the importance of suffering in his work, evil, not being a substantive part of the individual, can be washed away by suffering.

The classical novel is possibly unique among art forms in that it is obliged, if it is to attain genuine greatness, to incorporate a vigorous opposition to the very social class which makes use of it as a means of imposing upon human existence a form of coherence indispensable to the supremacy of that class. From this point of view Dostoevsky would have to be regarded as the greatest of the 19th century novelists; while he much increases the effectiveness of the explicit level by refusing the reader the consolation of attributing evil to certain people so as to rid himself of responsibility, Dostoevsky keeps the balance by increasing proportionally the presence of the Divine. Tolstoy, paradoxically, arrives at the self-evidence of God through a process of reasoning,[29] while in Dostoevsky the reader is made to feel the beyond as an almost constant presence in the humiliation which nearly every character feels sooner or later and which, since it is not the consequence of class oppression (as in Stendhal's *Le Rouge et le noir,* and in Malraux) can only be the result of a universal though unspoken acknowledgement of the "moral law within."

But while it was a noble achievement to have partially restructured the novel so as to prevent the reader from sitting in judgement, the result was fiction very much less "perfect" from the esthetic point of view than that of Tolstoy; and there may well be as Goldmann suggests a close relationship between formal perfection in art and the perfection with which art gives expression to the mental structures of a particular group or culture.[30] Tolstoy is the supreme craftsman of the novel because it is in his work that the two levels of discourse are as fully developed as is compatible with their being tightly interwoven. And yet it would appear inaccurate to attribute to Tolstoy the fullest and most coherent expression possible of the bourgeois vision since we associate with that vision an important element if not of atheism at least of anticlericalism. We shall have to turn now to French Realism after Balzac.

CHAPTER III

We know that in the classical novel man is simultaneously thing and value; in showing a man the novelist can, at the same time, point a moral. The importance of a literary work of this kind will clearly depend upon two factors: first the novelist's ability to "bring his characters to life," an ability which will tend to be a function of the breadth of view of the novelist as spectator. That is, the identity of the hero is put to the test most convincingly where he is made to confront the truly vital issues of his time (explicit level). But, secondly, since the hero is being tested, the reader must be in a position by the end of the novel to conclude, to judge; otherwise the moral of the tale escapes him. However, if the judgement is to be more than a manifestation of middle class morality (always held in contempt by the more honest or humane elements of bourgeois society itself) then the novelist must in one way or another render the Divine (without which a *final* moral judgement is not possible) as real as is compatible with the essentially scientific nature of thought and perception in bourgeois culture.

If these elements are not perfectly combined and balanced the result will be a lesser, but by no means a necessarily insignificant novel. Ordinarily in the classical novel the beyond is kept quietly but firmly in its place; event is discreetly adjusted to identity (in *Vanity Fair,* for example, ridding us at Waterloo of the unworthy George Osborne to the advantage of good old Dobbin); otherwise the novelist can fall into the vulgarity of Dickensian coincidence or Balzac's spiritualism unless, as we have seen with Dostoevsky, an attempt is made to remove identity as a given-proven from its central, dominant position, in which case a whole series of more or less minor structural modifications become necessary. For instance, in *Moby Dick* and *Wuthering Heights,* as in Dostoevsky, the novel as a spectacle is somewhat diminished; again the first person is used to bring the reader closer to what is intended to be less a view of the real than a more intense experience of the beyond achieved by causing the hero (Ahab, Heathcliff) to be a kind of personalization of nature and the elements (the sea, the moors). The naivety of identity as ordinarily used is avoided in this way but only at the cost of entertaining the reader by means almost as debatable—by trying to create the eerie impression of some extra-human presence which, however, is achieved not only by the use of the natural environment but by the almost complete elimination of the explicit level. It is this, of course, which constitutes very largely the inferiority of such novelists to a man like Dostoevsky.

The artist added harmony to the landscape, but the nature of the medium made it seem that he had found it already there. Part of the genius of Dostoevsky and Tolstoy consists in their giving the impression that religious values are already there and require simply to be copied. Balzac, in most of his work, was far less successful in keeping the explicit level unobtrusive, and subsequent realists laid it down as a principle that the novelist would have to be much more scrupulous about removing himself from his work. Vautrin may be impressive, but he is not "real." Anything to be told, in the future, would have to emerge of itself from what had been copied. The novelist was to become, finally, an absolutely irreproachable spectator.

The artist does not give only form to a landscape; a painting is an object we have come to understand as an equivalent for, or a sign of, something else. What gives these particular equivalents a special importance is that they contribute to the reality which, nonetheless, inspired them; so the perspective which the early Florentines invented we can now "perceive" as a part of the real. So it is with identity; it is there, but it was also invented. And just as the artists who preceded Cézanne "copied" perspective, so the classical novelist "copied" identity, but in so doing he implicitly contributed to the nature of "perceived" reality.

But apart from Marx the notion of reality receiving its meaning and, to a considerable degree, its very appearance as a function of the praxis of the group (in more technical language, the identity of subject and object) was foreign to 19th century thought; so there could be no question of the Realists eliminating identity as a given, susceptible to being "placed in perspective" (proven) by reference to some principle of order. There is a cultural subjectivity from which exceedingly few ever escape and then only in part.[1] Flaubert and Zola, whose contempt and dislike for the bourgeoisie can hardly be impugned, nevertheless succeeded only in providing the Voltarian and somewhat more progressive section of that bourgeoisie with exactly the novel it needed, one which achieved its universality not through recourse to more refined and genuine Christian values but simply through the author's self-effacement. In the absence of his "subjective" interference (explicit level) reality can impose itself imperiously and be recognized universally for what it is. The critics have always pointed out that reality being too vast to be encompassed by one man the novelist makes a choice which is necessarily subjective. Thus, some critics held that Zola's choice of the working class as subject matter for his two best novels (*l'Assomoir* and *Germinal*) was biased, while no mention was made of the possibility of bias in Flaubert's choice of the petty bourgeoisie. Perhaps this was because Flaubert had no pretention to being scientific, but perhaps, especially, it was because beneath a certain level of income, sheer brute need (as among the miners of *Germinal*) usurps a place which might have been occupied by that individuality which is the nodal point of the classical novel. At any rate, the real question is not how subjective an author may be (as though there could exist an objective one) but how he positions himself within that cultural subjectivity which he will almost certainly share with everyone else. The question, in other words, is what were the reasons for and the consequences of the attempt of Flaubert and Zola to suppress the explicit level?

The quality of 19th century fiction depends as we know upon the existence of an explicit level, or more accurately—since the explicit level can never be entirely eliminated—it depends upon the willingness or ability of the novelist to elucidate the basis upon which identities are established as a consequence of which he is able to test his hero more effectively. At one extreme there is Tolstoy, the most perfect of the classical novelists because his elucidation of the beyond is not only very thorough, but, since it proceeds from a religious sentiment considerably deeper than that of a Balzac, it can be used simultaneously to denounce bourgeois society and to render characterization more impressive. At the lower extreme there is no elucidation whatsoever; the beyond intervenes mechanically wherever necessary to bring about the triumph of our friends (the good) and the overthrow of our enemies (the evil). One could argue that, in popular entertainment, the explicit becomes the conclusion the reader is obliged to draw on the basis of what he has been shown; namely that the self-regulating universe of bourgeois rationalism can be relied upon to operate infallibly not only in the movements of the planets and the economy but also in the accuracy with which the fate of each of us is adjusted to his worth as an individual. On the other hand, such a message remains implicit in the sense that to examine it is to be obliged to marvel that authors could be that stupid or that cynical. To put this differently, identity is implicit in the classical novel because it is at once fact and value, while for 19th century thought the two are necessarily separate. The best classical fiction deals with this difficulty by testing the hero through the use of moral standards so elucidated or universalized that the reader finds himself accepting bourgeois values as part of reality; much time and effort are required for the hero to become what he already is. In low-brow art the values were very much the same (chastity, honesty, frugality) but they were taken to be so indissolubly and indubitably associated with "fact" (the character concerned) that event could never be too grotesquely providential (last minute arrival of the hero to prevent foreclosure of the mortgage).

What the realists did essentially was insist that fact and value be more conscientiously kept apart; that the novelist stop assuming that the story of a man's life is going to be morally intelligible; that the beyond, in short, is necessarily religious in nature. But this was not enough to bring about a structural change in the classical novel, for what the realist questioned was the results of observation, he did not doubt the ready-made nature of reality and hence the practicability of observing it from an uninvolved eminence. He did not question one of the most fundamental categories of bourgeois rationalism, the concept of the autonomous individual which in the practice of fiction takes two forms: the author himself as omniscient spectator (that is, individualism as ignorance of the fact that the objective observer is the peculiar product of a temporally and geographically located group) and the hero as entity, susceptible therefore to definition and judgement (that is, individualism as ignorance of the fact that identity is not a *fait de nature,* but is produced by others, among them the novelist as spectator).

What happens in the novels of Flaubert and Zola is that not only does identity remain as a given, it is *this* aspect of identity—its inertness—which will be "proven" without exception. Identity, to be sure, is always inert; in any classical novel the hero can prove to be only what he already is. But since his identity—in the work of a Balzac or a Tolstoy—will have a "universal" moral significance it is important that it be accurately established. The resulting evidence presented by the novelist and the testing he causes the character to undergo (which must be painstaking since appearances deceive, since identity can be concealed) constitute the depth and animation of character portrayal. The realist holds the moral significance of a biography to be an unwarranted intrusion, to be unreal; but since for him too reality is a spectacle, since for him too there has to exist a principle of order (without which we get the literature of a Samuel Beckett), that order could only be scientific in nature, it could only be the determinism that regulates the movements of the "atom-individual" of bourgeois society, and the most casual observation of that society reveals those movements to have nothing whatever to do with the wishes or efforts of the person involved. We have seen that in fiction where the beyond is a religious one the novelist had to be careful not to offend too openly his readers' rationalist susceptibilities. Flaubert and Zola had no need for concern in this respect; however, space which in Balzac or Tolstoy would have been taken up by character elaboration is, instead, filled in by the implacable operation of a law which condemns all the characters, rich or poor, to defeat and disillusionment.

There is, in Realism, a diminution of identity—since everyone is a victim—and consequently of the novel itself. To express this differently, identity is "sociological" rather than moral. Emma Bovary proves herself to be a romantic young woman throughout the novel, but she is neither good nor bad; and Homais has come to epitomize 19th century scientism. Anna Karenina is more complex and memorable a woman than her sister adulteress Emma because of the "cosmic" importance of the moral issue. Anna can only prove herself to be evil, but until almost the last moment the reader gives careful attention to everything she thinks and does since it is always possible an error has been made. The novelist consequently must provide as much information as practicable because, although such information can be fully reliable as in the case of a character like Balzac's miser Grandet, it can just as easily be totally and startlingly misleading (and therefore insufficient) as in the case of Balzac's other miser Gobseck, not to mention Vautrin, Anna Karenina's husband and, of course, many others. But when the role of the beyond is simply to pursue indiscriminately all men-objects to their destruction there is no point to concealing an identity, and neither Flaubert nor Zola ever do so to my knowledge in any important work.[2]

The absurdity of the classical novel (apart from the "impersonal" Realists) lies in its conception of man as being at one and the same time morally responsible and an object. Thus, as we have seen, Anna Karenina is doomed from the outset (this being her inertness, her evil identity); yet the reader is expected to condemn her morally, as she condemns herself. Flaubert and Zola proposed to relieve their characters of responsibility. How Emma Bovary is judged will depend upon the temperament of individual readers, and there seems little point in attempting to judge any of the other characters of Flaubert and Zola since whatever they are no meaningful connection can be established between their identity and their fate. Whether a character is "good" (Flaubert's Félicité, Zola's Gervaise, in *l'Assommoir*) or "evil" (Zola's Chaval in *Germinal*), he will be infallibly destroyed, while people like Homais are singled out to be honored for their services to mankind. The death of Balzac's Chabert is almost as grim as any to be found in Zola, but Chabert chose to end as he did, and in his way of dying he simultaneously denounces bourgeois society and attests to the existence of absolute moral values.

We have considered the possibility that fiction's lower reaches explicitly assert the existence of a moral order actively and intelligibly intervening in human affairs, but such a notion is so idiotic it cannot be baldly stated and must be shown through a carefully expurgated reality; it therefore remains to a large extent implicit. Something similar happens in the case of Realism which takes a far more courageous and comprehensive view of the world; for although what is discovered there is not idiotically unreal it is, for other reasons, just as unacceptable. Sartre remarks that Flaubert's work could be called a "discourse on fate."[3] The same could be said of Zola's best novels except that fate is more "scientific," less malevolently determined that not only shall no man meet with his just deserts, but there is a great likelihood his fate will be unjust or even ironic. Realism, therefore, creates an unlivable world; those values our culture theoretically holds in highest esteem (a selfless concern for others, in particular) are precisely those most apt to bring grief upon the people who practice them. One is tempted to argue that in trying to abolish individual responsibility, Realism (Zola, in this case, not Flaubert) makes it clear, in a sense explicitly, that the poor do not go hungry because they deserve to, because their condition is proof of an inferior or vicious identity. This was the source of the French bourgeoisie's sometimes pathological hatred for Zola: not so much what he revealed about the conditions in which the poor lived as his refusal to justify those conditions on grounds that a man's position in society is an accurate reflection of his value as an individual. If the poor do not deserve their privations it follows that the wealthy do not deserve their privileges. But, on the other hand, if the poor are not responsible for their misery, neither are the rich; so if this is to be regarded as the explicit level in Zola it is a feeble one for it grants the bourgeoisie all it really needed—no responsibility for social evils.

After 1789, when the bourgeoisie finally came to exercise that political power which was the natural complement of its economic power it brought openly into being the war of each against all, a war in which each is required to wrest from his fellows by whatever means available the wherewithal to make a material display serving to announce an identity which will be favorably judged. Popular entertainment takes it upon itself to show that there is only the appearance of "warfare" and that, in reality, what happens is that a certain lapse of time (purely formal) is required before the various identities can be properly sorted out and a providential conclusion arranged. This is the implicit level of all classical fiction; one can therefore appreciate the importance of the explicit level which alone distinguishes novelists like Balzac and Tolstoy from the feuilletonistes. For that level consists not in doubting the intelligible adjustment of event to identity (the good, like Chabert and Prince Andrey, may die—something that cannot happen in low-brow art where death is reserved for the villain—but their death has an exhilirating moral significance), but in stating the question: what if there is a discrepancy between goodness in the genuine sense (selflessness) and goodness as generally envisaged by bourgeois society (the careful observance of rule and convention). It is in Dostoevsky's *The Idiot*, of course, that the question is put most forcefully and insistently.

Such then being the importance of the explicit in classical fiction how could two novelists of the stature of Flaubert and Zola afford to dispense with it? The answer is that they did not. The explicit in Flaubert becomes estheticism and in Zola a documented, incontrovertible reality which all men would be compelled to acknowledge. The facts could be established, and they would speak for themselves without the novelist having to intervene in any way. Do the Realists, then, at last resolve the greatest difficulty of the novel, that of inseparably showing and telling in an unfragmented narrative?

Balzac's solution, identity, involves a more or less surreptitious recourse to middle class morality; the spectacle is more or less noticeably interfered with. The paradox of identity is that it should be indispensable to classical fiction, to the art form of the bourgeoisie, and yet, when elucidated, reveal a dependence upon a religious beyond, which that same bourgeoisie had struggled to supplant with an order heterogeneous to mere "subjective" (for instance, religious) values. But when the naturalists tried to eliminate everything extraneous to the real they simply closed themselves up all the more securely within the historical subjectivity of that form of bourgeois rationalism—scientism—which dominated the latter half of the 19th century. They made use of value twice over: first, in their uncritical acceptance of a spectator's universe on the very eve of the coming into being of a "new scientific mind" (Bachelard) for which the manner of carrying out an experiment determines in part the results obtained, and secondly, if the explicit level were to have any effect whatever, the reader would have to respond with an indignation utterly nonsensical if the real unfolds itself in complete independence of our merely subjective wishes in respect to it.

The explicit level then, once again, is both unavoidable and futile: unavoidable because bourgeois society violates as a matter of survival its own political ideology; futile since man, being a knowable object rather than a praxis determining what shall constitute the knowable, is condemned at best, as at the end of *Germinal,* to wait until "progress" brings into being a world more to his liking.

It was said a moment ago that no meaningful connection can be established in Realism between the identity of a character and his fate. But because identity remains as a given-proven (given, since the character is "visible" and, for scientism, manipulated by "universal natural law"; proven, since when the novelist writes he takes an initiative some degree of which he is obliged to grant his characters, otherwise he would differ from them in kind, a notion utterly incompatible with bourgeois humanism[4]) the reader is compelled to weigh the hero's degree of responsibility for what happens; and yet in Zola and Flaubert this is practically impossible, and as a result one is unsure as to what the novel has said. Let me compare typical novels from the work of Balzac and Zola.

There are the usual confusions in Balzac's *César Birotteau,* not only the contradiction between explicit and implicit levels (is it the money-lust of bourgeois society which destroys Birotteau or his character), but also the fact that in preferring death to the dishonor of bankruptcy Birotteau is as much a part of the whole sorry system as are the conspirators who outwitted him. And yet, in another sense, there is not the slightest confusion. We are being told the story of a man who has his weaknesses—he is ambitious without business acumen; he is often fatuous—but he is also probity itself; this is his "true nature," as a consequence of which he devotes his last years to the payment of his debts. On the day of Birotteau's rehabilitation he appears at the stockmarket accompanied by two other irreproachable businessmen, and there, by a strange coincidence, they encounter the villain of the novel, du Tillet, who, in the face of such a concentration of probity is condemned to confront his own evil, while shortly afterwards the gates of heaven open to Birotteau, that "martyr to honesty in business."[5] Beneath the apparent chaos of bourgeois civilization, therefore, beneath the war of each against all, there reigns a divine order guaranteeing that in one way or another everyone will be dealt with in a manner appropriate to the kind of person he has proven himself to be.

It is disconcerting to think that a work in which this sort of nonsense is largely eliminated—Zola's *Rougon-Macquart*—should occupy, and quite properly no doubt, in the history of fiction a place well beneath that of *La Comédie humaine* and the novels of Tolstoy and Dostoevsky. Ours is a society in which the only form of opposition left to the artist is to render himself unintelligible, at least until his death. Zola would have had to restructure the novel entirely; he would have had to do away with identity. Instead he tried to resolve his difficulties in the spirit of the scientism of the day by secularizing the beyond, with the following consequences:

Reality in Balzac constitutes an environment from which a given character "naturally" emerges; the more exhaustive the description of reality the more secure the immediate or eventual identification of character. This identification is of course at the same time a moral judgement made indispensable because rational scepticism overreaches itself leaving us in an uninhabitable world unless we reintroduce the absolute moral values of Christianity. In this scheme reality concentrates itself manageably at certain points (the principal characters) which the novelist can then "show" and in so doing "tell"; because middle class morality is part of the nature of things, it can be seen in physiognomy (Balzac) or in comportment (Tolstoy), or both. Unfortunately reality could not be honestly concentrated at the "point" of a working man or peasant without disappointing results, without revealing that the bourgeois economic order had destroyed its own moral order, that practically the entire human race was unsuitable for treatment by the art form most closely associated with Western humanism.

Zola was not free simply to ignore characterization since this would have left the novel with the explicit level alone;[6] that is, fiction would have disappeared into sociology, philosophy or whatever. His solution (if we take the *Rougon-Macquart* series like *La Comédie humaine* as a whole, as we must) was to convert the beyond into a progressive historical process making a more or less spectacular use of certain individuals. But then characterization, which cannot be simply dropped, falls into a neglect which damages the novel; a classical novel being primarily (implicitly) an account of what happens to people of this kind. It is very much to Zola's credit that he should have made it difficult or impossible for the reader to morally condemn Nana; on the other hand neither can he condemn Saccard the financier nor his brother Rougon, one of the most influential politicians of the Second Empire. On the explicit level of his novels (the "impersonal" showing of a reality so appalling that showing and telling become one and the same) Zola reacts *morally* to social conditions, and he expects the reader to do the same. Yet these values which are so important that without them there would have been little point to Zola writing novels, do not exist in a fictional world which is a copy of the real one! For if Saccard is simply the implement of progress (as is clearly stated in the concluding paragraphs of *l'Argent*) then so is one of Zola's supremely good characters, Florent in *Le Ventre de Paris;* otherwise we owe progress to evil. How do we know, though, that it is not his identity, this very goodness (his unfitness for life in a criminal society) that destroys Florent? How do we know it is not Saccard's devouring ambition of which we learn in *La Curée* that makes him rich? The goodness we are undoubtedly expected to recognize in characters like Florent and Gervaise (*l'Assommoir*) can be neither a sort of "visible extremity" of some natural law of historical evolution (by definition value free) nor can it reasonably exist inside the characters themselves (as in Balzac and Tolstoy) where it would remain necessarily unknown without reference to a creator and a divine order which presumably could have no place in the naturalists' view of things.

Balzac and Tolstoy combine a virulent attack on bourgeois society with reassurance for everyone; for although evil is given and consequently must be proven and eventually, in one way or another, destroyed, no one in real life is evil for himself, least of all the reader seated in remote and innocent omniscience by the novelist's side. Nevertheless religion in Balzac and Tolstoy constitutes a kind of negative perspective upon bourgeois civilization; for although an alternative exists only for the individual (so that the system itself cannot be touched), an alternative at least is there.[7] It has gone from Zola, and in its place we find that weird universe of 19th century scientism (and, in the last analysis, of present-day positivism): a gradually emerging beneficience without a benefactor. No intervention of any kind is possible; one can only abide in faith. Even Zola's explicit determination to tell the truth through what he showed derived from a moral concern which, in a mechanistic-evolutionary universe, could be no more than a personal vagary. The capacity to take initiatives in given circumstances (the more or less conscious choice of spectatorship being an example) which defines the very humanity of Zola and his readers is transferred in the novels to things (the mine in *Germinal,* the department store in *Au Bonheur des dames,* a sexual "instinct" which "inhabits" man and which therefore is usually uncontrollable, etc.) which, in turn, make use of the characters of whom nevertheless we necessarily approve or disapprove since there is no point in identity being a given if it is not also to be defined, however cursory the manner in which this is done. The reader finds himself obliged to morally judge an impersonal historical law, although to do so is impossible. But if he is to judge a person he should have the amount of information provided by a Balzac or a Tolstoy.

We can see then that the contradictions and confusions of naturalism are greater than those of less "scientific" fiction.[8] But Zola was not, for that, deprived of the highest honor the bourgeoisie can bestow—its hatred. It is as though Zola's readers knew better than he did, as though they knew that the iron laws of capital accumulation did not relieve them of all responsibility for the working to death of women and children, that immorality and crime could not exist without *their* morality and *their* legal system, that a better future (or even heaven, as Dostoevsky insisted) could never result in so much suffering not having taken place.

The paradox of Zola is that his finest novels constitute an appeal for a revolutionary praxis which, nevertheless, cannot exist anymore than can the "free" proof of an identity. In *Germinal,* Zola seems to deplore Etienne Lantier's constant temptation to rise, to represent (that is, to betray) the workers in parliament. Yet at the end of the novel, there is nothing else he can do, the alternative, unimaginable even for Zola, being to lose his individuality, to fall into the "bestiality" of the rioting miners. *Germinal* makes it clear that while the importance of a classical novel depends upon the explicit level, its very existence, like that of the bourgeoisie as a class, depends upon the implicit, upon identity, upon an individualism apart from which life is as inconceivable for the bourgeois as the pious Protestant family life of the 16th or 17th century merchant must have been for the feudal lord.

The classical novelist had the choice of working with either the known and the knower or God and the believer, and his choice was both illusory (since the known or God are the products of historical praxes determined to remain unaware of themselves as such) and partially real because the believer is more free to express and act upon values which the realist is obliged to consider subjective. Where such values are those of our society as a whole, where they are, in other words, those to be found on the explicit level of the novel Zola is at one with his great predecessors, the difference being, as we have just seen, that in naturalism value all but disappears from the real which it is the business of the novelist to copy, and it goes to reside in the author and his readers alone. Naturalism, however, being a manifestation of the classical novel, is compelled to identify its characters, some of whom are going to be good; but then we are doomed to living in a world where the good (since, in the best instances, goodness consists in revulsion from bourgeois society) are punished for their admirable qualities unless these qualities are shared by evolutionary laws which in the fullness of time will be able to work their miracles.

Zola's difficulties arose from his understanding that something would have to be done about social conditions, yet since he could not see violence for what it was—working class praxis combating bourgeois individualism and the *pratico-inerte* of capitalism through which it works—he was obliged to imagine a preposterous community of interests between his wishes and historical progress. This naivety (at which Martin du Gard pokes fun in *Jean Barois* and Gide in *Les Caves du Vatican*) did not suit everyone; for the more subtle, for the more refined, Flaubert offered the total indifference to social questions made possible by estheticism. The novel—and, *a fortiori,* all other art forms—does not show in order to tell, but to create beauty; its only "message" is that there is none.

The miracle of bourgeois rationalism is that it enables the educated to inhabit a world of which they are not a part. The historian is not himself historical;[9] the anthropologist is not himself seen by the people he investigates; the "pluralistic" statesman is not himself part of a particular political system. The picaresque novelist, in contrast, is not entirely disengaged from the spectacle; he is not readily distinguished from his hero with whom he had to travel widely to see reality, and his view was contested at every turn by one Sancho Panza or another. With the classical novel, however, the novelist radically divorces himself from the hero who becomes the focal point of a spectacle which can now be viewed in its entirety from an immobile position above and outside reality. But if it is honestly presented, the spectacle is going to be intolerable (since we believe that all men are fully men and then act as though only property holders were human) unless we see in it manifestations of a divine or scientific order, though to do this is to embrace a system we are obliged to find loathsome. Flaubert "resolves" these contradictions by placing the spectator at so great a distance that what he sees is dwarfish and inconsequential, so much so that the only reason for looking is the possibility of esthetic pleasure. The esthete is the astronaut of literature; having left the earth with nowhere to go all that remains to him is to find his former home beautiful.

For Hegel, the spectator *is* the spectacle itself. The whole, consequently, absorbs the observer who achieves perspective not, as in all preceding philosophy and in scientism, by correctly identifying a given from a distance, but by awaiting the end of history (that is, the philosophy of Hegel) at which time the observer, having reviewed the historical sequence of "spectacles," concludes that each represented a different form of alienation. Philosophers and scientists supposing they were discovering a real foreign to them were, instead, bringing the real to self-awareness, the existence of a mind separate from the object being a rationalist myth. Hegel bequeathed to us the very stuff of contemporary thought: time and history having become praxis, and the whole, structure. But he bequeathed to us as well the problem of finding a perspective without stopping history. One solution—that of Lévy-Strauss, Foucault and Althusser—is to suppress the subject, leaving only a structured reality. But then the dialectic, that is, the existence of an historically located and therefore self-interrogating subject determining what shall constitute the real, which one would have supposed a definitive acquisition of Western philosophy is lost to view, and we are back with the illusory whole of scientism created when the subject, by an initiative which he is unable or unwilling to elucidate, places himself at an impersonal distance.[10] The only genuine whole (which is therefore more appropriately referred to, as in Sartre, as a *totalisation en cours*) includes the subject defined as praxis; so perspective derives from the difference between what a free praxis could achieve and the sterility to which it is condemned by the weight of existing economic and political structures, themselves the half-organized petrifaction of historical praxes.

It is the existence in Balzac's work of something like a genuine whole which, for Lukács, constitutes Balzac's superiority over the naturalists. It is true that the "intrusion" of Balzac the "subject" (the explicit level of discourse) is indispensable; however what threatens its effectiveness is certainly not, as Lukács thought, another and negligible element of the explicit, Balzac's royalism, but the implicit to which criticism has always remained astonishingly blind and which can cause Balzac to fall to the level of Victorian melodrama or which at least enables the reader to partially ignore the words of Vautrin and Gobseck on grounds that Balzac's real concern is a more striking character portrayal. But the reader might have argued, as well, that disquisitions such as those of Vautrin and Gobseck do violence to realism; they introduce a contentiousness which has no place in a work of art. The notion that all art is "contentious" (and the novel more overtly than any other) in that it is one of the means by which a society, or a reigning class, causes an inexhaustible reality to render the meaning it needs, could not have occurred to Flaubert or to Zola. Their only option, as they saw it, was to try to eliminate two forms of subjectivity which could becloud the real: that of middle class morality upon which identity more or less narrowly depended; and, of course, what they regarded as their own subjectivity. This latter led Zola, as we have seen, to exclude from the real what he knew to be an inescapable element in the lives of all of us and therefore a part of the real, namely, a concern for others that follows naturally from the rationalists' destruction of the medieval castes and the vastly improved technology in agriculture and manufacturing which made it conceivable for the first time in history for everyone, everywhere, to be provided with at least the necessities.

Flaubert's solution was more elegant: whether inside (Balzac) or outside (Zola) the novel, the expression of wish or opinion on the part of the author is absurd because the beyond is not only indifferent to man, it exists to insure his individual or collective defeat. It was not sufficient, however, that Flaubert establish this "irrefutably" with painstaking attention to accuracy of detail; for the reader might suppose that Flaubert was "subjectively" currying sympathy for his characters, hinting, perhaps, at a kind of passive human solidarity against a malignant overlord. Flaubert had somehow to convey to the reader explicitly, so to speak, the fact that his work was not about anything at all, and he does this by looking upon his novels as works of art, the story existing simply because the artist requires material with which to work. In this way Flaubert arrived at "absolute impersonality." Thus, estheticism is the explicit declaration that the human comedy is foreign to the observer; it is a means of dealing with life without noticing it except for the beauty which is everywhere if we are sufficiently unconcerned to see it.

Although there is no eluding one's historical subjectivity it has been open to the writer since the end of the 18th century to achieve a partial perspective from ahead, to use the "subjective" aspirations of his time, that is, to use a possible society to throw light upon existing society. The work of Balzac marks the advent of the bourgeoisie as the reigning class, and this is reflected on the implicit level of his novels. But, in addition, the ever increasing dominion of exchange over use value (which had begun to spread to the countryside as Balzac shows in *Les Paysans*) was destroying any hope that the triumph of the bourgeoisie might be that of man himself. This is the explicit in Balzac, that subjective protest (or negation, as Hegel termed it) which "totalizes" the real, there being no totality where the real is deemed to exist apart from mind (which is absurd since mind—that is, praxis—determines the nature of the real by organizing it as a function of the historical goals being pursued) or mind apart from the real (which is equally absurd since our habits of thought will seem almost as strange to our descendants as our manner of dress). In a society where men are "equal" but where class distinctions are carefully established and maintained we have grounds for a subjective protest which is also "universal."[11] Our attempt to still that protest in order that the real "in itself" may be made more clearly visible is an initiative the effect of which (and consequently the *goal* of which since the bourgeois ethic of honest intention is really too convenient) is the preservation of a system in which the positivist and the esthete enjoy a privileged position. In brief, since our only choice is between praxes, the objective choice will be that which seeks to suppress the contradiction between a universal awareness that the extremes of need are no longer tolerable and the existence of economic and mental structures (for example, the implicit level of the classical novel) which prevent our using modern technology to satisfy those needs.

There are two "realities" in Balzac, that of scientism, the real as an environment "naturally" producing a person of this or that kind, and the real as it appears on the explicit level, the real as self-evidence, as simultaneously subjective and universal. This is a real totally divorced from any beyond (Balzac's Vautrin is a contemporary atheist in the sense that the religious question does not exist for him) which means that, in some way, it is essentially man's doing. Balzac's subjective protest was to be taken up by Marx and Sartre on grounds that the real is no more than ossified praxis, a *pratico-inerte* which, in our era of multinational corporations, serves to enable an infinitesimal minority to determine the health and standard of living of practically the entire population of the globe outside China.

The explicit level in the classical novel is necessarily, as we have seen, outweighed by the implicit. But it exists, and it is progressive because it replaces the essentially philosophical problems of the picaresque with much more immediate social and political issues. The reader is then free to be so impressed by the words of Vautrin and Gobseck or so nauseated by the life of Tolstoy's Ivan Ilyitch as to wonder whether the beyond in bourgeois society might not be simply an alibi, since the more obvious it becomes that the urgent problems are of our own making,[12] the more desperately the bourgeoisie needs to persuade itself and everyone else that they spring from the working of divine or scientific law, or, better

still, from a combination of the two, from a deity free to adopt his scientifically inevitable persecutions to each individual case. This was
Flaubert's contribution, and it was immense. It enabled the "intelligent"
and the "sensitive" to remain snugly closed up within the system whilst
giving the impression of being elsewhere. Flaubert altered the novel
without touching it. He removed the silliness of petty bourgeois morality
from identity (Emma Bovary's adulteries are not to the point) but otherwise left it intact (Emma is a Romantic and she "proves" this with a
thoroughness every bit as impressive as that with which Balzac's Grandet
proves his miserliness). Similarly, while the explicit level is still there (in
the sense that, for the bourgeois mind nothing is more incomprehensible
or irrelevant than beauty), it is as though it were not since one can read
Flaubert—as most of his contemporaries did—without seeing it. The explicit as protest, having taken the form of literary style, disappears even
from the private realm where Zola had at least retained it.

When scientific questions are extended to a different object—man
himself as well as nature—there is an indispensable preliminary question
which needs to be put: which men are to be the observers and which the
observed; who is to exercise the extraordinary privilege of never having
to inquire into his presuppositions so as to be certain that the question he
puts is not already the answer he wants?[13] In the classical novel the question as to what kind of person we are dealing with is of little consequence
compared to the unquestioned assumption that there are kinds of people
rather than simply kinds of questions.

If men are equal in the eyes of God, equal before the law and before
science (there is no blue blood for science, only red) why must a few of us
have too much and the rest nothing? The bourgeois does better than explain; he shows in dress, manner and speech that he is somehow different
from the common run. But that difference cannot be one of kind (as in
feudal society), nor can it derive from any vital contribution the merchant or industrialist makes to his society (since the bourgeois can and
must be concerned only for himself).[14] The difference must consist in a
portion of "exteriority," a foreign element with which one is born and
the existence of which is proven not only by property but by the bizarre
forms of self-constraint peculiar to the 19th century bourgeoisie. The
bourgeois is that strange creature which takes initiatives—he is therefore
human—but they come from elsewhere, from that piece of nature or of
God imbedded within him, and he is therefore a thing.[15]

One of the most striking aspects of Western culture since Balzac has
been this conception of man as a being at once empirical and transcend-

ental (to borrow Michel Foucault's terms), that is, a creature which is simultaneously an object of study—in the novel, in history and in the "sciences" of man—and the inquiring subject in the form of the novelist, historian or social scientist, although it is not clear how the observer succeeded in placing himself outside his particular class, culture and historical period in order to gain an unbiased view.

During most of the century which invented history, science and Christianity remained ahistorical, and these two extra-temporal points of reference enabled the novelist to regard people scientifically as things and then, in many instances, to judge them thanks to a morality which (whatever the case with the analytical approach to society which made it practicable for the novelist to miss the group for the individual) every educated man had to know was historically and culturally relative.

But the greatest of the 19th century novelists also accepted their historical responsibility to denounce on the explicit level of discourse the abuses of a political system which, unable to invoke divine will as could the *ancien régime,* had unwittingly rendered itself *accountable.* Even though the explicit level is easily discounted when viewed primarily as a demonstration of identity it could, as Zola showed, be disturbing. What was needed—since the criminal selfishness of middle class government and culture is too overwhelming to be ignored—was an opposition which no one would notice, and in estheticism Flaubert provided just that. The sense of beauty became and remains, in every university course in the humanities, a very successful means of critical collusion.

The foregoing paragraphs provide us with the criteria we need to decide what happens to the novel at the end of the 19th century and the beginning of the 20th; in other words, which authors introduce changes structural in nature and which find themselves able to work within the traditional form. Here again, more succinctly, are those criteria.

First, picaresque fiction takes for granted an order entirely separate from man and progressively "discovered" by him. In these conditions ethics can be given only in negative terms; it consists in inquiring into or ridiculing dogmatic and premature assertions as to the precise nature of order. The individual mind, that of the spectator, can be sure only about what will not do; while the primitive group can produce tangible, even "visible" evidence of the beyond and, consequently, a positive ethic.

Second, the classical novel, on the explicit level, retains this awareness of what obviously will not do. But from Balzac onward, the society which the novelist is obliged to criticize is his own, and since for a considerable part of the century the bourgeoisie remained the "universal class"[16] the result was a hopeless contradiction: the necessity of condemning the only conceivable social order. What the novelist did, as we have seen, was to suggest that reason (which was, in reality, the simple acknowledgement of the evident—we shall return to this in connection with the novels of Stendhal) oversteps itself into the absurd or inadmissible. Fortunately, however, there must exist an order (religious or scientific or both, depending upon the author) since we can "see" it in kinds of people. The fundamental business of the classical novel therefore becomes the revealing of identity as a given-proven and as the guarantor of the entire middle class system of values.

Despite wide variations in personal taste critics need seldom hesitate in choosing the very few indubitably great novelists of the end of the 19th and beginning of the 20th centuries; so in dealing with the period of transition between the classical novel and Kafka one's choice falls with little difficulty upon Joyce and Proust. But first it might be useful on the basis of the theory just summarized to see what may be done with an author—Henry James—who it is sometimes said anticipates important aspects of contemporary fiction.

CHAPTER IV

For some, Henry James is to be placed among the greatest of our novelists; for others he is unreadable. Must the matter be left at that? Is the work of the critic necessarily merely that of teaching appreciation in a world from which an appreciating leisure class has largely disappeared, or is it conceivable that he be able to *prove* that James still is or is not readable. Such proof will obviously be very different from the kind one expects from the physical sciences since the object of inquiry is a human being like ourselves, that is, a man engaged both as an individual (although this aspect of the question does not concern us) and as a member of a given collectivity in pursuing certain goals about which, however, he will not himself be all that clear since, like all of us, he will work not only consciously, but also in part nonconsciously or unconsciously. In examining the writings of such a man, therefore, we must try to determine what his goals (as a member of a given social group) were. In doing this we must bear in mind, of course, that his work can never constitute a "fixed object," a given, in the scientific sense; we inevitably view it in the light of the goals we ourselves are pursuing. The only conceivable "objectivity" in these circumstances is to be certain, first, that our goals are shared by the great majority of people living on this planet (or would be shared were people fully informed about such matters as the way in which the multinational corporations operate), that our goals are comparable to those of the Enlightenment, that is, imperiously suggested by the historical conjuncture, and, second, that we are scrupulous in respecting the facts (which, in the present case, will be largely the text). However, an interpretation based on these facts *must* be proposed otherwise we fall into the stultifying quasi-scientific fact fetishism of the academic which, of course, is by default an interpretation and which holds that the greater our fund of information of whatever nature about a writer and his work the deeper our esthetic pleasure will be; in other words the purpose of art is beauty, and this, mysteriously, is not regarded as an interpretation peculiar to a given group.

Here is the first sentence of James' *Portrait of a Lady* (which I have chosen because it is often referred to as his masterpiece). "Under certain circumstances there are few hours in life more agreeable than the hours dedicated to the ceremony known as afternoon tea." I read this to a class and one of the students said, "He's being ironical." Were he to read the novel he would discover that it continues in this vein, but that James is not being ironical. How am I to explain to a class exactly what James is doing? Every university teacher knows that students arrive at the university today having read precisely nothing except, which comes to the same thing, what is forced upon them in high school.[1] Is the teacher then to decide, heroically, that his job is to raise these deprived people to his own level of universal appreciation? To assume, in other words, that he is right and they are wrong, that their contemptuous irreverence blocks their understanding rather as the 19th century working class perversely refused to understand the iron laws of economics? Or, inversely, is the teacher to see that the teaching of anything but irreverence for the values of our civilization is a betrayal of his responsibilities as an intellectual?

Teacher and students alike have their vision distorted and its range restricted by their historical and cultural anchorage; however, no one can, with any honesty, fail to see that our very "anchorage" forces upon us a certain number of perfectly natural, inescapable convictions which then enter into conflict with the way in which our political and economic system functions. There is a universalism we derive from science (discoveries in medicine are made for mankind) which is severely cramped by the "particularism" of middle class civilization (such discoveries benefit a tiny minority of the world's population).[2] We know that in the greatest works of 19th century fiction this contradiction (between explicit and implicit levels) must be found otherwise the novelist is not seeing really whole. How is it with James? Referring to his heroine, Isabel Archer, in *Portrait of a Lady*, he writes:

> In the current of that rapid curiosity on which she had lately been floating, which had conveyed her to this beautiful old England . . . she often checked herself with the thought of the thousands of people who were less happy than herself . . . What should one do with the misery of the world in a scheme of the agreeable for one's self? It must be confessed that this question never held her long.[3]

If it "must be confessed" then the question ought to have preoccupied her more. In any case, the inevitable liberal acknowledgement that all is not perfect having been made, James is free to return to what really matters—the kinds of people we are dealing with. One of them, Mr.

Touchett, appears to be blessed with all the qualities we find admirable; he is wise, kind, generous and so forth. But he is only incidentally a wealthy banker; so the way in which he functions within his society, the way in which he most deeply affects the lives of others is of no consequence. The unspoken assumption of the whole classical novel is that a distinction is to be drawn between what a man is and what he does; so that, in the present instance, what James calls the "misery of the world" can have nothing whatever to do with banking since that is the calling of such sterling figures as Mr. Touchett. (A banker can of course be a blackguard, like Balzac's Nucingen, but this is a matter of the chance distribution of identities.)

If one holds that the novel cannot deal with banking, this is perfectly true, and this is also why the novel is, or should be, looked upon as an art form which has contributed enormously to the domination of our society by middle class culture. We have been led insensibly to regard as normal the astonishing fact that middle class art should be, by its very nature, unable to deal with those activities (it can only deal with people divorced from their genuine social roles) to which it owes its very existence. It is as though, in the *chansons de geste,* a warrior could have existed somehow "in himself," quite apart from his prowess in battle which would have had little or nothing to do with either his social station or his quality as a man. The study of the economy requires specialists of course, but so did the manufacture of swords and chain mail, without it being argued that warfare should be left to the artisans. The difference is that the economy functions to the advantage of a very few private individuals whose culture, nevertheless, in its struggle against feudalism brought into being the idea that men everywhere (for reasons to do with the universal nature of scientific thinking and the universality of human labor upon which—well before Marx—the wealth of nations was seen to rest) are the same. It was therefore indispensable to be persuaded that the few who occupied the commanding heights of the economy never took initiatives that might reinforce and perpetuate the inequalities and injustices to be found throughout the system; they were simply the instruments of economic law. Consequently, in their private lives the novel, to be consistent, could not represent them as taking genuine initiatives (as being free) but only as manifesting qualities of soul which would make it "natural" that they enjoy exceptional privileges in an egalitarian society.

With the exception of *The Princess Casamassima* (which we will come to in a moment) the explicit level in James is far less the "miseries of the world" than it is the threat of conventionality. This theme has great possibilities which, however, can only be realized on condition the novelist see identity itself as convention. Needless to say this is not the case with James (Stendhal alone in the 19th century, as we shall see, achieves this); so what happens is that the explicit becomes trivial and leads in turn to triviality on the implicit level. James uses the basic structure of the classical novel as it existed even before the modifications brought about by Flaubert and Zola; he simply infects it with a strange elephantine *légèreté* by trudging about interminably within his characters' "inner realm" for the purpose of determining not so much their moral quality as their degree of intelligence, sensitivity and general refinement. The reader then naturally supposes that James had taken from Flaubert and Zola at least their contempt for middle class morality (a morality one accepts in Balzac and Tolstoy because of the superb development of the explicit level) and that his explorations of character are intended to suggest a certain scepticism as to the likelihood of our being able to judge with absolute conviction. Nothing could be further from the truth.

The Portrait of a Lady is just that, a human being presented (as in pre-cubist art) as though time and movement did not exist. For in the classical novel time elapses and people move about so that a timeless and inert identity can be either confirmed as originally "drawn" (Isabel Archer, Ralph Touchett) or so that what at first appears to be a portrait of this kind of person can eventually—and dramatically—be shown to have been the portrait of someone very different, the difference usually being no less than that between good and evil, as in the instances of Osmond and Madame Merle. Except that from James we get only the secondary manifestations of good or evil (independence or conventionality), as though their grounding in the Christian religion did not exist or was of no consequence. It is primarily this refusal to elucidate or even to mention the necessary basis in religion of the moral judgements of character which gives James' work its massive emptiness; for to honestly confront the religious question involves, as we have seen, confronting the rationalist alternative, and then, even though reason is shown to overstep itself, it at least gives the novelist the opportunity to see his society whole.

If the explicit level in James is, for the most part, a criticism of conventionality, this relative trivialization of the explicit is precisely what makes a conventional novelist, and James is a conventional novelist except for his incredibly irksome adventures in characterland where, from time to time, the reader must be offered a moral monster if the trip is to be worthwhile. Yet if James gives the reader this, he falls into the vulgarity of melodrama (since a full development of the explicit was closed to him) unless he simply suggests the existence of unspeakable evil while concentrating the readers' attention upon its fair envelopment.[4]

I have argued that Balzac brought into being the classical novel by discovering, in identity, a means of simultaneously showing and telling. James carries on, in *Portrait of a Lady,* by warning us that people who appear to be of a kind capable of happily and quietly transcending bourgeois society through estheticism (Flaubert's invaluable contribution) may, in reality, be merely seeking its recognition; they may be, as in Osmond's case, vulgar fortune hunters rather than universal appreciators. The heroine, Isabel Archer, is exceptionally intelligent and sensitive (that is, accurately and sincerely appreciative) without (as is usual in the classical novel—Rastignac's "superiority" for instance) the reader being able to see what is particularly intelligent about anything she says or does. In fact she does a stupid thing by marrying Osmond, by being taken in by a very elaborately, it is true, concealed identity. James appears to be saying that reluctance to conform is a good and courageous thing but extremely hazardous; witness Daisy Miller's death, Hyacinth Robinson's suicide and Isabel's marriage. After Flaubert and Zola the explicit could no longer figure as blatantly as it had in Balzac; and although "impersonality," as we saw, simply opens the way to the expression of other forms of the writer's subjectivity of culture and class (estheticism in Flaubert, scientism in both him and Zola) at least it eliminated the silliest manifestation of that subjectivity, middle class morality. James however retains even that with the result that the explicit and implicit levels at times almost coincide; for of course it was difficult for the most priggishly conventional of 19th century writers to denounce the life-quenching potential of conformism. For example this, presumably, is what is wrong with the two villains of *Portrait of a Lady,* Madame Merle and Osmond: "Her [Madame Merle's] great idea has been to be tremendously irreproachable—a kind of full-blown lily—the incarnation of propriety. She has always worshipped that god" (p. 446). Yet how can the reader not see that much the same can be said of our heroine: ". . . they were married, for all that [Isabel and Osmond] and marriage meant that a woman should cleave to the man with whom, uttering tremendous vows, she had stood at the altar" (p. 441). In Isabel's mind, ". . . he [her husband] was her appointed and inscribed master" (p. 379). ". . . almost anything seemed preferable to repudiating the most serious act—the single sacred act—of her life" (Ibid.). "For the moment Isabel went to the Hotel de Paris [to visit Ralph Touchett] as often as she thought well; the measure of propriety was in the canon of taste, and there couldn't have been a better proof that morality was, so to speak, a matter of earnest appreciation" (Ibid.). Ralph Touchett says to Isabel that she thinks a great deal about "what seems right," to which she replies "of course one must" (p. 471). Is James on Touchett's side here? He can't be, since according to James' own notes (p. 485) Isabel falls innocently into Osmond's trap. She is our heroine with whom almost all the men in the novel are in love. She must, therefore, as in the novels of Balzac and Tolstoy, represent a recommended alternative, a means of throwing into greater relief whatever is being morally condemned. And yet, obviously, Touchett is right; so if James is to avoid the preposterous situation into which his pusillanimity has led him—the risk of the reader seeing there isn't much to choose between Isabel and her husband—then Osmond has to be evil in the old, naive, brimstone sense, and so he is.[5] But what of Madame Merle? On page 424 we read: "She [Isabel] asked herself, with an almost childlike horror of the supposition, whether to this intimate friend of several years [Madame Merle] the great historical epithet of *wicked* were to be applied." Yet in the same chapter we find Madame Merle saying: "I don't believe at all that it's [the soul] an immortal principle. I believe it can perfectly be destroyed. That's what has happened to mine, which was a very good one to start with; and it's you I have to thank for it. You're *very* bad" (p. 427). Madame Merle eventually acknowledges her "wickedness" to Isabel and punishes herself by voluntary exile to America (p. 456). But is her "evil" an act or series of actions, or is it her identity ("soul")? It is necessarily the latter, or, alternatively, she is an example of a concealed good identity. James is vague. In any case an original good identity could not have been "destroyed" as Madame Merle suggests, or identity could not be a given. And if it is not given, then the classical novel becomes unintelligible. For if an identity can be destroyed (and, therefore, presumably, created as well) by whatever means, then the moral of the implicit level of the classical novel necessarily shifts from the manner in which identities are confirmed or revealed to an examination of those forces creating or destroying them. Thus, the classical novel would have had to be about those social, political and economic conditions which produce or destroy identities (which, consequently, could not have been given).[6] But then, of course, the classical novel would have been reduced to its explicit level, that is, it would not have been a novel at all.

James, then, trivializes the implicit level of discourse by using a criteria for judgement, propriety, intelligence, sensitivity, and so on, rather than genuine Christian virtues as they appear in Balzac and Tolstoy. But since James also and necessarily trivializes the explicit into a criticism of those who allow themselves to be "ground in the very mill of the conventional" (as is said of Isabel, p. 470) he is unable to create sufficient contrast between his kinds of people and has to fall back upon good and evil in the absolute sense. He does this however "without noticing it," without a thought to elucidating the grounds of his judgements; so paradoxically there is in James a streak of low-brow sensationalism since evil is an inexplicable visitation. Osmond who in real life would have been a pathetic nonentity becomes frighteningly sinister, almost someone strayed from *A Turn of the Screw.* The good also, stepping out of the *bibliothèque rose,* may well figure blandly and unaccountably in, of all places, millionaires like Touchett and Verver.

James' achievement in the history of fiction is to have introduced taste as a vital criterion while retaining morality in the trivialized form of the diabolical at one extreme and, at the other, a petty, punctilious moralism very close to the conventionalism of which he is alleged to be very critical.[7] Fleda Vetch, of the *Spoils of Poynton* is an excellent example. It is thanks to Fleda's impeccable taste that Mrs. Gereth raises her from unmerited obscurity to a more fitting social position. But then Fleda's equally impeccable sense of what constitutes honorable conduct brings about the catastrophe of Owen Gereth's marriage to the tasteless Mona. What then is the significance of the burning of Poynton and all its treasures? It cannot be that Fleda's moralism was stupid (as it would appear to the ignorant student and which, of course, it was) since James, as he makes clear in his preface, fully approves of everything Fleda does. The destruction of Poynton indicates that Fleda was right to place honor above "things," but this cannot be the essential message, otherwise *The Princess Casamassima* and much else in James becomes almost meaningless and the weakness of the explicit in his novels very difficult to understand. So the real significance of this event is that, while Fleda's meticulous morality had unhappy consequences, at least Poynton's beauty would not be desecrated by entering into the possession of people unworthy to live there. The beyond, in Dicken's *Little Dorrit,* causes the Clenham house to collapse upon the villain Blandois so that moral evil may be destroyed. James' deity is more refined, and he burns down Poynton so that the tasteless, ungracious, unvirtuous Mona, along with the too "unscrupulous" Mrs. Gereth might be punished.

It will be recalled that the only hope of achieving some degree of objectivity in the study of literature is for the reader to be sure that the conditioning he has inevitably undergone as a member of a privileged social class (his particularism, one example of which would be identity and all it represents in the classical novel) does not becloud the universalism which he owes to that same social class and which finds one form of expression in the explicit level of the best classical fiction. Ours is a culture which simultaneously produces racism (that is, a means for the feeble-minded to effect infallible identifications) and moral revulsion from it. But if that revulsion is not to degrade itself to the hypocritical indignation of the liberal then it must seek allies in the "universal" camp of the underprivileged which is represented in some degree at least in the university by increasing numbers of barely literate students. But can the novel be made to make more sense from their angle of view than from any other? Is their position the most objective one? In brief, who is right, Lionel Trilling explaining that James' *The Princess Casamassima* is one of the world's great novels or the deriding or befuddled illiterate student?

That a man should devote his life to the study of one or another of the physical sciences could teach us something about his personality and a great deal about the culture to which he belongs. But those subjective elements which the scientist inevitably brings to his inquiry are of no importance since the results, given in terms of quantity, will be irrecusable. It is true, of course, that primitive peoples do not understand scientific procedures. Even if they could (without ceasing to be primitive) they would find them grotesquely irrelevant to everything that really matters, and they would be right to do so were it not for the tragic fact that no primitive culture is any longer viable, or will be for very long. Science, consequently, although unintelligible to some, remains universal in the sense that it has made itself indispensable to the survival of the race. The question is not whether to do away with science and technology, but rather who is to use them to what ends. It is at this point that literature has a word to say since the question is no longer a scientific one.[8] That being the case, there will be no possibility of universal agreement on the basis of the quantifiable inert, but there will remain a sentiment, as easily obscured as it is widespread, even—or perhaps especially—among the ill-educated, a sentiment derived from the incredible achievements of scientific technology that there are no *a priori* limits to human praxis except those fixed by ideologies (themselves derived from science: positivism, scientism, liberalism) the effect of which is somehow always to preserve the system as it functions and however it functions at a given moment.

Thus nothing could be done about conditions of working class life in the 19th century because of the iron laws of economics, and similarly, according to James and Trilling, nothing much can be done about our political system since "the monuments of art and learning and taste have been reared upon coercive power." So the hero of *The Princess Casamassima* "finds that he is ready to fight for art—and what art suggests of glorious life—against the low and even hostile estimate which his revolutionary friends have made of it, and this involves of course some reconciliation with established coercive power."[9] When one thinks that Trilling's essay appeared shortly after World War II his "of course some reconciliation" is priceless. "Coercive power" in the shape of German and Italian fascism had just produced some forty million corpses across the world or, more accurately, Western industry in its imperialist phase[10] confronted, as it frequently has been, by the breakdown of parliamentary cretinism had recourse to overt coercive power to guarantee itself a stay of collapse. Trilling's essay reminds one of Chiang Kai-Shek trekking off to Formosa with crates of art treasures salvaged from his own country whose ruin he had done so much to bring about. However, little could be salvaged from Coventry and Dresden; so the liberal esthete sends his art off to war as the industrialist proudly sends his son.

According to Trilling, "we of today can say that they and their relationship [that of Paul Muniment and the princess] constitutes one of the most masterly comments on modern life that has ever been made"; or again, *The Princess Casamassima* is "an incomparable representation of the spiritual circumstances of our civilization."[11] If, as we have seen, objectivity can be attained only to the degree to which an observer is able to liberate himself from the grip of an ideology which is class- or nation-serving, then Trilling's preposterous judgement of *The Princess Casamassima* follows from his confinement to a subjectivity which becomes more aberrant as the historical period which produced it (the Enlightenment, entrepreneurial capitalism) recedes further into the past; so the more unmanageable contemporary reality becomes, the less of it the liberal is prepared to see. A good part of the greatness of *La Comédie humaine* lies in its denunciation of the anarchy of bourgeois society. For James, anarchy threatens the existing capitalist order from outside and it ought not to prevail because our cultural heritage, the world of art, is part of that order. James and Trilling consequently have it all backwards: *their* art and *their* culture become universality, while genuine universality is turned into the particularism of a small group of people whom we can understand (the liberal always understands) but who should do as does Hyacinth Robinson the hero of *The Princess Casamassima* and decide in favor of "what art suggests of glorious life." Hyacinth, therefore, is exactly the good poor in Dickens; not a tragic figure as Trilling would have him, but a dupe.

It is frequent for the pseudo-scientist to discover an aggressive instinct in man which is simply the centuries long aggressiveness of European man. When James and Trilling find in culture a supreme value, they find what has been, since Flaubert, put there by a society which, when it comes to esthetic spontaneity and inventiveness or any of the forms of sensuous creativity, is probably the most sterile in the history of humanity. Its only *original* art form (the novel) is addressed to a specific class within an "egalitarian" society; and this contradiction is dealt with by arguing that, while men are equal, they are of different kinds, and since a particular kind is always a determinable given, it is permissible to start with identity and work outward to the collectivity (to political issues) which, necessarily, is simply a conglomerate of identifiable particles. It is therefore possible, as we have seen in examining the work of Balzac and Tolstoy, for the classical novelist to make political statements on the basis of an analysis of character. By virtue of never questioning the assumption—which by now has become childish—that the individual precedes the society to which he belongs, the intellectual can function happily within *any* society, including the Nazi.

According to Trilling, Paul Muniment and the princess are what we would today call political activists not because industrial society renders life intolerable for the great majority but for reasons to do with their characters: the princess suffers from guilt and self-hate; Muniment seeks power.[12] The impression given, consequently, is that men are driven to revolt not because there are excellent reasons for revolt (which we all understand, otherwise the explicit level of great classical fiction would be unintelligible to us) but because their characters are defective. In contrast, those professors who quietly pursued their appointed cultural rounds while McCarthyism reigned over a stupefied America and while international CIA thuggery consolidated the American Empire had no defects of character; they were simply understanding coercive power. But since that power might easily have destroyed Ruskin's Venice, James' bric-a-brac and Trilling's research facilities, culture exists not merely as a more effective distraction than most but as the means of establishing qualities of personality which are innate (though proven) and which consequently justify social and economic privilege.

Fleda Vetch's taste is regarded necessarily by James as inborn; otherwise man must be redefined as praxis, dealing as best he can (in some instances by the development of taste) with a situation in many respects unique. The structure of the classical novel forbids such a view since not only could the novelist not have used a "situation" for the purpose of simultaneously showing and telling (only Sartre has attempted this, in his book on Flaubert) he would have had to regard *himself* as praxis (rather than entity, rather than someone with the "gift" of language and of omniscient insight into "character"). That is to say, he would have had to ask himself what practical goal he had set himself in his fiction: given that ours is a class society, which group had he chosen to work with against which other groups. In the same way Trilling, as an educator, necessarily looks upon students as the classical novelist looked upon character: the acquisition of culture by the student confirms an inborn identity. At a very early age a child—depending upon the cultural level of his parents—either does or does not acquire an effective use of syntax. If he does not the educational system eliminates him. Logically, in an egalitarian society, the function of school would be to eliminate inequalities of home education, not people, but if people are to be eliminated it can only be done on the assumption, which is that of the implicit level of the classical novel, that it is people rather than situations that are defective.

Hume's contribution to philosophy consisted in raising doubts as to whether a clear line can be drawn separating the "spectacle" from what thought and perception may do to it to make it assimilable. It was not yet possible, given the promise of science and the work of Newton, to question the existence of a separate, ready-made meaning which the mind, ideally, would simply record or reflect. But that is the difficulty: if there takes place a mere reflection or reduplication, we are no further advanced; we are left with reality alone, though this is absurd since we are *aware* of reality. But if that awareness cannot be a reduplication what is the nature of the alteration it effects, and how could any alteration be made compatible with 19th century science for which the real is what is progressively discovered and consequently something that pre-exists and is unaffected by the manner in which we take cognizance of it. The two solutions to this dilemma—materialism and idealism—were so clearly unsatisfactory that there was room for a school of thought whose basic tenet was that no solution should be attempted. But positivism, despite itself, is an historical phenomenon; what it did was simply to borrow from materialism its confidence in science and from idealism a readiness to acknowledge that what science discovers may not have any objective existence "out there." Science could easily be no more than a scheme for saving the appearances, but, according to the positivists, it at least does that more satisfactorily than any other conceivable scheme.

To put all this differently, is science something men do (somewhat as, according to Feuerbach, man created God only to imagine it had happened the other way around) or something they "receive"? Despite the prestige of science, the enthusiasm and unanimity with which middle class intellectuals have always clung to the latter option is surprising in view of the extraordinary contradictions to which it leads, the first of them being the necessity of denying that an option even exists, even though denial would appear to be a choice. This is not so, however, according to the positivist; for there exists, if not an "objective" world, at least a "verifiable" one; there are the facts, which every reasonable man acknowledges or will acknowledge when they are established by research or experimentation. But the facts that eventually emerge from the progress of science must be of a nature such as to enable us to deal successfully with increasingly desperate social and economic problems; otherwise the abstentionism of the positivist in respect to these questions becomes incomprehensible. The facts, in other words, must reveal us to ourselves; they must make possible an ethic.

But a "discovered" or scientific ethic is a contradiction in terms since what is discovered would have to be obligatory in the deterministic sense, in which case men must have always operated in accord with it. Alternatively, that ethic is chosen, in which case positivist abstention is already an ethic, and one based on class interests. We cannot turn around upon ourselves and "see" what "produces" us, for that would constitute an historically situated initiative from which whatever was "seen" would receive its significance as a function of praxis operating as best it can within a given structure of the *pratico-inerte*. Man must therefore be entirely free (except, of course, for the limitations imposed by the freedom of others and by the *pratico-inerte* which that freedom, through time, brings into being), or we are left with that preposterous hybrid which is the subject of the classical novel: man as a free object. He (or it) would appear to have his origin in Protestantism for which a man discovers, or proves, his election in his wealth and high moral standards. But with the development of the factory system and of free thought, it became increasingly awkward for the well-to-do to attribute their prosperity to God. Luckily scientific determinism was there to explain that even though wealth would appear associated with the

wholesale exploitation of women and children—that is, with *free* enterprise—the fact is that the entrepreneur was impelled by an opacity within
him over which (fortunately for society as a whole, the alternative to
capitalism being anarchy, the squandering of our cultural capital) he had
no control.

The existence of the classical novel depends upon the novelist not seeing the absurdity of his conception of man as being free, but free only to
demonstrate or to try to conceal an in-dwelling, pre-established identity
which is therefore a thing, yet one susceptible, unaccountably, to moral
judgement. At the very core of the art form we associate with the
bourgeoisie there is that confusion of "is" and "ought" which the
bourgeois intellectual attributes to degenerate obscurantists and
troublemakers like Marx and Sartre. How can the literary critic, as he
commonly does, urge his readers to be edified by the career of a fictional
hero whose moral decisions flow automatically from the kind of person
he is? How can there be a moral lesson concerning courage in *Lord Jim,*
for example, when it is Jim's nature to be courageous? The only lesson in
this novel is that fate may be capable of so arranging events that a man
can have the wrong identity thrust upon him; so Jim may appear to be a
coward, but Conrad makes it clear in describing the abandonment of the
ship that Jim stood apart from the others, was horrified by what they
were doing and found himself in the lifeboat by error since, as Marlowe
repeats: "He [Jim] is one of us"; that is, a white man, and therefore
necessarily courageous, unlike Orientals and half-breeds.

When the critic discusses moral decision in the classical novel he places
all the emphasis upon an imaginary freedom in the characters; Flaubert
and Zola were able to be more real simply by reducing the exercise of that
"freedom" to almost nothing. Why, in the "rationalist" middle class
scheme of things must man be, unintelligibly, both a thing and free?
Surely it is because, a pre-Marxist economists saw and proclaimed,
human society rests upon labor. But then, if bourgeois society (that is, a
society based upon the elaboration, both material and cultural, of the
private realm through profit) were to survive, labor had to be at once free
(the worker had to be free to sell or withhold his labor from the market)
and a form of merchandise (a thing), so that the capitalist could pay for
it in full.

This is Marx's starting point; for if labor can be paid for in full, as we
pay for an object, then it is impossible to explain how—since the
capitalist has of course paid in full for his machinery and raw
materials—at the end of the manufacturing and marketing process there

can be a surplus of value from which the capitalist draws his profit. The answer is that man is not a commodity, not a thing; so he cannot be paid for in full unless the entire surplus value is returned to him—in which case, of course, capitalism disappears. Marx expresses this differently by saying that if labor is to be looked upon as a commodity then we must assume that it, like all commodities, has a use and exchange value, but then its only conceivable use value must be that it is the source of value. Since the worker cannot be both the origin of commodities and a commodity himself, we are obliged to drop the bourgeois conception of man as a free-object (as a given-proven) and assume him to be free. If man is the unique and universal cause, if he is the creator of the very notion of causality, if, that is, man's activities and achievements cannot be considered to flow from a pre-existing, definable nature, then we can explain both the sense in which mankind is one—man *is* praxis, which is to say his only nature is to be without one—and how he can differ profoundly from one culture to another since in the absence of a resistant inner core of identity men more or less passively become the products of their own achievements.

Nineteenth century working people shared certain obvious characteristics deriving entirely from the conditions of life imposed by capitalism, but the bourgeois preferred to regard these characteristics as manifestations ("proof") of a defective or inadequate personal identity; inversely, the educational system (to take only that example) fostered the development of a language for the reigning class which was somewhat different in vocabulary and accent from that of the masses and which could be looked upon not as the perpetuation of family privilege, not as an aspect of the system, but as the expression of an individual and innate distinction. This scheme was, of course readily adaptable to the requirements of the colonial period: natives all over the world were free to become Christians and businessmen (that is, the color of their skins concealed rather than revealed their true nature). However, in the immense majority of cases skin color marked these unfortunates as belonging to the "lesser breeds without the law"; so forced labor became a perfectly natural and understandable institution. Perfectly understandable also is what must be one of the most revolting practises ever devised by a "civilized" society—lobotomy. If, as we have just seen in Trilling and James, opposition[13] requires that we think in terms of defective individuals rather than in terms of a defective society then why not as an alternative to institutionalizing these individuals cure them permanently by destroying a certain quantity of brain cells? Would it not be preferable, in the interests of social harmony, that we all resemble the Skinnerized, robotized cretins capable of conceiving and performing such operations? One can be the keenest "viewer" imaginable and yet be viciously stupid simply by refusing to view oneself, that is, one's social and historical "position."

Marxism divides all societies into three levels: the means of production, the political-legal system and the ideology. The first may be referred to as the "material base" and the remaining two as the "superstructure." While these three levels probably exist in primitive societies they should perhaps not be referred to as levels at all because such societies are so much more closely knit structurally than our own that it is usually very difficult to make clear distinctions. However, in what concerns our own society we have possibly been too quick to assume that these levels, while they would undoubtedly appear to exist, do not share a certain number of basic components, one such being the contradictory bourgeois conception of man as a free-object. We have discussed the significance of this notion not only for fiction, but for philosophy where it occurs throughout the 19th century as the impossibility of understanding how consciousness or mind can be both produced by agents exterior to it (and therefore a thing) and also that which gave rise to this very conception of the nature of mind (and therefore historically situated praxis). As for the political-legal level, our degree of freedom is directly and exactly proportional to the extent of our material and cultural property while all emphasis (as in the novel where, apart from naturalism, our attention is drawn to the free proof of identity) is laid upon constitutionally guaranteed freedoms which in practice diminish as we descend the social scale until, toward the bottom, we reach the great majority, produced almost unresistingly *by* the system in order that they may produce *for* the system. Finally, as to the "material base," capitalism could not use a work force made up of slaves since they would have had to be fed, clothed and housed; they would consequently have cost considerably more than the self-saleable citizen, the free-slave of bourgeois democracy.

We have learned from the novel that man is an object unlike others not only because he is obliged to prove what he already is, but because determining what he is constitutes a value judgement even though, for 19th century philosophy and science, "is" and "ought" are two realms separated by an unbridgeable gap. Even though we are here on the implicit level of discourse the novelist cannot be unaware of appealing for approval or condemnation of characters defined in certain ways; he is therefore obliged to take for granted a beyond, religious or scientific, which will assure his objectivity. The substantive portion of man would have to be judged by someone who, thanks to the unquestioned existence of God and/or scientific law, need not fear having his vision distorted by bias of class and culture. In brief, if the notion of man as free-object is a basic component of all three levels, then so must be the means used to carry out accurate and indisputable judgments as to what kind of object is being dealt with. This need hardly be dwelt upon: to this day there appear books on economics whose authors take absolutely for granted that Western industry and commerce represent "achievements" toward which mankind has "progressed." But since peoples of other cultures are insensible to these achievements we conclude, with Conrad, that such people are not like us (that is, they are lesser forms of humanity) or, alternatively, that progress is an aspect of the operation of some natural law. On the political-legal level there is the notion that no man is above the law (which therefore must be conceived as having been handed down from "outside," rather than as the praxis of certain social groups pursuing certain goals), and, similarly, our "pluralistic" society is not simply one more historical form which must therefore change or decay but rather a final achievement since it provides means for all to be heard. In what concerns ideology it is sufficient to remark that for a large majority of English-speaking philosophers at least philosophy is, as it always has been, a quest for extra-temporal truth and value, or it ceases to exist.

It would appear then that while Western society may be readily divided into three levels it is also powerfully cemented into a totality by a cultural vision at once impalpable and all-pervasive. The tragic history of the Soviet Union has left no doubt but what changing the material base, rather than leading to a chain reaction of revolutionary changes throughout the system, has led instead to the confiscation of the means of production by a band of petty bourgeois tyrants. We can then argue that Russian backwardness in 1917 meant that an absolute priority had to be given to industrial productivity which in turn meant a centralized bureaucracy and consequently the growth of a privileged elite. Men become the captives of their own tools, there is no doubt about that, but why the willing and even delighted captives? There is an interpenetration of base and superstructure which needs more attention. The 18th century bourgeoisie, for example, conceived of such notions as freedom, equality and universality so that commerce and industry might break out of the restraints imposed by what was left of feudalism. But with the 19th century growth of the proletariat the bourgeoisie discovered it had meant its own freedom and equality, not just anyone's. It therefore without appearing to do so and as a matter of survival had to subvert its own political ideology; implicitly, its praxis had to be converted from the universal to the particular, and this it achieved in part through the novel by putting forward the confused and confusing notion that while men are equal, they are of different kinds. This idea of individual quality and the manner in which it is proven survived the Bolshevik revolution to the point where the greatest Russian novelist of the moment—Solzhenitsyn—is a reincarnation of Tolstoy.

However, with the waning of large, exclusively family fortunes and the ever decreasing importance of totally unskilled labor, innate superiority is demonstrated less through conspicuous consumption than through an alleged bureaucratic, technological or artistic competence. We are beginning to see now that what characterizes capitalistic or bourgeois industry is not only the expropriation of surplus value by private interests but the hierarchical organization of industry on the basis of "competencies." In other words, owners, overseers and engineers are not set above common laborers (the division of labor is simultaneously a division into kinds of men—the intellectual and the manual) so that work may be carried out more quickly and efficiently, but so that the worker will imagine himself incompetent to understand why the system has to function in such a way as to transform him from a human being into a blindfolded animal turning in a circle. The system must function mysteriously, or else the worker would quickly see that, for it to work at all in its present form, it is he who must be sacrificed.[14]

The change from private to state ownership of the means of production left intact a "superstructure" sufficiently resistant to guarantee that even after the revolution the masses would remain minors in need of instruction and guidance. After as before we have a principle exterior to praxis (and consequently not differing in essence from the 19th century combination of God and scientism) with the "dialectical laws of history" implanted as an opacity in some men who prove its existence to themselves and others by a blind and automatic functioning in accord with orders handed down from the ultimate competencies. Other men, unable to provide through obedience a convincing demonstration of what they are, have to be eliminated in one way or another. Competence, like 19th century virtue, is reduced to being primarily a demonstration of identity because it is not the natural response to self-evident social problems, it is fundamentally the way in which the system (private or state capitalism) copes with problems to which its own functioning has given rise. The bridge builder does not work for his fellow men but to expedite thc circulation of merchandise; the heart surgeon and psychiatrist attempt to repair bodies and minds broken down because the needs of capital or of bureaucracy are more urgent than those of men.

If the bourgeois vision of man as an entity susceptible to being defined and judged by reference to a beyond survived a revolutionary redistribution of power in Russia, the reverse appears to have happened here in the west where the breakdown of the superstructure had no effect on the distribution of power. The consequences of the passage from entrepreneurial to monopoly capital have been enormous, but the underlying structure of capital as Marx defined it is unchanged. In contrast, contemporary art and thought since Kafka bear no resemblance at all to what preceded them. One of the ways in which to approach this phenomenon would be to see in it the suppression of what we havc bccn calling the implicit in the classical novel.

Both levels of 19th century fiction are expressions of historical subjectivity; the explicit, however, is legitimate in the sense that it derives not from the consequences of reflection but is the stuff with which reflection operates. It is those presuppositions which, whatever the confusions and conflicts to which they may lead, we cannot do without on pain of ceasing to live in our own age. For example we know immediately and necessarily what Balzac means when he declares it to be intolerable that all human relationships should be mediated by money; we know, with Kafka, that it is intolerable that we should, out of moral cowardice, allow our lives to be rendered nonsensical by historical debris (the castle). These truths which are always "already there" are clearly to be associated with our mastery of the physical environment which becomes conspicuous with the steam engine and manufacturing, but one of the great dates of which would be the first circumnavigation of the globe. At any rate from the end of the 17th century onward it became possible for exceptional individuals to wonder whether man might not be "alone" (Pascal's "silence of infinite space"), whether God and, eventually, scientific law might not come from him rather than the reverse. But if, for the first time in human history, men were to *genuinely* free (not free to understand reality and therefore, as in stoicism, to accept it, but free to change it) then the whole tradition of Western metaphysics would have to find a radically different form of coherence. This was the work of Marx, for whom man became praxis, and reality the structured, congealed "wake" of that praxis. On this basis one can "legitimatize" the explicit level of the novel which is no longer a subjective impression, however generous, but the indignant reaction of a frustrated collective praxis to "true reality," that is, to a social and economic structure animated, though not entirely dominated, by the praxis of a small group within the collectivity. But on the implicit level the novel has a built-in security device in the sense that what we know self-evidently as members of a collectivity engaged in an historical praxis (the universal abolition of physical want made practicable by technology) is nullified by the class-serving notion that the collectivity is the negative or even destructive gathering together of people deficient in inner substance.[15]

A combination of scientific rationalism and the bourgeois labor theory of value made human "sameness," or equality, axiomatic in our culture. But that sameness was also the dignity, honor, and utility of individual pursuits, those of merchants or artisans freely engaging in different trades in which they displayed different degrees of individual ability. However, when these men became the entrepreneurs of the factory system they found themselves confronted by groups (what Marx called the socialization of labor) in which human sameness had become absolute because factory workers lived in conditions so harsh that all individual initiative was exhausted in the attempt simply to survive. The danger then arose that someone might see in the new group not the animals the French bourgeoisie tried to see in the Communards but the only form in which human equality can genuinely exist. Such a person might then proceed, as did Marx, to show that the very concept "individual" is historically produced by a particular group the members of which made use of private property, both material and cultural, to give the appearance of separateness one from the other. These "separated" people can then (as in the novels of James, where we never find Touchett or Verver at a board meeting) conceal their roots which stretch down into an unbelievably rapacious and unscrupulous mob infinitely more dangerous than the mob of rioting miners whose destructiveness Zola deplores in *Germinal*.

In the higher reaches of the classical novel the explicit level of discourse is part and parcel of the form; this would seem to mean that opposition to the regime through language alone (the domain of the liberal) is an essential aspect of the functioning of the system. In the absence of an alternative culture which would have, by force of circumstance, replaced the bourgeois social order (as that order had replaced feudalism) it was necessary to show how (since verbal opposition had always been part of the system, that is, the manifestation of an identity) revolutionary opposition, the constant exercise of freedom to both bring into being and destroy the *pratico-inerte,* could constitute in itself an alternative culture. It was necessary to show how, now that man dominates the natural environment, all culture, in the sense of ideology, is an attempt to justify authority or competencies for which there is no longer any metaphysical basis, individualism having broken down into praxis and reality into the *pratico-inerte.*

I have just described the progressive solution (that of Sartre developing and supplementing Marx's theses) to a cultural crisis which by the early years of the present century had grown acute: how could individualism honestly be preserved in the face of the disappearance of entrepreneurial individuals before the growth of monopoly capital on the one hand and, on the other, the ever increasing socialization of labor? How could extra-temporal principles be retained in the face of the enormous amount of historical work carried out in Germany and France tending toward the complete relativization of man's knowledge, including the scientific? Yet how could these principles be given up without it becoming apparent that bourgeois society is precisely the vicious struggle for private wealth and power it appears to be, with nothing "behind" or "above" it except a structured political, social and economic apparatus which is the instrument of power of a tiny minority?

By the time we reach Joyce and Proust the classical novel had become virtually unusable and was to survive only in the painfully debased form of socialist realism in the Soviet Union and mass entertainment in the West. And yet if we accept the criteria I have proposed, Joyce and Proust undoubtedly prolong, however briefly, the life of the classical novel.

Until now, for our purpose, it has been possible generally to consider Balzac and Tolstoy together. Both condemn bourgeois society with a ferocity so single-minded that Marx had to admire Balzac, and Lenin Tolstoy. These novelists however, as we know, had erected nonconscious barriers against the contagion of the self-evident, that is, against human equality derived from what the bourgeoisie itself liked to call the "dignity of labor" and from science proclaiming that all men belong to the same species. For the classical novelist, while men may be the same in a sense, they differ qualitatively as individuals, and these innate differences are established through recourse to principles held *a priori* to be extra-historical. If Realism in France after Balzac marks to some degree a falling off of the novel it is largely because the principles just mentioned (widely accepted notions as to what constitutes evil and virtue) were brought to bear by the reading public in an attempt to judge characters no longer as "free" as they had been to demonstrate their worthiness or lack of it. Emma Bovary is neither good nor bad as far as

Flaubert is concerned, but she is possessed nevertheless of an identity, that of a Romantic; so—since she exists as entity rather than as praxis—the reader is perfectly justified, within the context of the classical novel, in attempting to determine exactly what she is by using standards loftier than the merely sociological. But *Madame Bovary* does not offer the information needed for this purpose, and Emma must therefore be judged by default. Where a judgement is easily formed, as in the case of the supreme goodness of Félicité in *Un Coeur simple* or the good characters of Zola, it ought not to be, in the value-free universe of scientism. Tolstoy eliminates these inconsistencies by accepting the essentially Christian origin of the judgements readers in a bourgeois society will inevitably make given the substantive basis of fictional characters. But since Tolstoy comes toward the end of the reign of scientism rather than at the beginning, as had Balzac, his heroes do not merely believe in God, as do those of Balzac, they have a direct experience of Him, an experience which, since it cannot be perceptual, must take place "inside" the charcter. So subjectivity, which throughout the 19th century had been looked upon as an obstacle to man's attempts to know, is transformed into exactly the opposite: a means of access to the beyond.

It is as though, for a brief period around the turn of the century, Western thought struggled in desperation to keep itself from dissolving into simply one more Weltanschauung. The difficulty was that scientific rationalism itself (because of the work of men like Boutroux, Duhem, Meyerson and Poincaré) could no longer be relied upon to lead "outside" to something totally unaffected by a cultural angle of vision. However, what if one were to assume that subjectivity *is* the mode of existence of something supra-historical? Bergson with such ideas as involuntary memory in which duration manifests itself is the most characteristic thinker of the period. But others as well, far more important than he, were doing something comparable in that they increased the importance of "interiority" with a view to reaching the intemporal all the more securely. For Edmund Husserl, the perceptual world is in a sense "constituted" by human intentionality, and yet that process is ahistorical and consequently, in theory, susceptible to a scientifically rigorous description.[16] Freud often talks of neurosis as a means of coping; but then, contradictorily, he appears always to have hoped he might find a somatic basis for it. One could even cite Einstein in this connection, for although he relativized the scientist's point of observation he insisted as well that the traditional view of determinism was inseparable from science itself.

Joyce and Proust give the impression of having studied the history of fiction since Balzac and of having decided the form could be saved, but only on condition of changing everything. The hard center of the novel was identity, and by the end of the century it seemed that it could be neither maintained nor abandoned. It had come into being as the true subject matter of fiction when it was decided that man is the spectator not only of nature, of reality, but of his fellow men as well. However, in determining what kind of "human thing" we are looking at we have to refer ourselves to a morality and a religion already seriously undermined by rationalist scepticism and universalism; so if the novelist were to be so obtuse as to see in virtue as practised by the bourgeoisie anything more than a class privilege, then to save himself he would have to be especially lucid and courageous on the explicit level of discourse. The greatest of the classical novelists (Balzac, Tolstoy, Dostoevsky) then alleged that reason oversteps itself into chaos unless the values employed on the implicit level are restored and respected, and in this way they were able to give more countenance to a morality tending to conserve a system which was, by their own admission, intolerable. Flaubert and the naturalists attempted to deal with the problem by much increasing the weight with which brute reality presses upon people's lives so that judgements of them would have to be attenuated. But, as we have seen, one cannot improve a form by weakening its foundation, and, in any case, scientism is as historically subjective as are the moral criteria used on the implicit level, in fact more so. James took the opposite course. He converted identity into an interiority—this being his historical significance—in which he could elaborate upon relatively superficial traits of character, often as a means of concealing identities arrived at on the basis of middle class morality as its most conventional.

Such then was the situation when Joyce and Proust arrived on the scene. The naturalists had shown that reality could not be allowed to destroy identity, and James had shown that identity could not be allowed to destroy reality. Only the greatest of the classical novelists had managed to keep a balance between the two—but at a price (confidence in middle class values and in religion) impossible for most of us to pay.[17] Identity is at once the focal point and the *secret honteux* of the classical novel. Would it be possible to keep that identity and yet rid it of what is most objectionable, that is, first, that it should invite us—absurdly—to condemn individuals rather than the society which produced them and, second, that the judgement we are compelled to make should be effected with reference to a religious or scientific beyond which, for the many reasons we have given, cannot be accepted.

What if identity were transformed into an inner realm which would become the very heart and substance of the novel without there being any question of a moral judgement of the individual concerned since, although he remains substantive, that substance, or realm becomes the mode of existence of a beyond which therefore cannot be scientific in nature. If, furthermore, such a beyond is not regarded as sacred, then it need not be ineffable as it was for Tolstoy. Yet it will be sufficiently awe-inspiring to make the fixing of the moral quality of individuals seem of little account.

One is tempted to regard all this as rather silly on grounds that no one reads Proust for his Bergsonism nor Joyce for his version of Vico's circular history. Yet one of the many respects in which Joyce and Proust remain classical novelists is the attempt they make to assign to the novel responsibilities it is ill-equipped to meet. Only picaresque fiction did not strain to exceed its grasp. Balzac and Zola wanted to assist science; Dostoevsky and Tolstoy religion; and Flaubert's estheticism would have been better left to arts more successfully eternal, like painting and music. The English novel alone found reward enough in reflecting the lesser values of the new master class; on the continent, fiction achieved far more because it sought universality not only through the explicit but through "science" or genuine religious sentiment as well. It was perhaps too late for contemporaries of Kafka to be seeking asylum outside humanity, but if the work of Joyce and Proust, as I shall try to show, extends the classical novel into the 20th century, then the always unthinkable alternative to one absolute or another was bourgeois humanity—the bourgeois moral and social order, the world of the Verdurins in Proust.[18] In Joyce, there is perhaps no better reason for the modern Ulysses being a Jew, that is, a man at once part of modern urban culture and yet not altogether belonging to it. The beyond in Joyce and Proust is therefore functional, and although it is also extravagant, it is far preferable to James' God, holding shares and presiding over afternoon tea parties.

If we are to understand the importance of Joyce and Proust we must concentrate upon their conception of man as primarily an inner realm and then try to determine the place that reality is going to occupy.

Mass entertainment simplifies identity to absurdity, and it does so by simplifying reality to absurdity; so that a great classical novelist (that is, essentially, a great creator of character) is necessarily a great realist in that the complexity of a character is in direct proportion to the complexity of the real which both "produced" him and which will submit him to a series of tests to determine who he is. However, the classical novelist shares with the creator of low-brow literature the same position outside reality; and the question put by Joyce and Proust is: what if reality is not what the novelist as spectator sees, but what the hero himself sees? Or, to put it differently, the existence of a spectator presupposes the largely passive enregistering of a self-contained meaning about whose existence, however, philosophers and scientists toward the end of the century were increasingly sceptical. What the novelist had to do, therefore, was to see and to know nothing except what came to him through the eyes and mind of the hero; he was to cease being omnisciently outside reality. Then, any discoveries which might eventually be made would not have been presupposed but would have emerged from experience itself. Joyce and Proust revive the picaresque quest, but with two fundamental differences: it is undertaken on the level of perception and experience not that of rational discussion, and it is "successful." Proust-Marcel is finally able to satisfy himself that man can transcend his individual life, and Joyce-Bloom incarnates, presumably, the "eternally human."

Joyce and Proust, in proposing to reach reality through the self rather than despite it, gave their work a deceptively revolutionary appearance because the self in question remained essentially the knowing, transcendental self of Kantian thought, except that what it contained enables us to know not the universe of Newtonian mechanism but that of everyday life. Although the real as it appears in Joyce and Proust often gives the impression of having been strangely tinted, it is not in the least altered (as it would be in the work of men like Céline and Henry Miller), for both authors had a thoroughly "naturalistic" concern for accuracy. So the subjective real of Joyce and Proust is that of all of us; even the dream world of *Finnegan's Wake* is, preposterously enough, intelligible for the most part to anyone with the patience and cranky erudition to work it out.

Reality then, in Joyce and Proust, is still that of 19th century literature but with a difference which enabled them to exhaust the classical novel. For although reality is the same, its "principles of organization"—as in Kant—are inside rather than outside man; so to explore reality is at the same time to explore identity. In learning of Odette and Albertine, Venice or Balbec, we learn far more of Swann and Marcel; the same is true for Dublin and Bloom. But what exactly is learned; what is there "inside" in addition to reality; what are the "principles of organization"?

Balzac considered that he was doing very much what I have just mentioned, that is, in describing the reality of Paris, of the market place and the law, he was simultaneously providing the Birotteaus and the Gobsecks with their identities. But then, mysteriously and unaccountably, the characters are transmuted from fact into value; they lend themselves to an infallible moral judgement. It is with this illogicality that the author's class affiliations mark the novel most heavily. The unique achievement of Joyce and Proust was to have created some of the most remarkable characterizations in the whole history of the classical novel without the reader being able to assign any particular moral quality to these characters, in other words, without Joyce and Proust having to stoop—as did James—to the silly hypocrisy which asserts there can exist a private morality without a public one. To be sure Flaubert and Zola had given little attention to private morality, but with the consequence that identity tended to become "sociological" and hence less exaltingly ethical, or else it became simply weak.

The paradox of *Ulysses* and of *A la Recherche du temps perdu* is that Bloom and Marcel should have as full and vivid an existence as any character in the whole of fiction without it being at all clear what sort of men they are. They are simultaneously dispersed into everyman and concentrated into recognizable individuals. Natalie Sarraute never departs from the stream of consciousness of her characters, and yet even if she were to devote an entire novel to recording the consciousness of one person, that person would remain totally unknown because it is a matter of principle with her that character as moral or sociological identity does not exist. Something of the sort could be said of Joyce and Proust (except that they would not have made it a matter of principle); so the problem remains, where does the presence and substance of these characters come from?

It comes from our authors' obsessive devotion to their past. Not the past of anecdote or event, which would have formed the subject matter of one more autobiographical novel (like the *Portrait of the Artist*) of a kind our literature produces in such quantities, but the *existed* past with its sounds and odors, feelings and sensations; the past as Marcel revives it with the help of his grandmother's tisane and madeleine or as Joyce often reproduces or embodies it in the very lilt and sound of his language. In what Bloom does publicly, where he goes and whom he meets, he is simply the plaything of the gods as had been Ulysses, as are we all presumably in Joyce's mind; similarly, the events of Marcel's life are merely pretexts for cultivating what Proust, in *Sodome et Gomorrhe,* calls: "Ce jardin intérieur où nous sommes forcés de rester toujours." The paradox of a nameless identity in Bloom and Marcel is therefore to be explained in this way: each has received the fullness and consistency of his creator's affective past.[19]

But a further difficulty immediately arises. If Joyce and Proust are major novelists, as they undoubtedly are, then what has become of the explicit level we have learned to associate with the best classical fiction?[20] The question could be approached in this way.

The classical novel makes recommendations no one can possibly heed; we are obliged to assume that the only conceivable remedy for the social conditions denounced on the explicit level is the reform of individuals, and yet this is unthinkable since identity is a given. Individual reform furthermore, in Balzac and Tolstoy, although unthinkable is nevertheless, in view of the retribution usually required of the evil in this life, and in view of the Christian afterlife, "compulsory." Zola brought no fundamental change since not only does identity remain, but any recourse to violence on the part of the oppressed (as in *Germinal*) entails both a breakdown of individualism (that is, "chaos") and interference with the law of historical progress. Flaubert somewhat reduces the confusion by inventing an explicit (estheticism) which involved no recommendations, no injunctions, but simply the opportunity to feel contempt for most of the human race and for the bourgeoisie in particular for its insensitivity to "what art suggests of glorious life."

From a strictly theoretical standpoint of course the beyond in Flaubert, malevolently pursuing the destruction of each individual life, renders the esthetic explicit as absurd as Zola's mechanical historical progress renders the indignation he strives to excite in the reader. In practical terms, however, there was a critical difference since one can respond to the explicit in Flaubert by adopting various ways of life: from that of the misunderstood artist (like Joyce during the greater part of his life) on the periphery of society to that of the comfortable professor submitting articles to reviews devoted exclusively to the work of a specific artist formerly misunderstood. The explicit in Flaubert is one the reader can act upon without the necessity of genuinely transforming his life as he would have to were he to be deeply influenced by Balzac, Tolstoy, Dostoevsky or Zola (although logically, because of the nature of the implicit level, that influence cannot operate). Flaubert has been enormously influential because he offers us the opportunity of elaborating a superb identity (that of a Swann or a Marcel in the best instances) entirely apart from the stupidity of middle class morality and the vulgar servitudes of the moneymaker. To be sure, for one half-blind poet in exile like Joyce there are a million playing the rôle; for one Swann a million Madame Verdurins. But that is precisely Flaubert's contribution—the relative success with which such rôles can be played. Everyone knows what to think of the statesman's integrity, the old maid's virtue or the industrialist's yacht as outward shows of inner distinction, but how can we be sure that Madame Verdurin does not really get headaches from the intensity of her response to Vinteuil's sonata? We know what to think in her case of course since, being a fictional character, she is known to us exhaustively (she is identified); but in real life we could do no more than strongly suspect that esthetic exquisiteness might not be as life-filling as some claim.

On the explicit level the classical novel appears to demand a response from the reader (something must be *done* about a social system that is viable for only so long as it is able to ignore historically relative but, for that very reason, self-evident notions of right and wrong) which he cannot and need not give because on a deeper level he is the spectator of a universe in which a benevolent beyond makes all desirable adjustments either now, in the hereafter, or in the future (Zola). In Flaubert alone the beyond, with a strange meticulous persistence and oblivious to identities, works out the undoing of humanity. Consequently the explicit as beauty, as contemptuous indifference to the affairs of us human insects, receives a kind of justification. On the other hand, in conceiving a beyond of such a nature, Flaubert deprived himself of all serious motivation for the elaboration of morally significant character upon which the quality of the classical novel, in the last analysis, depends.

Flaubert demonstrated that the explicit level could be in appearance maintained but in reality suppressed on condition it offer a practicable model of comportment.[21] Anyone (anyone well-to-do, of course, that being why the explicit is maintained only in appearance) can have or at least pretend to have a sense of beauty so delicate and vigilant as to make for a different and higher life like that of Swift's Laputians wandering about on their levitated island. We need now to see how Flaubert's hint of identity as an "inner initiative" which one might take without consideration for any of the accepted absolutes helped Joyce and Proust solve some of the problems of fiction as they appeared around the turn of the century.[22]

One of the most remarkable characteristics of the 19th century novel is the fragility of the timeless principles set up to arm the reader against the disheartening effects of the truth concerning the society of which he was a proud and prosperous member. That fragility is easily conceived when one considers that Stendhal—for whom religion and science were not issues in respect to which he entertained advanced ideas but issues which for him did not even exist—was sixteen years older than Balzac. By the end of the century, therefore, the eternal verities had become so worm-eaten that no self-respecting thinker or artist could continue to work with them unless he could manage somehow despite their absence to restore to identity its central place; alternatively, the classical novel would have to be replaced by some other.

Roger Martin du Gard's novels are an interesting historical example of the consequences of doing neither, of an attempt made by a very gifted and intelligent novelist to prolong "artificially" the life of the classical novel without recourse to the baroque extremes of a Joyce or Proust. The great classical novelists tried to be clear about the absolutes which served as safeguards against the corrosive effects of the explicit (Balzac's *Avant-Propos,* Zola's *Le Roman expérimental,* and Tolstoy's numerous meditations on the religious question.) But those absolutes at a deeper, nonconscious level dictated certain preconceptions and procedures of which the two most important are identity and the novelist as a non-situated observer. The most striking single characteristic of Martin du Gard as a novelist are his attempts to do away with the metaphysics of the classical novel using fictional techniques which were the products of that metaphysics. *Jean Barois* offers the clearest example, and our conclusions in respect to this novel would apply as well to the far more important *Les Thibault.* On the explicit level there is the Dreyfus affair and on the implicit a group of characters whose identity constitutes a critique of either religion or scientism (as Emma Bovary and one of her lovers, Léon, were a satire of Romanticism). However, Martin du Gard retains that "impersonal" vantage point of Flaubert and Zola which makes sense only if one presupposes the existence of an outside to humanity which one reaches, naturally, by striving to place oneself outside in perfect objectivity. But since Martin du Gard rejects the idea that a knowable outside, or beyond, exists, does this not clear the way, finally, for an explicit the reader would not be able to discount? No, since reduced to the explicit alone a novel, unless it is a thesis novel, is not a novel at all, and this is certainly not the case with *Jean Barois* since the basic structure of classical fiction is unchanged: there exists an observer focusing his attention upon human beings who, since that observer is omniscient, become knowable entities; the goal of the novel is then to establish the nature and quality of those entities and even where the novelist makes a judgement almost impossible (there is no way of deciding whether Barois dies a freethinker or a believer) the reader has no choice but to attempt to identify the characters. Basically the classical novel cannot be about anything else.

Once the explicit has been given the place it deserves in a novel the author is bound to meditate upon what ought to be done, and in the classical novel the self-evident abuses of our society are explained in terms either of the Christian or scientific beyond (that is, by the existence of evil individuals or by determinism or both) so that none of us can have any responsibility. Unable to provide an explanation of this kind Martin du Gard appears to be saying we should emulate Luce (more the hero of the novel in a sense than Barois) who, at the risk of his career and possibly even of his life, chooses to fight for Dreyfus since no self-respecting person in possession of the facts of the case as then known could do otherwise. Does this mean that in Martin du Gard we have, finally, a novelist willing to see that the condition of our society is the responsibility of each of us? Yes, but that responsibility is one we can exercise only as individuals and is therefore one that cannot be exercised at all. The injustice done Dreyfus was eventually redressed, at least in part; but the culture that breeds anti-semitism was left to proceed to the achievements of the Nazi era because the way in which the problems are posed is part of that culture. The form of the classical novel, and of the mentality satisfied with it,[23] is such that Luce's decision is primarily an indication of his quality as an individual upon which the quality of his action will depend (he has a reputation for probity, he is above party politics, etc.), and in fact that action consists almost entirely in the offering of an example of civic responsibility. But it is an example which cannot be widely followed since even intelligent and sensitive people (like old Gerlach in Sartre's *Les Séquestrés d'Altona*) will act as they are dictated to by the social and economic structure of their society, by the *pratico-inerte*. One of the most formidable obstacles to altering that structure is the unwillingness of novelists and intellectuals to admit that their non-partisan position above society was prepared for them well in advance so that it affords no perspective whatever even where the writer, as in the case of Martin du Gard, can see that the philosophical underpinning of his objectivity has rotted away. Vision from a distance is a class privilege even where all that one can see is absurdity, and what Paul Valéry says of death and eternity applies equally to the absurd: "Meditations on death (like those of Pascal) we owe to men who do not have to struggle in life to earn their food and to support children. Eternity occupies people who have time to waste. It's a form of leisure."[24]

We can argue that the classical novel serves a particular social class not only in what the narrator-spectator sees essentially (man proving himself with a greater or lesser "freedom" to be a thing of this or that kind) but in the notion that vision ranges over a field where, given sufficient keenness, it will discover features which although always there, had been underestimated or passed by. For even where there is little or nothing to discover (as in novels like *Les Thibault* and Mann's *Der Zauberberg*), where identity exists largely by default but necessarily, and where events are no longer the expression of concealed supra-human forces (as in Flaubert and Zola), there is at least *that* discovery, namely, universal meaninglessness, which however is "visible" only to the individual solitary observer, the creature of scientific rationalism unaware he is producing meaninglessness by the very isolation which he takes to be a precondition of clear vision. In the world of *Les Thibault* there is little room even for a *belle-âme* like Luce, and Mann's magic mountain is, in reality, his own position as narrator, a position which magically reduces humanity to a scurrying little cluster of beings seriously discussing matters of life and death much to the amusement of Mann and his readers who have thoroughly sounded all these questions. And although there is no explicit conclusion the message is clear enough: look at humanity from a great height and through the big end of the telescope; it will then appear to you a different species from your own and of little consequence that the hero Hans should leave death on the mountain top for death in the trenches of the flatlands. One of the marvels of contemporary Western culture is that the spectacle should have become a vast cemetery without that having in the least discouraged the spectators.[25]

In writers like Martin du Gard and Thomas Mann the classical novel keeps its form but loses its content. Since one is a function of the other, this does not mean that a new content was found but simply that content is gone; there is nothing left for the observer to observe except what is there by default. It is silly that the reader should be encouraged to note Vautrin's words for the purpose of arriving at a moral judgement; and of course this is not the case with Naphta, Settembrini or Peeperkorn in *Der Zauberberg,* who presumably are there to represent the various views one can take upon the problems that plague us. But then why read *Der Zauberberg* rather than a much more important book (because it is the work not of an *impossible* observer, but of a partisan) *Geschichte und Klassenbewusstsein* by George Lukács whom Mann is said to have had in mind in certain passages of his novel?

Joyce and Proust alter the form of the novel so as to make possible a last full flowering of its "natural" content, and they do this by working from the inside outward; they abandon the necessarily magic mountain top and disperse themselves over the terrain. We are not given a bird's-eye view of Dublin in *Ulysses;* the city builds itself up gradually, but the end result is still an accurate enregistering of an objectively existing place.[26] Thus, the traditional relationship between inner and outer realms is not radically affected in either Joyce or Proust (as it will be, as we shall see, in Kafka), it is simply that the former becomes a vastly more self-contained area in which both a personal and historical past occupy far more space than does the directly reflected exterior world. This being the case the novel, with Joyce and Proust, becomes openly static. I say openly since, as we have seen, time in the classical novel is merely that elongated space through which an already existing identity is confirmed or revealed. So that, once again, Joyce and Proust bring no fundamental change in replacing a gradually unfolding narrative with a series of tableaux. There is no need to test the quality of identity through event where identity has become a domain for the reader to explore, an uncertain domain shading off into the surroundings, perhaps, yet unmistakeably a separate area because we are concerned far less with events than with their affective—and therefore deeply personal—impact and resonance. What actually happens to provoke jealousy in Bloom and Marcel is of little account; our attention is drawn to how jealousy is lived in each case: very well by Bloom, it so happens, and very badly by Marcel.

But then what is the reader expected to get from the succession of tableaux out of which *Ulysses* and *A la Recherche du temps perdu* are constructed? What are we to look for? Where is the high seriousness which was assured in the classical novel by religion and science? It has been my argument that only the explicit level in the classical novel is genuinely universal because it marks the at least partial acceptance on the part of the novelist of the ineluctable and universal rooting of the observer in a given time and place; and while, as a result, absolute truth disappears from view (although, of course, this nowhere happens in the classical novel) the self-evident nature of certain social and political tasks can then be revealed. The classical novel survives in the work of men like Martin du Gard and Thomas Mann because, although religion and science as absolutes have vanished, the non-situated position from which they had been viewed remained with the result that their place was filled by a meaninglessness which the next generation would call the absurd. One could say that the explicit level in Martin du Gard and Mann becomes this announcement that timeless meaning is an illusion, but then their explicit becomes far more class-serving than that of Balzac or Tolstoy since it constitutes the "objective" discovery of something supra-historical while Balzac, Tolstoy and Zola denounce abuses associated with a specific culture and class. The more the capitalist yahoo—for "sound economic reasons"—girds himself to go forth to do slaughter, the more "meaningless" becomes the spectacle for the cultivated observer.[27] The consequence for the novel, as in the case of naturalism, is an impoverishment of identity since moral earnestness, natural in the fictional world of Balzac and Tolstoy, can be no more (as in the case of a Jacques Thibault) than one of the ways in which people differ.

The fictional Kantianism by which Joyce and Proust open new but short-lived possibilities for identity had nothing to do with the recognition of our cultural subjectivity, which constitutes the explicit level and access to genuine universality in the greatest of the classical novelists. How do they then avoid becoming even more transparently class-serving than those working on the "outside," than the absurdists? How could they safely turn their backs on all the great issues to fall complacently into what Sartre, with his usual verve, called the "malodorous brine" of the bourgeois inner life?[28]

To understand this we have to appreciate to what extent Joyce and Proust prolong a tradition which goes back far beyond Balzac. However, in examining more closely the fiction that preceded the classical period we will have to take into account, as well, the Lukács-Goldmann theory of the novel, the usefulness of which is restricted to the picaresque era, although, a we shall see, Goldmann attempts to apply it to the contemporary novel.

According to the Lukács-Goldmann theory, the novel is essentially an interrogation of reality carried out by a problematic hero, and this makes of it a bourgeois art form because in replacing use by exchange value the bourgeoisie created a world which does not make sense in terms of general human welfare. But Goldmann is then obliged to wonder how the art form of a particular class could fail to propagate or to reflect its values.[29] I believe this to be a false problem since scepticism played a vital rôle in undermining feudal and theological dogmatism, and even where it operated against middle class morality, as in Fielding, it did so within a framework of universal rationality which no one at that time was in a position to dispute; that is, it did so from within bourgeois culture. The Protestant artisan or merchant might have been very different men from some of the scientists of their time; but the same could be said of the medieval cleric and the warlord. In neither case were either kept from representing, each in his own way, the values of the same culture. A 16th or 17th century artist might have painted a picture of disorder, a problematic picture in Goldmann's language, but men and objects would nevertheless have been in perspective. Perspective, or hidden order, manifests itself in the classical novel by the position occupied by the principal characters when the tale is ended, for that position will be appropriate to the quality of the person involved (except, as we have seen, where a more purely scientific order supplants the moral order). This being the case the disorder generated by the novelist's own culture can then be vigorously denounced on the explicit level without bringing anything fundamental into question. Even after moral and scientific order have gone, as in Martin du Gard and Mann, there will remain the spectator, and because he persists in staring, he succeeds in transforming an unintelligible picture into a picture of unintelligibility. So, as in all of classical rationalism, the world remains what we contemplate from a distance, or what we succeed in discovering.

It is impossible to derive an ethic from scientific rationalism; it is equally impossible to find any common ground between the bourgeois war of each against all and any imaginable interpretation of the Gospel. The solution to this predicament was, and still is, to assume without further discussion that what is right is what is done by good people, wrong being what is done by evil people.[30] All that remains is to distinguish one from the other by a series of tests while the historical and cultural relativity of the criteria used for these tests passes unnoticed. In some picaresque fiction these criteria form part of what Goldmann calls the implicit values of society about which the problematic hero alone is dubious. But there is another very important group of novelists from Defoe through Marivaux, Richardson and Rousseau who never for a moment question those criteria and whose work constitutes an attempt to establish bourgeois legitimacy on the basis of Christian virtue and, in the cases of Marivaux and Rousseau, a kind of general refinement of soul as well.

One of the main purposes of Rousseau's *La Nouvelle Héloïse* is to demonstrate through Saint-Preux the existence of a category of human beings for which, in English, we have a term: nature's noblemen. This is the exclusive concern of Marivaux in *La Vie de Marianne*. This novel is unfinished, and Marivaux might well have intended to reveal at its conclusion that Marianne was of noble extraction. Nevertheless, even though no one knows who her parents were, Marianne is suitable for marriage into one of France's most aristocratic families, the reason for this being stated very clearly by Madame de Miran: Marianne has a nobility of soul which "she owes neither to her experience of the world nor to the education she received which was of the simplest. It must therefore be in her blood; and that, to my mind, is the essential."[31] Valville then explains there exists a true aristocracy based upon the "merits of mind and heart" which might not correspond in all cases to the actually existing aristocracy. There are other passages in which this point is made (on page 354, for example, and pages 427-28) but what really matters is that the entire substance of the novel, its events and characters, exist simply to enable Marianne to demonstrate her inner quality (her beauty, as Madame de Miran remarks on the page just quoted from, is what distinguishes her least). The same point could easily be made in respect to Richardson's novels where the supreme test becomes an assault upon chastity.

Defoe is far more important a novelist than Marivaux, Richardson or Rousseau. *Robinson Crusoe* is scarcely less illustrious in the history of the novel than *Don Quixote,* yet Lukács and Goldmann barely mention it. Defoe is not easily disposed of; it is a simplification to say, as I did a moment ago, that his work helps establish a "new legitimacy" in the sense that there exist people not necessarily belonging to the aristocracy who manifest innate qualities of soul such that their fitness to rule cannot be reasonably doubted.[32] Yet it is equally difficult if not impossible to maintain that Crusoe is a problematic hero assimilable to Don Quixote. The fact is that just as Western philosophy since the Renaissance has never been able to show how the inner and outer worlds created by scientific metaphysics can be related, so the novel has tended to move either in one direction or the other; there would appear to be little in common between a novel like Le Sage's *Le Diable boiteux* at one extreme, and Richardson's *Pamela* at the other. In the former, character—insofar as it may be said to exist at all—is a function of the particular anecdote of which there are literally hundreds, and the overall meaning of which may be said to be problematic; in the latter, event or anecdote all but disappears, giving place to a situation created by the interaction of characters whom we identify by reference to moral absolutes taken entirely for granted. It is a simple matter to place most pre-19th century novels on one side or the other. In one category one would have those novels which appear to conform to the Lukács-Goldmann theory, novels turned "outward" toward an interrogation of reality, where character, if it exists at all, is incidental: *Don Quixote,* Smollett, Fielding, Voltaire, Diderot (*Jacques le fataliste*), Le Sage, and so forth. In the other category one would list those novels turned "inward" toward an interrogation of people caught in situations which constitute a test of quality (Richardson, Rousseau) or where event is carefully shaped to meet the needs of the identity of the hero (*La Vie de Marianne*). There are novels needless to say containing elements of both categories, but there is seldom doubt about the main emphasis: Blifil, for example, in *Tom Jones* is a villain (but nevertheless a figure of fun as well, and therefore very different from the Dickensian villain), while in *La Nouvelle Héloïse* Rousseau often discourses upon problems having nothing to do with the quality of soul of his characters. Sterne's *Tristram Shandy* is a notoriously wayward work, but the reason for this is clear enough: basically the novel presents a group of characters (and therefore belongs to our second category), but they are all characters who would have played a secondary role in a 19th century novel. That is, they are approached not with the moral earnestness of a Richardson or a Rousseau or a Balzac, but with a humor confined ordinarily to the first category of novel. (At the end of the 18th and beginning of the 19th century there appear a small number of transitional novels of which the three most notable would be *I Promessi Sposi, Les Liaisons dangereuses* and *Wilhelm Meister*.)

In traditional Western philosophy materialists and idealists are in a sense at opposite extremes, and yet since each took for granted the timeless and universal validity of scientific knowledge the disagreement concerned merely the means of travel, not the direction to take. Similarly, with our two categories in pre-classical fiction: what is problematic in one is not the existence of universal order, but our ability at the moment to understand how it manifests itself in day-to-day human commerce; while in the other the novelist insists that, after all, commerce takes place in a reasonably satisfactory way, and this is possible thanks to the existence of moral imperatives and the conscience which reveals them to each of us. Sterne is rarely serious, but if one were required to find in *Tristram Shandy* an earnest passage an excellent choice would be the sermon on conscience with its concluding paragraph in which we learn that "God and reason made the law" and that conscience gives us access to it.[33] The fictional hero in the Lukács-Goldmann theory is doubtful about values which everyone else in his society easily takes for granted. However, in Robert Chasles' *Les Illustres Françaises* (1713) exactly the reverse appears to happen. In it, a very convincing case based upon reason and common sense is made for women's right to the sexual freedom our society accords only to men.[34] But while this passage renders "problematic" one of the most transparently unfair and tenacious practises of Western society, almost every one of the stories in *Les Illustres Françaises* makes it clear that sexual infidelity is the most dreadful crime a woman can commit. This novel, belonging very clearly to our second category is interesting for the way in which here and there on a small scale it anticipates certain important aspects of the 19th century novel; in the present instance the contradiction between explicit[35] and implicit levels and the use of concealed identity, most conspicuously in the case of Silvie. But Chasles serves also to remind us that identity as it exists in the classical novel evolved over a long period: the villain of *Les Illustres Françaises,* Valeran, is motivated—though insufficiently no doubt—by his passion for Silvie, while the "authentic villain" of a century or so later would commit evil largely for evil's sake. (Two of the earliest real villains are probably Madame de Merteuil and the Comte de Valmont in Laclos' *Les Liaisons dangereuses.*) Dupuis and Gallouin furthermore, in Chasles' novel, appear to undergo a change which in the classical novel would have to be a revelation of concealed identity.

It is as though these two types of novel mark the negative and positive positions of pre-revolutionary bourgeois culture: the problematic novel serving to undermine the dogmatism of church and throne, the other to assert the existence of a clearly defined moral code to which the noble of soul effortlessly adhere. If the sceptics sometimes made fun of the moralizers the mockery abruptly ceased with the French Revolution, the new rulers having discovered that much—especially property—was sacred after all. Stendhal alone continued to be sceptical with, as we shall see, surprising consequences for the history of the novel.

It is as though, before Balzac, the explicit and implicit levels of the novel could exist only in different works; the two not being consummately joined together until Tolstoy whereupon they immediately fell apart again with Joyce and Proust on one side, Martin du Gard and Mann on the other. If the second category of novel manipulates the real, often shamelessly, so that its kinds of people may be thrown into the clearest light,[36] the first prefers not to look too closely into the "nonconscious" foundation of all bourgeois life: men are equal of course but, rather mysteriously, they are also of different kinds, and the differences are qualitative. Balzac was the first to effect a reasonably satisfactory conversion of our two categories of novel into two levels of discourse within the same novel and he achieved this by turning reality first into milieus which with pseudo-scientific precision would produce identities of a given kind and, second (by making use, in the best instances, of the explicit level), into a relatively convincing testing ground for the identities involved. The only pre-classical novelist to do something of this sort, that is, the only one to put his characters genuinely to the test—and who is, consequently, by far the greatest novelist of the second group—is Daniel Defoe.

One sometimes finds critics suggesting that Defoe might not have written novels at all, and the context usually makes it clear that there is doubt because Defoe, unlike Richardson, does not sufficiently "explore" his characters. (In feeling this way the critics reveal that no one yet knows exactly what a novel is, but it is at least suspected that "depicting the human heart" is essential to it.) Yet how much probing into character does one find in books, presumably novels, like *Les Liaisons dangereuses* or *Les Misérables*? Does not the real difference lie in the fact that Laclos and Hugo "honestly" inform the reader about whom (or more accurately, about what) in the way of protagonists the story is being told so that he may securely and comfortably pass judgement? Madame de Merteuil and Valmont are villains (but not Roxana, the fortunate mistress) and meet with an appropriately terrible fate; while Jean Valjean is only a thief and convict in appearance (but not Moll Flanders), an appearance which conceals a thoroughly good identity. But while Defoe refuses to let us know exactly in whom (what) we are being invited to take an interest, that is, while it is difficult (but by no means impossible as we shall see) to place him in our second category of novel, it is certainly not practicable to see in the heroes of Defoe "problematic" men and women seeking a truth which forever eludes them. Quite the contrary, his characters begin their careers in a state, not of scepticism to be sure, but of almost total indifference to what were taken to be the vital questions. Sooner or later in the course of their adventures those questions *and their answers* are thrust upon them, in the case of Singleton, for example, by an awesome clap of thunder which is the beginning of an awakening and an eventual conversion. There is consequently an important filiation between one of the very earliest of Western novelists who is still readable (in fact Defoe is more readable than most of the English Victorian writers) and the man who brought the classical novel to its highest perfection, Tolstoy. In both novelists the protagonist is a person living in a state of moral and intellectual torpor until the beyond contrives to reveal itself (while remaining hidden, of course) as a result of which the hero undergoes a kind of conversion.

We know that identity in fiction implies the existence of a set of moral conventions which cannot be recognized as such by the novelist or his readers without their being forced to see that fiction is not just literature; it is literature of a given class struggling to persuade itself that class doesn't exist. The best fiction therefore will attempt to legitimatize its moral law by relating it clearly to the beyond from which it derives. Failure to do this, as we have seen even in the case of a "sophisticated" novelist like James, causes goodness to fall into bourgeois respectability and evil into melodrama. But then another and far more serious threat arises, that of causing the beyond to intervene so forcefully or having the hero seek it out so earnestly as to provoke a change of identity which would destroy the novel and the concept of bourgeois legitimacy which is its raison d'être. If the beyond manifests itself too actively it suspends the operation of natural law, and we are back to primitive religion; if the hero is free to the point of bringing about a genuine change of identity under the influence of religion then identity as a given-proven does not exist, and there is nothing for the novelist as omniscient spectator to see or discover. More serious still, given the socialization of labor with the factory system a genuine conversion would have had to lead to a degree of social responsibility on the part of the bourgeois utterly incompatible with the maximization of profit, that is, with the very existence of the system. What happens, therefore, in Tolstoy's novels *Resurrection* and the *Death of Ivan Ilyitch* is not a change of identity but the emerging of one, since before their conversions both men were simply "anyone," living in limbo like minor characters until promoted to the rank of protagonist by their spiritual awakening. But what of Defoe? Moll Flanders and Roxana would appear to have led the lives of whores, and Singleton that of a pirate.

At the conclusion of *Colonel Jack,* Defoe writes as follows:

> I think it is just to add how in recollecting the various changes, and turns of my affairs, I saw clearer than ever I had done before, how an invisible over-ruling power, a hand influenced from above, governs all our actions of every kind, limits all our designs and orders the events of every thing relating to us.
>
> And from this observation it necessarily occurred to me, how just it was that we should pay the homage of all events to him; that as he guided, and had even made the chain of causes, and consequences, which nature in general strictly obeyed, so to him should be given the honour of all events, the consequences, of those causes, as the first mover, and maker of all things.[37]

And so by gradations Defoe comes in the next paragraph to talk of wickedness, good and evil, moral knowledge and the like, even though it is manifestly absurd to pass from a being who "governs all our actions of any kind," and from "chains of causes and consequences" to recommendations concerning morality. Yet so necessary is it to make that impossible passage that Pascal and Kant were obliged to take the first step toward a new rationality—the dialectical—with their notion of "laying a wager" on the existence of God and a universal ethic, while Dostoevsky was right to warn of the danger of ignoring religion if that were to mean our being left with scientific rationalism alone.

In primitive cultures metaphysics and ethics are usually one and the same; there is often little difference between a description of what is and a moral imperative. The Renaissance, however, gave rise to the idea of an "impersonal nature" in respect to which value became a secondary quality residing in the solitary spectator along with his intellectual faculties which enabled him to discern the rational operations of an invisible hand. This division of the inner man into the intellectual and the moral is reflected roughly in our two categories of novel; the first critical of any attempt (especially those made by the remaining representatives of feudal culture) to attribute value to the real until an indispensable period of objective waiting had borne its scientific fruit, the second obsessed by questions of private morality precisely because, in our system, public morality, or responsibility, whether in the form of the primitive group-self or of socialism, was at first the greatest single obstacle and became, with Marx, the greatest threat to one of the most grotesque developments in all of human history, the private ownership of land and, eventually, of the sea and air since private interests are destroying both. After two hundred years of progress it appears we have been progressing in the direction of global famine; capitalism and Western culture created one world and one human race for the purpose of starving it.[38]

To be sure, in Defoe's day nothing of all this could be foreseen, but the origins of the predicament (the conflict between the universal and the particular, the explicit and implicit) and the means of dealing with it—by private morality, that is, identity—are clearly visible. Robinson Crusoe, for example, is shipwrecked in the course of a slaving expedition, yet when he begins to wonder why such a misfortune should have befallen him all he is able to find is that, in going away to sea, he had disobeyed his father. To answer that slavery at that time was taken for granted is to beg the question. How could it be taken for granted in view of what we learn when Singleton discovers drifting at sea a slave ship whose white crew had been killed by the blacks? Singleton's men, incensed at what they had found, are all for the immediate execution of the slaves when William, the Quaker, intervenes and "with many persuasions prevailed upon them, by telling of them, that it was nothing but what, if they were in the negroes condition, they would do, if they could; and that the negroes had really the highest injustice done them, to be sold for slaves without their consent; and that the law of nature dictated it to them that they ought not to kill them, and that it would be wilful murder to do it."[39] There is a long passage in Defoe's *Roxana* with all the force and feeling of the best present-day pamphlets on women's liberation.[40] But if the "universalizing" effect of scientific rationalism is so effective in the case of women, how is it possible for Colonel Jack, without the slightest qualm, to use negro slaves on his tobacco plantation in Virginia? His slaves are very well treated, to be sure; nevertheless there are only two rational possibilities. Either blacks, like women, are part of the human race, in which case slavery is an abomination, or they belong to some ill-defined lesser species in which case the manner in which they are treated is of little consequence.

This whole section of *Colonel Jack* offers a glimpse of liberalism in its sturdy, naive early years where it can be studied more easily.[41] When Defoe argues eloquently and at length for humane treatment of slaves he does exactly as does the liberal industrialist of our own day concerned to humanize assembly line work by forming teams of workers who fix their own pace and see the same automobile through from beginning to completion. The concern of the industrialist is necessarily hypocritical since he could easily come to understand if he wished that whatever working conditions may be, money—wages, for example—can buy only commodities, but the worker cannot be a commodity, that is, a thing, since he would then be susceptible to definition, and it is inconceivable that a thing define itself. (The existentialists say that it is of the essence of man that he be unable to attribute to himself an essence.) The only possibility is that some men are qualified to define others, which is to say that men are of different kinds, in which case we enter into conflict with that universalism without which scientific rationalism is inconceivable. The difference between Defoe and the contemporary liberal is that Defoe, with a candor educated people no longer willingly display, continually reminds the reader that Colonel Jack is a gentleman *born,* that he never intended to do wrong and that consequently his early life of crime was a pure appearance beneath which the identity of a gentleman remained unaffected. But then it follows—very conveniently for a system based on the purchase, in one form or another, of men-objects—that when Defoe describes negroes as he does (they are of a "brutal and obstinate temper,"[42]) he identifies them in the sense in which I have been usng the word. For whatever their traits of character may be, such traits are not the perfectly understandable reaction to the conditions of life imposed upon slaves but, on the contrary, inborn characteristics. When, therefore, Defoe advocates humane treatment, he acts out of pure generosity. When Colonel Jack proves "that a negro can be grateful"[43] we are free to conclude that gratitude is an appearance beneath which a negro's "temper" is unaffected, just as Colonel Jack took upon himself for awhile the appearance of a criminal.

Colonel Jack is not one of Defoe's best novels, the reason for this being clear enough. As in the case of *La Vie de Marianne,* it is a story about how the hero becomes what he already is; and we know that part of the art of the novel consists in not allowing its fundamental subject matter (identity as a given-proven) to emerge too obviously.[44] *Captain Singleton* is also a lesser work, for although there is more doubt as to what exactly Singleton is, Defoe never allows us to suppose him to be indistinguishable from his villanous crew; at the end of the novel Singleton and William the Quaker rid themselves by a subterfuge of the "rogues" who for years had been their faithful comrades-in-arms.[45]

Our second category of novel is that which would eventually provide the implicit content of the classical novel, the crucial level of discourse, that which gradually rendered natural the extraordinary conception of morality as an almost entirely private matter. We have seen that tragedy in Renaissance theatre is brought about because the hero has a public responsibility which he cannot disregard without destroying himself. Oedipus committed his "crimes" in total ignorance of what he was doing, so that the contemporary reader is puzzled to know what all the fuss is about. Whereas in the case of Moll Flanders who also commits incest involuntarily there is no tragedy because the heroine's intentions were pure, that is, her quality as a private individual is unaffected. In the theatre of antiquity and of the Renaissance the hero has a public dimension in the sense that, like Christ, he is a mediator between the beyond and humanity. Needless to say there is no question in the novel of the hero transcending the private realm in such a way, but it is vitally important to see that while bourgeois rationalism had brought into being a new form of public responsibility (our planet is inhabited by a single human race all the members of which, whether men or women and whatever their color, are born equal) it was a responsibility which could be safely ignored since morality is essentially a question of demonstrating inner quality. It is true that such quality is sometimes proven in one's treatment of others, for example, Colonel Jack returns money stolen from an old woman, and Captain Singleton, at some risk to himself, spares the lives of the crew of a captured vessel. But, of course, in such a system there is always the possibility of an individual or a group failing to produce evidence they are people of an acceptable kind; so there is little difference in *Robinson Crusoe* and *Captain Singleton* between hunting natives and hunting game, and the bombardments of North Vietnam were not acts of senseless barbarism because the victims were not human beings but communists and Orientals.

The best of the classical novels make use of an economy of means in that a character is tested as it moves through a society which, since it is middle class, and since it is shown as fully and as honestly as the author knows how, is simultaneously denounced. Thanks to a realism which is impressive because the novelist is brought to acknowledge the vileness of his own society and class, the reader easily overlooks the unreality involved in adjusting event to identity by providing a conclusion which is morally significant in terms of individual quality regarded as a given. The realism of the explicit level could not be developed before full responsibility for social and political conditions could be attributed to the bourgeoisie (that is, not much before the time of Balzac); however, there was at least the possibility of attenuating the lack of verisimilitude that results when the novelist manipulates event as a function of identity, and this is Defoe's achievement in his two best novels, *Moll Flanders* and *Roxana*.

In cultures unaffected by scientific rationalism the distinction between fact and value, between science and religion, cannot be drawn. In primitive societies—including our own medieval—an individual was inevitably one of the faithful for the simple reason that reality would not have made sense otherwise. Individual morality was almost indistinguishable from group comportment since that comportment was dictated by the very nature of things, and any other would have been not so much immoral as anomalous and incomprehensible. However, as the concept "nature," a separate, essentially quantitative and impersonal entity, came into being a new and growing social group which assured its existence by engaging in activities (commerce, manufacturing, the purchase of formerly inalienable land) largely unregulated in traditional cultures seemed to be functioning not as a group but as individuals arriving at free decisions. But while these decisions and activities were free in that there was no place for them, except perhaps as strictly peripheral interests, in ancient orders, they could not be free in any real sense of the word in a world increasingly dominated by scientific mechanism. Hence the strange juxtaposition in Defoe of Protestant moralism (freedom), and such words as nature, law, reason and the like. We know that the "solution" was the invention of modern man: a creature both determined and free, a given-proven. But then what if a person's conduct were transparently dictated by his determination to survive? There are many passages in both *Moll Flanders* and *Roxana* where Defoe poses this question, but it was far too soon for him to be proposing the answer the naturalists would give: the survival of the fittest; man is a scientific rather than a moral thing, that is, something produced by the environment, like Taine's La Fontaine. On the other hand, it is even more unthinkable that Defoe had in mind the only remaining possibility: man not as the produced thing, but as the ultimate producer of all things including the bizarre notion of man we owe to scientism. In *Colonel Jack* and *Captain Singleton,* as we have seen, Defoe adopts the solution of his time. Good men may be driven to extremities without their "good substance" being affected; it is simply concealed.

But what if a whole way of life is at once an attempt to survive and morally wrong? The weakness of *Captain Singleton* is that we are obliged to imagine the hero a good pirate. It is just conceivable that Singleton had no bloody crimes to atone for at the time of his conversion, but it strains our credulity. What was needed therefore was a hero forced into a way of life (isolated misdeeds can always be said to have had good motives) incompatible with accepted notions of morality and yet at the same time not so criminal as to sacrifice the reader's sympathy. What was needed, in other words, was a woman living in sin; and that is what we have in Moll Flanders and in Roxana. Realism of this kind—that which consists in forcing the hero to choose between crime and survival, putting identity to a genuine test—would not recur until the 19th century. But there, as we saw, although an "isolated misdeed" (since it was a matter of coldblooded murder) could have served as the most conclusive of tests, Rastignac's name and influential relations made the crime unnecessary, so his identity survives without too great a strain. Raskolnikov, however, though in far more desperate straits, is really undone because his reason momentarily overrules the dictates of an infallible conscience. There are none of these refinements with Moll Flanders or Roxana; each is brought to the verge of actual starvation, and each slips into whoredom to save herself. Each is tormented by her conscience; but neither is there the unequivocal demonstration of innate goodness on the one hand (as in Balzac and Dostoevsky) nor, on the other, does the Lord finally rid the earth of bad women, as he does in the case of Anna Karenina.

Yet Defoe—in view of the period in which he lived, and the existence of *Colonel Jack*—was certainly not suggesting that it is out of the question to arrive at firm judgements of our fellow men. What he does seem to be doing (which is remarkable enough) is saying that conditions of life in our society are such that, in some instances at least, what a person does may not be an accurate reflection of exactly what he is without it being easy for us to wriggle out of the dilemma, as in *Colonel Jack,* by assuming there exists a concealed identity. Here and there in his novels Defoe looks wistfully toward the possibility of distinguishing between wrongdoing by inclination and wrongdoing by necessity.[46] But he is too honest to be satisfied with that, for Moll Flanders goes on stealing, and Roxana continues to whore long after each of them had become well-to-do. For Defoe property is sacred, and so Moll is a sinner and a criminal. Yet when she is finally caught and taken to Newgate, she refers to the "hardened wretches" she finds herself among.[47] And when she and her husband are condemned to be transported, she explains to the boatswain of the ship carrying them to Virginia that "we had been persons of a differing character from the wretched crew that we came with."[48] So despite the lives they lead (Moll's husband is a highwayman) they are somehow, like Captain Singleton, different from the others, and this confusion is the greatness of Defoe as a novelist for it compels the reader to suspect what he knows perfectly well but prefers not to know, that one does not survive in our society thanks to one's moral quality but to the lack of it. The choice is not between doing right or wrong but, as Vautrin put it, being hammer or anvil. The Protestant beyond was still too strong in Defoe's time for him to go nearly as far as Balzac, but there are, in *Roxana*, some astonishing anticipations. Roxana's maid, Amy, sometimes plays almost exactly the role which would one day be that of Vautrin in the life of Rastignac.[49] And it is impossible not to think of *The Brothers Karamazov* when Amy murders Roxana's daughter who threatens to destroy her mother's newly found legal and blameless position in society.[50] Roxana, like Dostoevsky's Ivan, is horrified at what happens, and although she is innocent of the crime since she had expressly forbidden it one cannot but attribute to her, as in the case of Ivan, a measure of responsibility.

Since Roxana's religious convictions are unshakable, she neither puts unanswerable nor unanswered questions to nature and society as should a problematic hero, nor does Defoe inform us "honestly" and fully as to what exactly Roxana is so that we may have the satisfaction of seeing confirmed once more the relationship between wealth and quality which is the basis of bourgeois legitimacy. On the contrary one might even be tempted to acknowledge, as Balzac did a century later, that wealth comes not as the consecration of inner richness but as the reward of crime more or less skillfully concealed. The reader may even, if he wishes, answer the question Defoe keeps posing: why do Moll Flanders and Roxana persist in their naughty ways long after they had acquired enough to support themselves for the rest of their lives? Might it not be that in a society where the law grants the wealthy the right of absolute irresponsibility toward the poor one is never sufficiently far beyond the reach of want?

If we bear this in mind I think we may come close to accounting for the extraordinary position *Robinson Crusoe* has always occupied in the history of fiction. Crusoe is a man who survives *innocently.* He is put to a very severe test in the course of which he displays a variety of admirable qualities which earn for him, eventually, a life secure from need. This he achieves without taking anything from anyone; even the "capital" with which he begins (what he salvaged from the wreck) he acquired innocently since the crew had been drowned. Nevertheless it would appear that Defoe paid far too high a price for all this, namely, the suppression of other people, the risk of writing a story for children, a sort of "real fairy tale." This does not happen for two reasons. First, the novel is already by its very nature condemned to solipsism in that the crucial "ontological" relationship (since identity is a given) can never be that between people but only that between an individual and the beyond. In fiction, other people exist to give the protagonist the opportunity to demonstrate all the more conclusively his "true nature," while, of course, in real life others (working through parents, initially) *constitute* a "nature" which is therefore subject in some instances to revision later on and which is consequently not a natural fact, but a social fact. Defoe therefore lost less than might appear by leaving Crusoe, before the appearance of Friday, with only God for a companion. A hidden companion but nevertheless palpable enough still, almost two centuries later, to kill Anna Karenina. Second, *Robinson Crusoe* is the first, greatest, and perhaps only novel of consequence about frontier life, that is, a life of struggle not against other people, but against the natural environment. Other people existed of course, but fortunately they were not human as we are, but "primitives," "savages" or, as in Crusoe's case, cannibals.[51]

However, again fortunately, certain of these creatures (Friday being a good example) are capable, with a little instruction, of conceiving a salutary horror of their own nature, and upon these we can safely confer the honor and privilege of serving us.

By Defoe's day the peoples of Western Europe were well on the way to the conquest of the whole planet. But they did not set out as entire migrating peoples seeking territories with sufficient resources to sustain them as *collectivities* which therefore would be held in common. The basic tool of primitive groups is their relationship to the environment regarded as a being who will provide abundantly on condition his integrity be respected, that is, in most cases, made sacred. Before the Renaissance this necessity the group was under to solicit or to negotiate with the natural environment as with a sacred being constituted a kind of equality of dependence among different human groups which made possible throughout history a more or less continual fusion or intermingling of people, a cross-fertilization which undoubtedly played a vital role in the origins of all the great civilizations of the past. The notion of racial superiority or of racial purity is very recent; it is part of the pseudo-scientific cultural baggage of the great white destroyer.[52] Needless to say it was invented not out of perversity but because for the first time in history the existence of one group meant the inevitable, more or less rapid extermination of all the others. There could be no cultural exchanges or territorial arrangements where the intention of one of the parties was the destruction of the territory; that is, its secularization, its privatization, the giving over of common land to individuals or to family units able to survive apart from the primitive collectivity thanks to their tools, weapons, and supply lines to Europe. Common land is the common use of territorial resources, the recognition of common rights, sometimes even where one group has enslaved another; private land is the inevitable starvation of the original occupants of the region.[53]

To say that private property, bourgeois civilization, inexorably destroys primitive collectivities (and would eventually enter into a life or death struggle against revolutionary solidarity) is to say at the same time that solitude, like some insatiable monster, waits for the stragglers whether rich or poor; the others try to protect themselves through associations of like entities: romantic love, cult of the family and the nation, innumerable clubs and organizations. But what holds the entities together is less a force operating from inside drawing toward the center, than a shrinking from what is outside—a hatred or contempt for others which reaches a hideous paroxysm in fascism, but which is the only "justification" (and we cannot do without one since rationalist universalism has to be counterbalanced) for the piratical sacking of a planet for the benefit not of men, but of a few individuals.

Robinson Crusoe is the enthusiastic account of the astonishing success a man achieved alone, with the help of God, of course, but as Defoe himself knew perfectly well, primarily with the help of his tools.[54] This would have been remarkable enough in itself when one thinks of the degree to which mass entertainment exploits the theme of the man alone (or men in very small groups) who thanks to his mastery of tools (usually guns and explosives) and, of course, his "goodness" which brings about providential intervention from the beyond at moments when the odds are particularly overwhelming, succeeds in ridding the earth of evil individuals (in *Robinson Crusoe*, the cannibals). But what is even more remarkable is Defoe's warning that success is at the same time failure. Crusoe becomes, through his own labor and therefore legitimately, the proprietor of a domain which provides richly for all his needs but which is, simultaneously, a place of solitary confinement. Throughout the novel Crusoe is unable to decide whether he is to be congratulated for having come into possession of a large and splendid estate or whether he is to be pitied for having labored so long simply to make his own prison endurable.[55] Such is, to this day, exactly the predicament of the free-enterprising Western individual who has labored for two centuries only to discover himself walled up within his own material and cultural individualism. Our half-witted, frenetic "progress" toward *individual* self-sufficiency had to produce gutted cities and a befouled countryside before we were able to see that, in destroying primitive "conviviality," we destroyed the essential, unless it can be reconstituted in the form of revolutionary praxis.

In the meantime, with Joyce and Proust, the novel comes full circle; we are back on Crusoe's island, having discovered that the *island itself* is *home,* that imprisonment is man's highest achievement, for through it alone can he hope to reach out, if not to God as with Crusoe, at least to something beyond, to some form of "eternity" without which we are all entrapped in an evil-smelling historical cul-de-sac. Crusoe could make sense of events only in terms of sin, only in term of his quality as a person. Joyce and Proust do something very similar except that it is not one's moral quality which is tested, but rather the resourcefulness one displays in turning the island (the solitude of the inner man) into a means of getting back home. Joyce and Proust lived in exile from their childhood and youth; but rather than go back naively, like Crusoe, after

twenty-seven years to find everything changed, they used their very isolation—an estheticizing, retrospective, encyclopedic culture—to restore it
intact, exactly as it had been.

It will be recalled that the problem I am trying to deal with is that of
understanding the importance of Joyce and Proust despite their having
largely ignored the explicit level of discourse which we had grown accustomed to suppose indispensable to a genuinely great novelist working
within the classical tradition. And we have discovered—coexisting with
the novel devoted to showing that reality as the hero encounters it bears
little resemblance to what the dogmatic, whether feudal or rationalist,
claim it to be—a second category of novel making a "positive" contribution (destined to become the implicit level of the 19th century novel)
which consists in saying that events are not meaningless provided they
are related to the identity of the hero; an identity fixed by reference to
certain commonly accepted religious and moral values all the more effectively asserted for having been put forward indirectly.

With the coming to power of the bourgeoisie after the French Revolution no novelist could see reality whole without being obliged to denounce what he saw since the new ruling class, while proclaiming a new
universal humanism, had set in motion a system in which things (money,
profit) take precedence over men and in which, therefore, men
themselves become things, manipulated by various "natural laws" borrowed from the physical sciences to establish the disinterestedness of the
reigning class. However, the more virulently the novelist was obliged to
criticize his own society, the more important it became for him to find a
"solution" (otherwise we fall into Goldmann's difficulty of explaining in
what sense the novel manifests a vision peculiarly bourgeois), and he
finds it, naturally, *within* the system by accepting that men are things,
but they are moral things, that is to say, "free" to prove what they are.
Because Balzac, confronted by the calamity of bourgeois rule, was forced to much increase the critical content of fiction, he increased,
simultaneously, the safeguards against it by making of the novelist an
omniscient observer, someone in a position to penetrate infallibly to the
heart of charcter so as to do away in this respect with the uncertainties
and special pleading to which novels of the second category could give
rise as a result of their use of the first person. Conditions are not
therefore as desperate as they appear: success in business or politics confirms and identity which, in this way, comes to occupy the position most
suitable for it. Where errors occur, the gimlet eye of the novelist is also
that of the magistrate and priest (in fact, in some of the nastier forms of

nationalism it becomes that of an entire nation directed against its neighbors), so the damage is never irreparable. In identifying his characters the classical novelist makes use of criteria which plain honesty compels him to elucidate, but since that involves looking *backward,* in a century of progress and science, to religious values, he is obliged to work indirectly by suggesting that the use of reason alone leads to the unthinkable: crime and revolution.

As the 19th century wore on, however, its "progress" lay in the elaboration of an industrial and financial apparatus of which individuals were increasingly the servants or victims; so it became ever more aberrant to attribute a social significance to individual quality.[56] Furthermore, with World War I (which plays so important a role in both *Les Thibault* and *Der Zauberberg*) the system itself "leads to the unthinkable," to crime on a colossal scale. We know that the structure of the classical novel is such that it cannot deal with social problems except in terms of kinds of people; so that, with the 20th century, the classical novel had run its course, and to persist in using the form (Martin du Gard, Mann) meant remaining in the position of an omniscient observer with nothing to observe except, of course, exactly that—reality as "pure" spectacle, stripped of its myths, reality as the absence of meaning. For the second time, therefore, the existence of the novel was threatened by what the novelist—where he considered his art to be something more than entertainment—had to show (explicit level). Balzac countered the difficulty by a reinforcement of the implicit level. In his best work each incident or episode either confirms an already established identity or offers clues (either deliberately misleading or quite straightforward) as to what those still in doubt might be, and the reader is not reduced to accepting the word of interested parties as in almost all novels of the second category. However, by the time of Martin du Gard and Thomas Mann, the explicit level (meaninglessness) had destroyed all the criteria formerly used for the precise estimation of human worth. Even the "collective identity" of naturalism (man as victim) no longer seemed useful since we are the victims not of natural law but of what would eventually be called the *pratico-inerte* which makes of us victims who at least partially consent and are at least partially responsible. We have seen that the "problematic" novels which preceded Balzac were complemented by a different novel in which certain values were asserted without possibility of doubt. But since these two categories of fiction were produced by the same culture, there could have been no fundamental incompatibility; it was simply that authors of first person and epistolary novels dealt with matters about which other writers preferred to remain noncommittal on the grounds that men were not yet sufficiently informed about certain aspects of the Divine plan to pronounce with certainty. What they objected to would have been certain Protestant excesses and certainly not Rousseau's noble souls; Richardson's Sir Charles Grandison, far from being a source of merriment as Pamela had been for Fielding, gave rise to great enthusiasm in his day.

Throughout the history of the novel therefore, while the outward gaze of the novelist falling upon society as a whole and men in general gave rise only to doubts and to questions, that same attention, when directed upon individuals, discovered them to be embodiments of an exalting, reassuring moral order that would no doubt eventually emerge clearly for all to see. And when, finally, in the early years of the present century a genuinely problematic novel comes into being (those of Thomas Mann and of Martin du Gard, for instance) one which presents reality as bereft even of potential meaning, it is written, nevertheless, by and for individuals occupying "objective" places outside and above society; and even though it is suspected that such places cannot exist, it was still practicable, for a very brief period, to convert them into inner domains subject to exploration. We consequently have a repetition in different novels of what the classical novelist managed to contain within single works: the "explicit" discovery of the chaos of bourgeois society was nullified by the assumption that people differ by innate moral quality (rather than simply by the peculiar location of the point at which they make their entry into life), and that there exists consequently a moral order of which we are all the bearers. In the same way the discovery of the absurd is nullified by a second reinforcement of identity arrived at by converting the position of the intemporal, absolute spectator into an inner realm through which we gain access to a mysterious, ill-defined netherworld capable of restoring meaning to our lives. The best classical fiction is that most rich in characterizations, but characterization (as in naturalism, as in Martin du Gard and Mann) lacks depth and conviction except where an author has maintained an historically retrograde and clearly class-serving set of moral values which must then be counterbalanced by a powerful development of the explicit level. The achievement of Joyce and Proust was to have done away with an archaic moral code while at the same time actually enriching characterization by placing the reader "inside" where he could participate in the hero's affective life. It is as though the classical novel, just before its disappearance from the scene, had contrived to suppress the division within itself (explicit and implicit levels) by causing the true subject matter of the novel to occupy the entire fictional space in the form of an inner life which the reader can share. The explicit level can safely be much reduced in importance because the reader is no longer at a spectator's distance from the hero and therefore no longer required to judge on the basis of "particularist" criteria.

It would have been difficult or impossible for a 19th century novelist to be perfectly lucid about that presupposition without which the classical novel could not have existed: man is object, but he differs from "real" objects in that he is required to prove he is this or that kind of object. We know that the greatest of the 19th century novelists (Balzac, Dostoevsky, Tolstoy) traced back to religion the origins of the criteria used in determining kinds of people, and they were compelled to do so since without a beyond we are left, on the explicit level, with a civilization which is, in reality, a jungle where only the most ruthless or insensitive survive. But we know as well that, from the beginning, strictly moral criteria were not the only ones the novelist could use: Marianne was not only virtuous but a lady; Colonel Jack was primarily a gentleman; Rousseau's characters are extraordinarily noble of soul; and Rastignac is to be congratulated for being "superior" as well as for having an infallible conscience. By the time we reach James high moral standards can be so taken for granted that the reader's attention is more often drawn to the hero's cultural refinement. Bourgeois legitimacy, in other words, derives not only from identity as the more or less spontaneous cleaving to the moral law (since even the poor can do that, at least if they are stupid enough, as they always are in the English novel) but from identity as Crusoe's island rendered supremely habitable thanks to the prisoner's spiritual gifts. In our culture (to misquote Donne) "every man is an island unto himself"; and Montaigne had already suggested that this might be where our true freedom is to be found.[57]

Crusoe still had the privilege of various signs from on high, but as the Lord became ever more hidden, and as the heroic age of the founding fathers receded, the need was felt to develop the cultural resources of the island. As Europe's civilizing mission drew near completion the time came to explain—since man does not live by bread alone—what it had all been for, and to celebrate. But how (unless one is Kipling) do scribes *fête* the triumphs of self-important tricksters sitting in countinghouses? The importance of the Lukács-Goldmann theory is to remind us that, for as long as bourgeois civilization exists, its principal art form will have to face the consequences of our having replaced use by exchange value: it will have to show reality as being this, while everyone who is sane and in the least informed, knows it ought to be something very different. This is the basis of Sartre's *Qu'est-ce que la littérature*? Literature is an "appeal to our freedom," our freedom to see to it that reality comes closer to what we know it can and ought to be. But, as we have just seen, the novel, from the beginning, took precautions: the "freedom" to which the explicit level of discourse appeals does not really exist since character is, in the last analysis, a thing defined by reference to a more or less elucidated beyond; and, when all that became a little too preposterous, character, without ceasing to be a thing, was converted into a sumptuous living area, the estheticized treasurehouse of memory, the island domain of those who, after Flaubert, knew how to transmute the selfish ennui of bourgeois life into the gold of beauty.

Culture, however, as our society defines it does not serve merely to render the inevitable solitude of the bourgeois individual more endurable. If it is hard to explain how private wealth can lead to public benefits, then one has forgotten the libraries, the museums and the galleries. No sooner had we exterminated the North American Indians than buildings were erected to house and immortalize their arrowheads and teepees. They would not have done as much for us. It is in the nature of primitives to sacrifice the real past to a mythological one so as to be able, like children, to live in the present. One would not expect them to understand the unselfishness of spending millions on saving ancient Egyptian monuments from water backing up from the Aswan Dam. It would have been more immediately satisfying to have given the money to terribly needy, living Egyptians; but we have a responsibility to posterity. It is unselfishly and joylessly that we intellectuals have become the soberly clad curators of everything and anything that has died. One can appreciate in this light the achievement of Joyce and Proust who worked out methods for restoring the past to life, for converting the present into a still living past.[58] (T.S. Eliot achieves something similar in his poetry where a grasp of the present as a wasteland is conditional upon one's having a gentleman's grounding in all things dead.)

By the early 20th century, then, the synthesis of explicit and implicit levels which the classical novel had brought about is no longer workable, and fiction "reverts" to the two categories which had existed before Balzac. In the first category, the novelist persists as omniscient observer even though there is nothing left for him to observe with any conviction: neither character in the grand manner as moral identity, since morals and religion are relative, not reality as envisaged by scientism thanks to which there could exist in varying degrees and combinations sociological identities, identity by default and the identification of mankind as a whole (man as "insect-victim"). For the first time, therefore, we have a certain number of fictional heroes who are "problematic" in the full sense of the word; their quest comes literally to nothing because there simply are no answers (whereas doubt as it exists in the novels of the first category is a formal one, like that of Descartes; one doubts so as to undermine feudal dogmatism and prevent the resurgence of other "metaphysics" until the great scheme, free of historical debris and despite human folly in all its forms, can stand clearly forth). But if, in some quarters, the spectacle had ceased to have any meaning, in others it was suspected that what we see might be a function of our angle of vision. If we see nothing perhaps it is because the position of the 19th century novelist outside and above both time and place was imaginary. The result was the attempt on the part of two great novelists, Joyce and Proust, to see reality as reflected through an ineluctable subjectivity, but that subjectivity remained the universal one of classical bourgeois philosophy, a "subjectivity-container" in which reality reappears substantially unaffected by its transposition to the "inside"; so the real goal of the operation becomes the cultivation of an inwardness which had been the unique province of the novel from the beginning.

But in the past that inwardness had always existed so that the reader might judge its quality through reference to a beyond. This is what Joyce and Proust change: inwardness is not there so that we may determine what kind of thing it is but to provide access to a new beyond, neither scientific nor religious. It is here we can appreciate that our four novelists, two of whom appear to have left work differing in nature from that of the other two, were contemporaries confronted by the same problem—the bankruptcy of bourgeois rationalism—to which they gave answers which were the same: the occupation of a viewing position which is, in reality, a means of evasion, and an attempt to face new problems by making use of deep-seated cultural presuppositions which the revolution in science and philosophy had already condemned to obsolescence. No one can take the beyond one reaches through interiority in Joyce and Proust seriously; their real purpose therefore was to fashion an inner dwellingplace to which we can withdraw from an increasingly insane reality.[59] Similarly, in Martin du Gard and Mann, since nothing much is visible any longer even from the God's-eye vantage point of the classical novelist, the real purpose becomes the preservation of a position-refuge which is the equivalent on the "outside" of an "inner garden" made fertile by a cultivated and encyclopedic memory.

The novel consequently, with our four authors, becomes more incurably bourgeois than ever. Previously there had been an explicit level on which the great 19th century novelists, although they could not address themselves *to* all men—since their readers had to be middle class to be literate—at least spoke *for* all men. Since the generalization of literacy had not been won by the masses in a revolutionary upheaval but granted by the system so that its increasingly complex technological equipment could be competently manned, entertainment was also granted from above, and it took the form, naturally, of the classical novel which, however, had to be modified to meet new requirements. It was intended not for cultivated gentlemen seeking, with the help of authors like Joyce and Proust, to furnish an inner retreat with beautiful objects salvaged from the past, but for weary employees who had to be convinced that, even though they enjoyed few if any of the cultural and economic advantages of individualism, they nevertheless existed normally and naturally as separate entities since an invisible hand reserved them a fate carefully adjusted to their quality. To transform itself into mass entertainment the classical novel therefore eliminated or trivialized the explicit level and inflated the implicit into sensationalism, that is, into the exciting, last minute triumph of good over evil. Mass entertainment is a readily available non-prescription drug taken with feelings of simultaneous relief and disgust which causes people to set aside their common sense so they may believe that a principle of order struggles endlessly and successfully to put things right.

The solution could lie only in the invention of a new novel. And if the structure of fiction since Defoe and Cervantes is as we have described it, then this work begins undoubtedly with Stendhal to whom we can now turn.

CHAPTER V

Stendhal was a contemporary of Balzac; so if he did succeed in creating a novel different in kind from all that had gone before and all that would follow until Kafka he could not have done so as the spokesman of a different culture. He could not have created a novel that was "new" in the sense that the 17th century novel had been new by virtue of giving expression to a culture offering different values and a different way of life. It must be, therefore, that bourgeois rationalism contains *with itself* the possibility of a revolutionary choice; a choice not between alternative cultures, but between the accepting of a state of affairs by common consent intolerable and working toward a future which the existence of scientific technology makes perfectly practicable.

To belong to bourgeois culture is to be divided against oneself; this is the significance of the contradiction between implicit and explicit in the classical novel. To be a revolutionary is to be determined that reality shall be altered in such a way as to suppress that division. But we know that in the classical novel there are two distinct realities: the reality of social conditions and the reality of the beyond with reference to which it is possible to establish the existence of different kinds of men. The reality of social conditions then takes on an entirely different significance. It is no longer these conditions which determine the quality of human life but the quality of individuals which, in the last analysis, determines the conditions. Since that quality is a given, then so are the conditions, and bourgeois society is permanently and justifiably stabilized. Yet conceivably the truth about social conditions was so appalling that simply to show them as accurately as possible (Zola) might perhaps in itself contribute to changing them? So there comes into being an absolute deadlock between explicit and implicit levels; a division within the novelist himself which Stendhal alone among 19th century novelists was able to surmount. To understand how he did this, let us look again at the process which gave rise to the contradiction.

We assumed at the outset that if the novel is a bourgeois art form, then there was a good chance it might contain, in addition to its criticism or interrogation of the real, a "positive" element; and this we discovered to be individualism, man defined as object but, incomprehensibly, an object which is free to establish through moral and/or cultural endeavor that he (it) is of a given kind. The classical novel brings about a synthesis of these two elements (social criticism and identity) in the following way: the novelist becomes an omniscient, impersonal observer, in a position, therefore, to view the "whole" of his society and times; this, in turn, enables him to "place" his character effectively, that is, take the first step toward establishing an identity. Thus, high society will "naturally" produce people like Anna Karenina and Vronsky while other kinds of people (Kitty and Levin) will find themselves more naturally placed in the country; commerce and finance will "naturally" give rise to people like Balzac's César Birotteau or Zola's Saccard. But Saccard is a very feeble characterization, and the principal reason for this is to be found far less in differences of "talent" in the novelists concerned than in the way in which they utilized the structure of classical fiction. Great 19th century novelists, having shown reality as fully as they knew how were obliged, at the same time, to denounce what they saw. But Balzac, Tolstoy and Dostoevsky do so far more openly than Zola, that is, they allow their characters, and sometimes they themselves, a criticism of bourgeois society so relentless and persuasive that there is "no alternative" but to reestablish ancient values if "civilization" is to endure. In this way these authors inconspicuously grant themselves moral criteria which, along with the infallible judgements that follow from omniscience, enabled them to achieve characterizations far more memorable than any in Zola.

One thing alone in all this was *indubitable*: social reality as it had come to exist since the French Revolution could not be tolerated (hence the explicit level could not possibly be dispensed with). But then the self-evidence of social abuses is immediately rendered inconsequential when it is pointed out by Balzac, Dostoevsky and Tolstoy, that reason, far from offering a conceivable solution, is part of the evil. So what then becomes "self-evident" is conscience, the religious sentiment, and of necessity, since only reason presumably might have led us out of the wilderness. These novelists were right, to be sure, to warn us there exists a rational insanity, a *délire logique* which, incidentally, is often that of the modern technocrat. But then, far from leaving things at that, far from remaining "problematic," they attempt to revive values which could no longer be "universalized." For while the peasantry of Tolstoy's Russia may have been medieval, the miners in *Germinal* were atheists. Similarly, in the case of Zola (and Flaubert and Maupassant) it was sufficient to show reality to be sure that every reader (including working class readers, had there been any) would know at once what was meant. But then, once again, as with Balzac, Dostoevsky and Tolstoy, the self-evident contradiction between what social conditions really were and what they were supposed to be is obscured when—by what we can only consider a class or particularist recourse—reality becomes pure exteriority which we can more or less objectively, more or less accurately observe, but which we cannot hope to change.[1] Novelists like Martin du Gard and Mann, as we have seen, although without interest in the traditional absolutes, nevertheless maintain a position (that of the vast majority of Western intellectuals) which is unintelligible apart from them. It is like some strange cargo cult keeping a lookout for the arrival of ships loaded with answers even though everyone knows the ships do not exist. The purpose of the rite is to enable the lookout to pretend not to know where he is, not to know he is divided against himself since he belongs to a culture which has created a universally unacceptable reality. We know also that subjectivity in Joyce and Proust was not that "indubitable awareness" which writers like Tolstoy and Zola knew they could count upon in the reading public when they offered a picture of reality as accurate and as impersonal as they could make it. It was, instead, a means of belonging to some other age.

"We can imagine a society in which reflexion would build up into a world of lies. We can all the more easily imagine such a society because it is our own."[2] If reflexion (that is, bourgeois ideology) is a lie, then it can only be that on another level of awareness, the pre-reflexive, we know indisputably something it is the function of ideology to explain away. If reflexion takes us away from the truth rather than toward it,[3] it is because reflexion (religion, philosophy, scientism) is, like growing food or building houses, something men do for certain reasons. It is a form of praxis, and in a class society it will, inevitably, be directed toward maintaining the supremacy of one class over the others. The truth then becomes the demand to know why praxis (since there is no position outside or above praxis) should not be directed exclusively toward implementing the self-evident proposition that all men are equal since we have the technological means of providing equally for all. Otherwise the notion of equality could not have existed in the first place. We know that the classical novel was able to survive the loss of confidence in its "reflexion" (scientism and middle class moral values) because the essential, identity, remained in the form of an intensified and elaborated inner life on the one hand, and, on the other, as a purely imaginary, disembodied, supra-temporal recording apparatus. However, if the explicit level of the classical novel is that of the pre-reflexive (there was no need for Zola to explain that living conditions among the poor were such that no truly civilized society would have tolerated them) then we know what is being shown us not because we are reasoning, objectively viewing, moral or immoral individuals but, on the contrary, because we exist only as praxis. The choice then is to acknowledge our historical subjectivity, our historical tasks (the explicit) or to attempt to erect ideological protective barriers the most effective of which has proven to be the notion that men are not simply what they do (praxis), but that they do as a consequence of what they are (identity).

The work of Stendhal makes it clear that even in the early years of the 19th century it was possible for a novelist to choose, to choose to attach himself to what alone was indubitable, refusing the ideological-particularist recourse to a reflexive beyond and the equally reflexive concept of the self as object. It was far too soon of course for Stendhal to make of these questions a matter of principle as we do today. As far as he was concerned he was, like Balzac, "holding a mirror up to reality." And yet any reader knowing very little about Stendhal's period, having taken care not to read the critics for whom Stendhal's work is "necessarily," given his dates, a rather strange mixture of Romanticism and Realism, would know at once, reading the first chapter of *Le Rouge et le noir* and comparing it to anything in Balzac, that he had entered a fictional universe different in kind from that of Balzac. Such a reader would sense that the tone of that first chapter is somehow unique in 19th century fiction even though Stendhal is saying there exactly what we get from the explicit level of all of Balzac's best novels. But the terminology we have been using is no longer of any help. There is neither an implicit nor an explicit level in Stendhal; the two have been fused into a unified discourse the narrator of which is neither an objective observer nor the first person of our second category of novel. In Stendhal there is neither a reality from which an observer could detach himself, nor a subjectivity-domain; so that there sets in a "confusion" which was not much appreciated at the time and which would not recur until Kafka, an ambiguity which arises when we see reality to be—like language—inseparably a part of us and apart from us. Reality, for Stendhal (as for Marx) is not pure exteriority; it is value-ridden. And, inversely, subjectivity is not thing-domain, but the *act* of attributing value and significance as a function of the goals which have been set.

Stendhal's tour de force in the novel consists in dealing exclusively with what everyone knows and cannot help but know by virtue of belonging to the same culture at approximately the same moment in its historical evolution. As a consequence Stendhal's heroes neither fall within our field of vision to be judged, nor are they problematic in the Lukács-Goldmann sense. They are simply, and essentially, the anonymous pre-reflexive acknowledgement of what no one in his right mind can fail to admit; they are, therefore, all the same person, and they are all Stendhal himself. Mosca is Julien Sorel grown to middle age, Lucien Leuwen is Julien born rich rather than poor; Lamiel is Julien as a woman, Fabrice is Julien as a young Italian nobleman. Stendhal's novels are all in the first person although he pretends they are not, and this is what gives rise to those extraordinary and very numerous passages in which he seems to appeal to the reader against the outrageous conduct or sentiments of the hero whereas, in reality, he is insulting the reader for not having the moral courage to sympathize fully with this hero-Stendhal who is "shocking" simply because he refuses to have recourse to the ideological or the conventional against the self-evident. Stendhal knew that the vast majority of his readers were the natural enemy, those important and respectable individuals he showed to be such fools in all his novels. When he addresses himself to them directly the result can be the few lines immediately preceding the opening chapter of *Lucien Leuwen* which begin "Gentle reader" and conclude, "Farewell friend-reader; try not to spend your life hating and being afraid."

There is a passage in *Le Rouge et le noir* where Stendhal describes Madame de Rênal giving herself over to the happiness of being in love with Julien Sorel and feeling fully alive for the first time.[4] But then suddenly the word adultery occurs to her and, for a moment, the joy of lovemaking appears to her as the "vilest debauchery"; so for Stendhal conscience is not the constant, undeniable presence of the beyond in each of us but the reflexive obtrusion into our lives of *other people* with their petty fears and hatreds. A life well and courageously lived (exactly as in Camus' *l'Etranger*) is one that concedes as little as possible to the tyranny of others disguised as morality, custom, usage and the like. The beyond does not make men; it is made by them and is therefore a purely social and political phenomenon. The same may be said of reality which is not, in Stendhal, scientifically productive of identities. It is, on the contrary, the consequence of what men do. If, as Stendhal writes, the novel is a "mirror held up along the road of life, and if it reflects mud-filled ruts, one does not accuse the mirror, but the road inspector who allowed the highway to deteriorate to such a degree."[5] If the good citizens of Grenoble (Verrières in *Le Rouge et le noir*) where Stendhal was born have never forgiven him his descriptions of their town it is because Grenoble, for Stendhal, *was* simply what the townspeople said and did. Whereas for Balzac a town (Issoudun, for example, in *La Rabouilleuse*) is its history, geography and climate; Saint-Petersburg, in Tolstoy's novels, is the aggregate of its important citizens defined individually in a given way. The reader easily removes himself from that society since, seated by the author's side, he is the judge and not the judged; in Flaubert and Zola the situation is much the same, the reader being invited to contemplate not so much men themselves, as that from which they derive and which "explains" them.

There is no better way to sense the strangeness of 19th century bourgeois culture than to see that Stendhal (and the same argument could be developed in respect to Marx) gave offense even though his intensely subjective manner should have made him incomprehensible. Had mechanistic views of the universe been fully convincing, the work of Stendhal would have been unthinkable. The whole middle class way of life is like a sandcastle that any child could kick over; this is precisely why it is so desperately important that children be "educated." They must be protected against themselves and taught to *think* rationally or mystically (the two have coexisted contentedly for a century and a half, sometimes in the same man, Balzac, for instance) so they will not be able to *see*. But since people continue to see more or less clearly depending upon the amount of accurate information accessible to them, and since what they see cannot be reconciled with what they are taught to think, our culture has become marvelously productive of psychosomatic illnesses and insanity. Stendhal's novels give an overwhelming impression of intellectual and moral good health almost unique in the 19th century. This impression is the result not of his being right and the others wrong, but of his being so constituted as to have been able to live with what was left after he had treated with contempt and derision all the eternal verities of bourgeois culture. I am thinking not only of middle class morality but of the notion of scientific objectivity which Stendhal brings into question not only by his use of the first person disguised as a third and turned outward but, occasionally, in other ways as well. In *Lucien Leuwen,* for example, Stendhal tells of the pleasure Lucien found in discussing science with one Gauthier. They talked of the work of Fourier and Ampère, and of "this fundamental question: was the analytical approach keeping men from seeing the circumstances in which experiments were conducted?"[6]

What can this mean if not that scientists should bear in mind (as they are obliged to do today) the possibility that the circumstances in which an experiment is carried out may predetermine the results obtained? To be sure, Stendhal very seldom talks of science; nevertheless he would usually bear in mind the absolute relativity of the observer's position implied in the remark just quoted (and which Hegel had introduced into philosophy) when writing of art, architecture or social custom.[7] In this light the scientism that gripped European culture during the second half of the 19th century appears less as the *episteme* that some structuralists might wish to make of it than a device enabling educated people to notice the increasingly obvious class struggle without seeing it, enabling them to take up social problems but in such a way as to make it impossible to really come to grips with them since the approach used (the perfectly "natural" division into intellectual and manual labor which any intemporal, absolutist form of thought authorizes) is an aspect of the struggle.

I said a moment ago that Stendhal was able to live with what little was left after making a mockery of everything the bourgeois believes or feigns to believe. What *was* left? What are Stendhal's novels about if not identity as a given-proven since, of course, they cannot have been reduced to the explicit level alone as it exists in the classical novel without turning into some nonfictional form of expression. I think we can say that only the explicit level survived in Stendhal, but it has been transformed because only the pre-reflexive element of the explicit is retained (that is, it is not so much the *fact* that money precedes men in our society as our immediate awareness of the insanity of such a state of affairs), and it is directed far less against social and political conditions than against what "justifies" and "explains" these conditions in the classical novel: the notion that men's actions flow from an identifiable source, that men will always prove themselves to be what they already are. Hence one could say that the two levels are fused in Stendhal. With astonishing single-mindedness, he comes back to this one point everywhere in all his novels; what other novelists of the century described as a thing (the self) Stendhal presented as manifestly a form of comportment, a product of reflexion and not a discovery.[8] Identity is not already there; it is produced. It is a rôle one can assume or refuse to assume, and upon that choice depends one's value as a human being.

Valéry writes: "One cannot deal with Stendhal without having the question of sincerity arise in one form or another."[9] True, if what one means by sincerity is the refusal of the distinction and importance which people who exist "substantively" confer upon themselves. But Valéry is taking the word as it is usually used: sincerity as the honest expression of what one really thinks or feels. He then points out that this is only feasible on condition of our knowing exactly what we are, which is not possible. So we are left with Valéry taking Stendhal to task for failing to see that one cannot express what does not exist, while the non-existence of the self is the underlying premise of all Stendhal's work! Although it is true that Stendhal's novels are more "personal in tone than any to be found in literature,"[10] there is no excuse for confusing this with the notion of a "natural self" and its display as found in Jean-Jacques Rousseau with whom Stendhal is compared.[11] "What does it mean to be sincere?" Valéry asks. "There is almost no difficulty where it is a question of relationships between individuals; but between the self and one's self?"[12] And yet in Stendhal's novels the hero could be defined in each case just as Mathilde de la Mole defines Julien Sorel in *Le Rouge et le noir* as one who: "Never has any attention for himself."[13] The critics have always sensed this in explaining that Stendhal's novels are those of "energy." But it is difficult to know quite what is meant by that if not simply that Stendhal's heroes are ambitious,[14] yet that is absurd since Lucien Leuwen and Fabrice are already "arrived." Being a woman, Lamiel cannot envisage "success" in any case, and Julien Sorel no sooner "succeeds" than he commits suicide by refusing to escape from the prison where he was awaiting execution. Rastignac's *à nous deux maintenant* at the end of *Le Père Goriot* is the remark of an ambitious man in the sense that Rastignac plans to force recognition from his peers by occupying as lofty a social position as he can manage. Whereas in Stendhal concern for the opinion of others, the seeking of a favorable judgement, in short, the putting forward of an identity, is precisely what best characterizes those who pass their time "hating and fearing." Monsieur Teste, at the opera, contemplating the "social order," remarks "*They* are devoured by others."[15] Presumably the added emphasis indicates that Monsieur Teste (Valéry) is not. But then how do we account for Monsieur Teste becoming a member of the French Academy, however ironically detached from that august body he may have held himself to be?

Valéry who, long before Foucault, knew that man does not exist, no doubt knew as well that we must go on from there to define him on the basis of what he does or fails to do, as being self-inventive. But, as Valéry also knew, men do nothing alone.[16] If we ask in what company Valéry carried out his life's work, we have to answer: in that of other anti-Dreyfusards, other academicians, that group most determined that man should not invent a new society and, along with it, a new race. We do not know what Stendhal would have done had he lived at the time of the Commune, but we do know the essential: he could not have stood with the Versaillais and the esthetes, with the Flauberts and the Valérys without finding himself in sharp contradiction with his own writings. I think this may account for the tone of pique and the extraordinary inaccuracies to be found in Valéry's article. For example: "Most of those who flatter themselves with having a thorough knowledge of the human heart fail to distinguish between what they are pleased to consider their clairvoyance in this respect, and their being unfavourably predisposed toward their fellows. . . . Nothing, of course, produces more successfully the appearance of *psychological keeness* than the habit of *depreciating*."[17] Had Valéry been talking of Flaubert he would have been perfectly right, but Stendhal had no interest whatever in psychological investigation, either from the inside (introspection) or from the outside (final moral judgements). There are no villains in Stendhal, only people who do villainous things; no one is stupid or contemptible except in so far as they do stupid or contemptible things. There are no studies of physiognomy in Stendhal, whereas they are indispensable in Balzac since, correctly interpreted, a face infallibly betrays an "inner nature." Rossi, in *La Chartreuse de Parme,* is as close as Stendhal comes to providing us with a villain. But Rossi does not look the rôle, nor is he concealing an identity behind particularly "handsome, intelligent eyes."[18] His villainy consists in what he does, and his motive is simple (it is that of most politicians): "be in intimate conversation with important people and seek to please them with whatever buffoonery suits the occasion."[19]

Strictly speaking Stendhal's characters are all the same; we distinguish between them on the basis of what today we might call their existential choice. The choice Stendhal naturally and invariably "depreciates" is that which consists in acquiring by any means (Valenod, in *Le Rouge et le noir,* appropriates funds intended for the poor) sufficient wealth to be able to propose to society the kind of self it expects from its members. Conduct is then dictated by the requirements of this reflexively elaborated self rather than by the situation. Stendhal's heroes are simply people who make the reverse choice, that is, they adjust their conduct to the requirements of a given situation, never to those of self-display. There are two fundamental "situations" in Stendhal: one in which people having made the second choice come together in love or friendship; or one in which people of opposite "choices" collide with one another. It is the conduct of the heroes in this latter situation which has given rise to so much talk of Stendhal's "immoralism," an immoralism which mysteriously vanishes in situations of the former kind where one finds only loyalty and generosity. We cannot therefore look to "ruthlessness" as a means of "identifying" Stendhal's heroes whose immoralism consists in their determination to defend themselves against a society bent upon their destruction (in the cases of Julien Sorel and Fabrice del Dongo, their physical destruction), a destruction they invite by refusing to pretend that the emperor is fully clothed. They do this not because, as Valéry would have it, they prefer to fall back upon some Rousseauesque natural self, but because they find no evidence within themselves—and they therefore refuse to grant it to others—of that individual merit (identity) which is the only possible legitimacy of the whole bourgeois system.

In *Le Rouge et le noir,* Mathilde thinks to herself, "I don't know Julien." She then goes on: "Julien refused to don the petty little *uniform* of the salons: this is his superiority and, at the same time, the very thing that makes my father unwilling to believe in it."[20] I do not think anyone could prove that, in Stendhal's mind, there exists beneath the "uniform" of bourgeois hypocrisy (what Sartre calls "distinguished comportment") a more natural garb which one could describe with reasonable accuracy. All he says is that this particular uniform will not do because it is worn out of cowardice and carefully nurtured stupidity; beneath it there is only an impossible nudity, a nonexistence with which the hero can live only on condition he avoid being deceived or humiliated. This is the "energy" of Stendhal's novels; it is not a "passion" flowing, as in Balzac, from a source in identity. It is rather a series of freely chosen goals (identity, being a given, can only set predetermined goals through which, inevitably, it will confirm itself) which the hero must reach since, despising the prefabricated selves his society attempts to impose, he has no other form of existence. The penalty for failure is self-contempt, even for Lucien Leuwen and Fabrice del Dongo, unable to regard their wealth as the outward sign of some inborn endowment.

Since the subject matter of Stendhal's novels is the nonexistence of identity he had no need of the beyond which he unceremoniously drops, hardly noticing he had done so except for a few very remarkable pages at the end of *Le Rouge et le noir,* pages which might, incidentally, be mistakenly regarded as confirmation of the Lukács-Goldmann theory of the novel. Julien Sorel's career is at an end. He had risen from the bottom to the very top of the social order only to find nothing there and to realize it would have been wiser to have stayed in Verrières with Madame de Rênal. But the picaresque novel (the second category) is essentially an interrogation of the universe, of reality, from which man in some way derives; whereas in Stendhal there can be no quest for an answer since there is no beyond. What is most striking about all Stendhal's heroes is that they already know, and their only "quest" (which is always successful) is for other people who also know, entirely apart from any "reflexive" demonstration that bourgeois (and, *a fortiori*, Restauration) self-importance is a hypocritical farce. The picaresque inquiry survives to some degree in the classical novel where rationality is seen to break down or to lead to crime, whereupon (though in the classical novel alone) the hero falls back upon conscience. There is nothing of this in Stendhal where "the happy few" are not the "good" but simply those who enjoy the happiness of never having cheated. But such happiness is rare and precarious because it makes a mockery of bourgeois legitimacy which, knowing itself to be vulnerable even to the unblinking stare of a child (Stendhal's Lamiel), will fight back with all its unleashed fear and cowardice. Where the hero is a plebian (Julien Sorel) the result can only be described as a story of the class struggle. In the whole history of Western fiction preceding Malraux's *La Condition humaine, Le Rouge et le noir* is the only novel of any consequence of which this may be said. For Marx, the class struggle is the motor of history (or, more accurately for us today, it is the form taken in our society by the struggle against scarcity). This means, in the last analysis, that it gives rise to class-serving ideologies of which the work of Balzac and Zola would be examples since in their novels the class struggle, where it exists at all, is the consequence of and not the reason for the existence of various extra-human forces. In Stendhal, on the contrary, there are *only* men themselves divided into two groups: the first, very few in number, capable of responding directly to the exigencies of a given situation (and then creating, inventing, themselves) refusing to pass reflexively through a self borrowed from others; the second made up of those anxious to reinforce a usurped authority by alleging the existence of an inner qualitative superiority leading to wealth and culture rather than being the consequence of those advantages.

Stendhal, then, created a number of characters who stand apart not because they voice a "natural self" (or some mysterious Gidean "authentic self") but simply through their acknowledgement of what everyone always knows. We are therefore left with the paradox of characters who are unique because they are anonymous. They are just anyone since their "characters" are no more than a crucial and self-evident negativity which is the very basis of the difference between the bourgeois and the feudal lord: there is no divine right authorizing the division of society into castes; a man *is* only insofar as he contributes through his labor to the well-being of his fellows. This notion is not the end product of reflection but the stuff with which reflection operates. It was, in the 18th century, simply the recognition of a state of affairs which anyone, at that time, could see to be progressive; the prosperity of a society had come to depend upon the practical activities—trade, manufacturing, science—of men who indiscriminately but understandably despised everything feudal. Men are therefore the *same* in that they all fulfill a practical function; man is defined as a maker and user of tools, and "honest labor" comes to be, in principle, the noblest attribute of the race.

This conception works reasonably well where it is a question of artisans, small farmers, village bakers and the like, but what of the mill hand and the entrepreneur after the socialization of labor? Why should the man who performs productive labor starve while another man, the capitalist, lives in luxury even though he produces nothing, even though he simply expropriates and distributes the surplus value resulting from the labor of others. The only conceivable answer is that men are not, after all, the same; even though, if the bourgeois is to be as good as the noble, if he is to have the moral right to rule (and, of course, if science is to be universal), then men must be the same, this being the contradiction between implicit and explicit levels. Men are the same—or equal, or "universal"—in appearance only; concealed inside there is a substantive core qualitatively different from one individual to another. Among the criteria used to judge that quality, honest labor (except in the feeble-minded mythologies of the lower middle classes) is of little importance compared to the degree of wealth necessary to high "moral" and cultural achievement. In the great majority of cases that wealth was already there; one was born into it. But then there is the danger of everyone seeing that a caste system based on birth had given way to one based on money—hardly an improvement.[21] Wealth therefore *had* to be a sign manifesting an inner goodness and superiority, and since these qualities had nothing whatever to do with the general welfare, since they were no sense practical, they could only exist by reference to another concealed entity, the Christian beyond, revived and revitalized for the needs of the moment. Where an entrepreneur claimed to be self-made, the situation was not much improved since he had made himself through a merciless exploitation of women and children. So again the pre-reflexive awareness of human sameness that scientific rationalism and the bourgeois struggle for equality had brought into being had to be ignored, this time by recourse to scientific metaphysics: there exists a law or mechanism which works toward the general good not despite but thanks to the fact that all individuals pursue selfish ends. In *Le Père Goriot,* Vautrin talks of those who labor quietly and honestly in the Lord's vineyard. It is among them one finds "virtue in its fully flowering stupidity."[22] It is among them as well we are obliged to number Rastignac's mother and sisters who, however, far from being stupid, are represented as being saintly.[23] So Balzac is forced to appeal to a retrograde beyond against Vautrin-Stendhal's "cynical" relapse into the self-evident. In *Germinal* we are at first free to suppose that if the Grégoire family lives so comfortably on the money they get from shares in the mine, it is because the miners themselves are not paid enough to be able to feed themselves; it is therefore perfectly understandable that, sooner or later, there will be strikes and rioting. Yet, when workers react with a necessary counterviolence against the violence done them by the rich, Zola, as we have seen, appeals against the resulting "disorder" to the bizarre theological-scientific notion of an historical movement which is value-free yet proceeding in the direction men want it to take.

The Enlightenment represented genuine progress, but the only way in which the advance from feudalism could have been pursued, the only way to avoid the hopeless confusions described in the foregoing paragraph would have been to allow an increasingly "hidden" God to disappear altogether as in Stendhal (and in Balzac, at least on the explicit level) and then understand that if God had vanished it could only be that man is not "made" (and therefore thing) but the maker of all things (and therefore praxis). This would have been the only way to elucidate our pre-reflexive conviction of human equality (without which such documents as the American Declaration of Independence and the French Declaration of the Rights of Man would not have been possible). The moral, physical and intellectual differences between men do not proceed from a definable, judgeable, internal source but are the consequences of a struggle to cope with a situation at once unique (circumstances of birth and family life) and general (cultural conditioning). But of course such an "elucidation" would have destroyed the very basis of capitalism: the assumption that labor (that is, according to the bourgeoisie itself, man in his highest manifestation, contrasting with the parasitical life of the noble) is a commodity like any other, put up for sale on the labor market and purchased by a salary. The contradiction between explicit and implicit levels in the classical novel reappears in the prattle of the humanists according to whom man is the measure of all things and who remain, nevertheless, the "organic intellectuals" of a society which can exist only on condition it regard man as a purchasable object.

Placed in such a context Marx appears not as the advocate of an alternative culture (in the sense that bourgeois rationalism constituted an alternative to feudal civilization) which, in any case, did not exist, but simply as a man determined to work out the whole logic of a situation which the bourgeoisie itself had brought into being: if man is to be really the measure, that is, if one is to suppress the beyond in whatever form, then one creates, simultaneously, an absolute historical relativity. If we are not to condemn ourselves to the impotence of the contemporary "absurdists" (who are not unable to choose because they can find no meaning; rather their abstentionism is, inevitably, the *choice* of existing conditions) we must be able to find within our own historical situation a "principle of disequilibrium," a means of producing a perspective (necessarily limited) upon ourselves. That "disequilibrium" exists in the contradiction between the two levels of discourse in the classical novel, but it is stabilized when the novelist "objectively" withdraws for the purpose of making sense of the spectacle before him by assuming that a man is an entity, and of a kind that can be determined with reference to a beyond.

Stendhal not only drops all this paraphernalia, he makes it clear that the total relativity that results, far from depriving us of all value and direction, (except of course for those intellectuals in whom contemplative paralysis is a way of life and a livelihood), on the contrary, clears away the ideological debris which can, if we wish, render the indubitable invisible to us. This indubitable (the "pre-reflexive" explicit level of the classical novel) is, to be sure, very largely negative but necessarily so since there is no alternative to bourgeois culture but only the possibility of compelling it to suppress the grotesque contradiction between what it professes to want and what it hypocritically declares to be the real in the old empiricist sense of something ineluctably given. However, since this contradiction cannot be seen to be repugnant and intolerable from the vantage point of a new culture, opposition must come from within, from a combination of middle class individuals repulsed by the sinister comedy of special competencies, of self-display and self-importance, and of those social groups—workers—to whom the system refuses the means of leading an autonomous individual existence on the basis of "merit." The worker, in Marx, is not, needless to say, a different and better kind of man; he is simply man as he exists "universally" *before* the reflexive, ideological invention of the self as a given and of a beyond in relation to which the self establishes its nature or quality.

In view of all this I believe that from Stendhal onward we are obliged to abandon the notion that important fiction is primarily a quest under-

taken by a problematic hero; this theory being of use only when applied
to novels of the first category. These novels, undoubtedly, leave the
reader with a strong impression of an ever recurring interrogation to
which it is impossible to find the answers; however, as we have seen,
answers are either given (by other novelists within the same culture and
class—novels of the second category) or anticipated. For it is understandable that a concealed, universal order (concealed because secondary
qualities constitute a veil of deceptive appearances) can be revealed only
progressively and that, while waiting, everyone can assist by observing
Descartes' first precept which he announces in the second part of his
Discours de la méthode: "My first principle was never to assume
anything to be true unless I had evidence it was so: that is, I must carefully avoid haste and preconception, while accepting nothing from my
judgements which did not present itself so clearly and distinctly to my
mind that I could never have occasion to call it into doubt."

This is the spirit in which the picaresque hero doubts and questions; in
so doing he, first of all, assists in the erosion of medieval culture which,
like all primitive cultures, refuses the scientific distinction between the
real and the imaginary so that physical reality can be leavened and
animated with a whole population of supra- or sub-human beings about
whose existence there can be no doubt. Secondly, by the beginning of the
19th century, an attitude which had served to discredit the anachronistic
dogmatism of the old order and which therefore had been in a sense
negative, became a positive aspect of the way in which the new regime
functioned. It became, and remains, the way of life of the bourgeois
cleric who serves a specific class and a specific culture by imagining that
his sceptical queries (which become the "objective" omniscience of the
classical novelist and, in part, the explicit level) constitute an opposition.
In reality, though, these queries constitute a wholehearted commitment
to a number of conceptions without which the system could not function,
that is, without which the writer or intellectual is left—like Stendhal—with nothing except a self-evident negation which, in the circumstances, is the only conceivable affirmation, the affirmation (in
Marx) that man is not thing but praxis. So given the existence of tools,
which enable him to master the natural environment, the only problem
becomes that of removing obstacles to the free deployment of praxis.
The bourgeois cleric is committed to maintaining those obstacles: one in
the form of an empirical or positivist real which makes of capitalism a
natural phenomenon rather than the "congealing" of the praxis of certain groups (that is, rather than structure, or *pratico-inerte*); and a se-

cond, following from the first, in the "natural" division of labor, the special competencies (in the last analysis, a form of identity) that enable some particularly "gifted" individuals to understand the functioning of a real entirely separate from men and therefore unintelligible to the common run. (For example, only the "educated" economist can understand how the economy works since it works in a way foreign to the mere wishes of the great majority, and thanks to the labors of the educated elite the ignorant and subjective worker need not be enticed into supposing himself a victim, into supposing the system works intelligibly.)

If my analysis of Stendhal's novels is correct, if he puts an end to all forms of transcendence[24] which involves, as well, the end of the problematic hero and of man viewed as identity, then that analysis will have to be confirmed by what is best in contemporary fiction. We have seen that from the structural point of view Joyce and Proust are not the innovators most critics imagine them to be. To my mind this leaves as the two greatest novels of the present century Kafka's *Das Schloss* and Malraux's *La Condition humaine*. My assumption of course will be that these novels cannot be fully associated structurally with any fiction, except that of Stendhal, earlier than Kafka. And yet two works of criticism, certainly among the most remarkable ever devoted to these authors, Marthe Robert's *L'ancient et le nouveau* and Lucien Goldmann's *Pour une sociologie du roman,* attempt to show that *Das Schloss* and *La Condition humaine* remain within the framework provided by the Lukács-Goldmann theory. In dealing, therefore, with these two novels we shall have to deal simultaneously with the thorough and impressive interpretations suggested by Robert and Goldmann.[25]

The novel, like everything else, has no existence in itself. We see it more clearly to the degree in which we are able to contrast it with whatever comparable forms preceded it, the novel constituting a "negation of these forms. Otherwise the novel "swallows us up," and the empiricist studies the perfectly natural existence of character-individuals circulating in a perfectly natural exterior world. It is Lukács' achievement to have made the novel genuinely "visible" for the first time by showing what it is not: the fictional hero, unlike the epic or mythological hero, is not the embodiment of an entire cultural group, a kind of emissary with little or no personal existence; and reality in the novel is not, as in all primitive forms, a living space so perfectly adapted to human needs that any enduring moral or intellectual dilemma is out of the question. If, in Hegelian fashion, we negate this negation, we are left with what Lukács took to be the basic structure of all fiction from *Don Quixote* to approximately 1920, the date of publication of his *Die Theorie des Romans*. According to this theory, the fictional hero is an individual in the sense that he has an inner life taking the form, in the best instances, of an "ethical" determination to know the world he lives in so that moral decisions may be made with reasonable confidence. However, that world is unknowable in any fully satisfactory way, or, as Lukács puts it, there is an "inadequation" between the individual and reality (especially social reality, of course) which can never be surmounted. So (again in the best instances) the hero's career terminates with the resigned understanding that his quest was doomed from the beginning. Hence, as Lukács repeats, the novel is the form of "virile maturity."

There can be no doubt that scientific rationalism has made of us inquiring observers or spectators of something that, during the Renaissance, came to be called nature; something of which, formerly, we were indistinguishably a part; something which was once a home and which is now a problem. But there the difficulties begin. In what sense exactly is the hero of fiction problematic? Does it mean that there often arise problems in converting one beyond or another into a safe guide to daily living? Or does it mean that the hero's "maturity" consists in his being alone in realizing, finally, that there is no beyond? Both Lukács and Goldmann refer to the novel as a search for the "absolute," for "positive values," a search which is, of course, never successful (except, possibly, in the case of a very mediocre work). But is it unsuccessful because the absolute does not exist or because, temporarily or permanently, man is unable to formulate it clearly?

This question is crucial, and yet it is surprisingly difficult to come by an answer. However, after a careful reading of Lukács and all the relevant texts in Goldmann I believe we ought to conclude that the theory requires the existence of an absolute, of what Goldmann calls "authentic values." He writes, for example, that toward the end of the novel the hero undergoes a kind of "conversion" resulting in his giving up the problematic search, but that renunciation "is neither a reconciliation with the world of convention, nor the abandoning of authentic values which, however, the hero knows he can never succeed in actually living."[26]

Assuming then that authentic values—what Goldmann, in the passage just quoted from also calls the divine—constitute a beyond, another difficulty arises which Goldmann himself discusses at length in this article. There is little or no reason to doubt a close structural relationship between the rise of the European bourgeoisie and that of the novel; yet if this means anything at all, it should mean that we can look to the novel for, in Goldmann's language, the fullest and most coherent—though non-conceptual—expression of the bourgeois view of man and the world. But if the existence of a problematic hero is the central structural feature of the novel, then the novel is "by essence critical and opposi-tional. It is a form of resistance to the development of middle class socie-ty . . . it is not the expression of a real or possible awareness in this social class."[27]

We have discovered that the novel before Stendhal and for more than half a century after him has nothing "oppositional" about it: in novels of the second category Protestant morality is taken very largely for granted; and in the first category of fiction whether or not the hero is confronted by "insoluble problems of which a clear and rigorous awareness is out of the question for him,"[28] has little importance for a reason which Goldmann himself mentions in an article on reification. He reminds us that economists used to hold (and still do, it seems, in many instances) that each individual, in pursuing selfish ends, works toward the common good. Goldmann then continues: "This notion, far from being peculiar to economists, expressed so perfectly the essential struc-ture of early capitalism that we find it already in the 17th century in a let-ter from Descartes to Princess Elizabeth where he writes: 'God has so established the order of things and so closely associated us with our fellows that even where a man is concerned only for himself, having no regard for others, he would nevertheless, in everything he did, be work-ing for them, provided he be a prudent man living at a time when man-ners and morals are not corrupt.' "[29] Goldmann then cites Leibnitz and Kant as having much the same view.

It is confidence in the existence of this scientific-anthropomorphic order which gives to 18th century writing its serene anticipation of better things, a confidence so complete there was no need to mention it; in fact Voltaire, in *Candide,* could even give the impression he was utterly lack-ing in it. But if we compare *Candide* with a book like Céline's *Voyage au bout de la nuit* the subject matter of which is roughly comparable (man's inhumanity to man) the contrast is startling and may be largely attributed to our contemporary inability to honestly suppose there is anything or anyone out there looking after things for better (Zola) or for worse (Flaubert). Voltaire, consequently, was simply applying what one can gather from Descartes' remark quoted above: things will be satisfactorily taken care of on condition men do their part; in the case of *Candide,* they ought not be so stupidly naive as is Pangloss in supposing that any event, however appalling it may seem, is actually the great scheme working its way toward fulfilment. In *Tom Jones* the great scheme is the province of Thwackum and Square, and all their conclusions are systematically ridiculed simply by bringing them into contact with reality, with Tom Jones' adventures. But, after all, Candide and Tom Jones are "right." That is, Candide and Cunégonde survive—which is preposterous—and live happily ever after, while thanks to the usual discovery of a birthmark and various other providential events everything is happily sorted out at the conclusion of *Tom Jones*. Is this really no more than the high-spirited tomfoolery so common in picaresque fiction? To be sure, Fielding is not saying that things always turn out beautifully in the long run; but, on the other hand, why is it never necessary that Tom Jones *answer* Thwackum and Square or that Candide *answer* Pangloss; why is a different metaphysics superfluous unless it be that the various qualities of the noble soul of the Enlightenment—common sense, tolerance, kindness, generosity and so on—are sufficient to see us through? They serve, in other words, who only stand and wait. But then there has to be someone at the helm.

If I am correct in assuming that the Lukács-Goldmann theory involves the existence of a beyond, then the foregoing remarks are not strictly speaking in contradiction with that theory, except that Lukács himself seems to attach great importance to the sad disillusionment of "virile maturity," a disillusionment which requires a beyond so tenuous as to be virtually nonexistent. As Lukács cheerfully admits in his preface of 1962 to a new edition of *Die Theorie des Romans*, his book is disastrously lacking in analyses of specific works or authors; and in the two instances where they do occur (Goethe and Tolstoy) it is interesting to note the importance of this question as to where exactly the beyond ought to be situated, if at all.[30] Lukács presents *Wilhelm Meister* as an important novel exemplifying almost perfectly his theory: "Its theme is the reconciliation of the problematic individual, guided by his lived experience of the ideal, with concrete social reality."[31] But then when the inevitable happens, when the beyond, towards the end of the novel, interferes in too barefaced a manner, Lukács is obliged to declare that Goethe had marred his work. Yet if there is one characteristic of fiction that endures stubbornly throughout its history, it is certainly this more or less discreet maneuvering of the great invisible hand. So one is tempted to feel that Lukács has defined the novel as it ought to have been rather than as it really exists. It is as though, with only *Don Quixote* in mind, he elaborated a theory which, for structural reasons, ought to have applied to the whole of fiction. But when he attempts to show that Tolstoy can be successfully accomodated by his theory, the results are little short of absurd;[32] once again, he is obliged to minimize the beyond, this time in the case of a novelist who, more than any other, is unintelligible without it. In other words, like the quasi-totality of the critics confronted by the classical novel he sees only the explicit level which, as we know, exists largely so that the reader will be thrown back all the more heavily upon the calculated stupidity of the implicit level.

Goldmann provides an indispensable complement to Lukács' theory[33] by making it possible for us to see why the novel should insist as it does upon the lack of adjustment, or "inadequation," between men and the world they live in. It is simply that, as men cease to produce by and for themselves everything they need (as in all primitive societies and in the manorial economy of the middle ages), as they gradually lose possession of their tools and skills and are obliged to sell their labor so that goods may be produced *primarily* for the market, in brief, as exchange value—be it a question of men or things—usurps the place of use value, the world becomes increasingly unintelligible or "problematic." This homology between economic and cultural levels in our society is striking and certainly of the utmost importance to an understanding of the novel. And yet, once again, vagueness as to the status and nature of the beyond and man's relation to it leads Goldmann to vastly overestimate the "oppositional" nature of the problematic hero who senses the slow, fatal occlusion of use value but is able to express it only indirectly through his inability to espouse any of the positive values of his class. But why should we not argue that the various values we associate with Protestantism and science while they are certainly negative compared to those of primitive societies are necessarily positive in that they alone existed during a considerable period? We have seen, in novels of the second category, how the beyond is utilized in a certainly non-problematic, Protestant fashion to identify individuals; and in novels of the first category preceding the French Revolution the inability to arrive at a final conclusion was simply the refusal of the "conclusions" put forward by Church and Throne. While after the Revolution, noncommittal, sceptical problematic-objective waiting became, and remains, the way of life of the bourgeois intellectual protecting his own social class by rendering the self-evident invisible.

Godmann appears to have held that the novel remained unchanged structurally from Cervantes until the end of the 19th and beginning of the 20th centuries when entreprenurial capital gave way to monopoly capital, thus creating a situation in which the individual would count to far less than he had before. Since, in our society, the economic level is always fundamental there occurs another homology in that the individual begins to disappear from fiction.[34] There is surely much truth in this; and yet why should we not hold that the transition from mercantile to industrial-entrepreneurial capital is every bit as important as the yielding of the latter to monopoly-imperialist capital? In fact, why should it not be considered more important when we bear in mind that it was accompanied by the rise of the bourgeoisie to political as well as economic supremacy? Furthermore, if it is conceivable that the problematic hero express indirectly and obscurely a natural apprehensiveness that use value be supplanted everywhere by exchange value, why should we not expect to find in great fiction an awareness that the medal had a reverse: the insane, degrading pursuit of exchange value had, nonetheless, with the agricultural and industrial revolutions, created for the first time in human history the possibility that man might, on a global scale, learn to master the natural environment so as never again to know physical need. But since, in our culture, it is the individual who relates himself to the beyond (group existence being "primitive" or "anarchical") and since it is only through the collectivity as sovereign that we will suppress need, the indispensable prerequisite to such an achievement is the discrediting of all forms of transcendance, secular (i.e., scientism, positivism, the "immortality" of art) as well as religious. This process begins in the novels of Stendhal and, at almost the same moment, in the philosophy of the young Marx.

At the beginning of the last century, consequently, there occurs very nearly the reverse of what the Lukács-Goldmann theory calls for. Instead of a hero unable to "coincide" with bourgeois values because he senses the growing alienation of humanity in the growing supremacy of exchange value we have a clear recognition of that alienation in the explicit level of the classical novel along with the simultaneous neutralization of it on the implicit level—that of the novel proper—where it is taken for granted there exist innate differences between individuals. Since (paradoxically, in a scientific culture) these differences are qualitative (and unchangeable, since given), making it natural that some rule while others starve, judgements of individuals have to be carried out with reference to a transcendent recognized by all (religion, science); otherwise the whole system becomes arbitrary. Or, as Stendhal puts it, "only the strength of the lion or the need of those who are hungry or cold is *natural*; only *need* in other words."[35]

If the Lukács-Goldmann theory obscures the critical importance of the rôle played by the absolute in the classical novel it also, of course, makes it impossible to recognize its disappearance in Stendhal along with, inevitably, the disappearance of identity and consequently the creation of a new novel.

with the decay of medieval culture and the coming into being of the hidden god of Protestantism and the hidden framework of universal natural law, the relationship between the fictional hero and his world becomes, certainly, in one sense or another, problematic. But is this notion really of much use from Balzac onward, especially when we bear in mind the omniscient viewpoint (more accurately, the impossible absence of any particular point of view) of the classical novelist? Neither Lukács nor Goldmann, to my knowledge, ever even mention this; yet if it is practicable for the novelist to occupy what can only be called God's point of view for the purpose of issuing a definitive and infallible judgement of the principal characters, it is difficult to understand how either hero or author can be described as problematic. The spectator is one who, by definition, *sees.* But then what of the explicit level? Here, as we know, the novelist accepts his historical subjectivity, but what he sees from that position is self-evident; the only question being how will the hero react to the discovery that his own society is profoundly and transparently corrupt? But even here the situation cannot be problematic in any real sense because the hero, reified and "named" in the omniscient gaze of the novelist, has no genuine freedom of choice.

With the suppression of the implicit level in Stendhal there remains only the self-evident, or pre-reflexive; one character can no longer be distinguished from another except on the basis of the choice we are all summoned to make. Either we can "authentically" acknowledge the end of transcendence in whatever form and consequently the intolerable nature of bourgeois civilization (since it can be the result only of human praxis), or we can refuse to see this in the interest, primarily, of clinging to the means of "knowing ourselves" apart from any effort to change an economic and political structure of which we are all the victims.

This gives us what we need to attempt a definition of the contemporary novel: it is one involving the existence of a hero who is alone and an outsider not because he entertains admirable but unrealistic ideals (*Don Quixote*) or because he is sceptical in the face of premature assertions concerning the great scheme (novels of the first category) but because the generally accepted forms of meaning and comportment in his society are so manifestly absurd or criminal that he is unable to conform to them and hence to lead a normal life. The most striking characteristic of this form is that the hero's own culture is incomprehensible to him, and while, in appearance, he is himself incomprehensible to the other characters, they understand him sufficiently to seek, in one way or another, to rid themselves of him. But what danger can a man alone, almost a pariah, represent unless he is insisting upon what everyone already knows? We are a long way from the interminable discussion of picaresque fiction[36] and the essay-chapters of Rousseau and Fielding. The only question now is who will acknowledge the self-evident, and who is going to continue to pretend it isn't there. How will those who have adjusted themselves to insanity (the villagers of *Das Schloss,* the counter-revolutionary oppressors of *La Condition humaine,* the silent majority of countless other contemporary novels) deal with those unwilling or unable to do the same?

The hero of the contemporary novel, in other words, is none other than the regulating or mediating third of Sartre's *Critique de la raison dialectique;* a person he elsewhere refers to as a "unique anyone."[37] Not "unique," needless to say, as was the hero of the classical novel by his "nature" which it was the function of the novelist to define, nor unique as was the problematic hero for the questions which, thanks to certain individual qualities, he was able to put to the more gullible or superficial; but unique by a "position" or "situation" which one occupies by chance and which anyone might have occupied. For example, a troop of soldiers chooses one of their number to mount guard; the enemy appears, and the lookout alerts his comrades so they can prepare to defend themselves. In the case of the hero of contemporary fiction, however, the sentinal's fellow soldiers are too exhausted to heed his warning (that is, they have material interests), and, in any case, they are absolutely sure that enemy troops cannot be within several hundred miles (that is, the debris of scientific rationalism and the Protestant ethic blinds them to what they would see "self-evidently" were they to place themselves by the side of the sentinel). Sartre defines contemporary literature as an "appeal to the freedom of the reader," and this is, in part, what he means. The great novel, today, appeals to our freedom to take up the author's position from which we would then see what in one sense or another we already know—first and foremost, the end of transcendence.

If the contemporary novelist can appeal to our freedom on grounds that we already know in a sense what he sees, it is because he no longer speaks from the vantage point of a viable alternative culture; rather he speaks from within a culture divided against itself.[38] It is a culture divided into the universal (where we all agree, so he is, therefore, anyone, or everyman) and the particular (where, if we prefer, we can allow class interests—both cultural and material—to render all the issues extremely "complex"). Between the Renaissance and the French Revolution the novelist spoke necessarily and inevitably from the critical and progressive viewpoint of bourgeois culture either to establish what we have called bourgeois legitimacy (novels of the second category) or to insist upon a self-regulating universe in which it is sufficient that the private realm not be interfered with for the public to function perfectly. However, by Balzac's day the public realm had fallen completely under bourgeois domination, and what resulted was clear for anyone to see: the universe was "regulated" in such a way that the vast majority of men became enslaved by what they had themselves created: by money and by those who, sometimes to their own detriment, manipulated it. It was then possible in principle—though only Stendhal achieved this—for the novelist to become, for the first time in the history of fiction, oppositional by insisting upon the explicit alone.[39] But this could be practicable only on condition the novelist refuse to take up the position of the omniscient spectator who, restricting himself to the explicit, destroys the form by producing a thesis novel. The explicit had to become the "subjective" experience of the hero-narrator who then, necessarily, lost all hope of establishing definitive identifications of other characters (we can only know with some probability what they are on the basis of what they actually do) and so had no need of a beyond. The alternative was to recognize that the reign of the bourgeoisie had produced chaos; that reason, far from assisting us to a progressive understanding of the self-regulating nature of the universe and of social phenomenon, could lead to crime or to a conformism which is often the same thing (Dostoevsky). However, for as long as the bourgeoisie could look upon itself as the "universal class" the novelist might hold that there existed after all a kind of regulation (and therefore a beyond) which would assure an adjustment of kinds of people to the fate that befell them.

The foregoing paragraph gives us a schematic view of the entire evolution of fiction the purpose of which is to help us deal with *Don Quixote*. Instead of regarding this novel as a foundation, as Lukács appears to have done, which would determine the shape of the structure to come, we will look back from what we know that structure to be in the hope of arriving at a better adjustment between the origins of the novel and subsequent developments. Marthe Robert, in *L'ancien et le nouveau* attempts something of the sort, but her conclusion—that *Don Quixote* and *Das*

Schloss are identical in structure—we cannot accept, since it is inconceivable that the best of contemporary fiction has simply revived a structure which had been supplanted during an entire century by that of the classical novel.

Robert's book may have been inspired by the fact that Cervantes and Kafka lived at times of cultural crisis: the former during a period of much accelerated decay of feudal institutions and values; the latter at the point of collapse of bourgeois rationalism. Therefore, both novelists might, theoretically, have posed themselves the problem of dealing with a disconcerting "new" on the basis of an "old" at once ideal, or at least enormously influential, and irrelevant. The novel consequently remains problematic, and in a somewhat clearer sense perhaps. Here is a passage in which Robert both uses the word problematic and describes what she considers to be the "deepest meaning of *Don Quixote*": Cervantes' hero sets out to "bring books down into the streets" at a time when

> specialized religious writings talk of goodness, truth, justice and salvation, but no longer have anything to say about decisions one has to take in daily life; they do not teach how one puts act and thought together without sacrificing one to the other, how one brings about a true reign of justice or how, where a man believes himself to be in possession of the truth, he can give it force of law. But Don Quixote has an absolute need to know that to be able to live; what he lacks is not abstract knowledge or spiritual principles or moral precepts, or the voice of a vigilant conscience (his is wakeful but perplexed); he needs precise rules of conduct, a code which would enable him to distinguish, on the practical level, order from disorder, the true from the false, and that not in general terms, but here and now, from one moment to the next. Since he is unable to find these norms in the channels through which they had been traditionally conveyed, he goes to look for them in literature which, although it is without legality, continues to produce for the use of individuals those figures, in a way familiar and transcendant, that the epic formerly created for the general good. So the book of Amadis becomes his guide to living, a sort of substitute scriptural authority to which he can serenely refer himself at critical moments.[40]

One final quotation and we shall have a sufficient grasp of Robert's thesis: "Which of these two voices, equally strong and clear, is right: the childlike soul demanding its right to dream, or the adult mind drawing its only hope from the dismal awareness of what is? Quixotism doesn't know, it doesn't even know from whence a decisive answer to this question could come, and it is precisely this ignorance which creates the urgency of its mission."[41]

We have seen that Lukács' theory gives the impression of having been inspired by *Don Quixote* alone. Yet even here it is too loose-fitting since surely it will not do to transform the hero's determination to revive a dead past into an "ethical quest," especially as that quest takes the form of slapstick comedy and not of some wry and melancholy humor. Robert's work, at least, does not compel us to overlook what is so obvious, that the past (or, more accurately, the literature of the past, since knight-errantry never existed), in one way or another, is playing a critical rôle in the novel. But then it is equally obvious that Don Quixote's attempt to revive knight-errantry is presented by Cervantes as something absolutely grotesque (in fact, insane) and very funny. Many generations of readers made no mistake about this, yet if someone who had never read *Don Quixote* were to try to guess at its nature on the basis of Marthe Robert's book, he would imagine a noble and solemn tract on the difficulty of being. Not much of the original funniness perhaps is left for the contemporary reader, but no one can doubt for a moment Cervantes' intention to make his readers laugh. Could this have been a more or less chance device beneath which a discerning and sensitive reader might have detected the "childlike soul demanding its right to dream" or a man seeking "precise rules of conduct"? All this is there, in *Don Quixote,* undoubtedly; but we know that different generations of critics will take up different angles of view from which they will discover what is genuinely visible. We also know however that the angle of view will be an aspect of a particular praxis (and, in our society, of the praxis of a given social class) structurally related to the totality of the society concerned. If this is the case with criticism, the same, of course, a fortiori, will apply to important works of art.

To reduce the arbitrariness of the angle of view adopted we must try to establish a connection between the immense popularity of *Don Quixote* during several centuries and the ideological requirements of the class which did most of the reading during that period: the bourgeoisie. Neither Lukács nor Robert attempt this, and we have seen that the homology Goldmann establishes between the novel and the gradual replacement of use by exchange value is not all that pertinent before the coming into being of the explicit level of the classical novel. Between Cervantes and Balzac the hero's "quest for the absolute" has none of the earnestness or urgency that Lukács and Robert attribute to it. In fact it is difficult for me to see in what sense a "quest" exists at all, since the hero does little more than reject (or, where he accepts, as in the case of Don Quixote, he is insane) whatever is offered in the way of a firm answer (especially when that answer comes from the past, from the feudal order) to the question at hand, and he does this with the utmost serenity knowing there exists an order as yet ill-defined and hidden (so much so that exploit reference to it is seldom made)[42] but also absolutely indubitable since it frequently intervenes (although not miraculously of course, as in the absurd tales of chivalry) to set matters straight through the use of whole series of all but impossible coincidences. In such a universe it is natural to wonder and to interrogate, but to conclude is not only superfluous, it could perturb the benevolent functioning of the new humanist beyond. Strictly speaking, however, one could never, on any scale, perturb a natural order; so the threat can be conjured with a little ridicule. However, when that threat takes the form of a whole way of life and of active interference (as in what is, I believe, the unique instance in picaresque fiction of Don Quixote's knight errantry), and when the interference is made in the name of the feudal past, then the ridicule must be merciless.[43] The immediate and seemingly conclusive objection to this is that Don Quixote is very sympathetic and, at least in the latter half of the novel, such is certainly Cervantes' intention. But let me try to show that this is no objection at all.

The classical novel has accustomed us to characters in whom a given trait dominates to the point where the reader can, without any difficulty (except, of course, where an identity is being concealed), establish qualitative identifications which will be unchanging. This may be one of the reasons why critics, including Lukács and Robert, have either overlooked entirely or given insufficient weight to something that Cervantes himself marvels at continually throughout the novel: Don Quixote (and, somewhat less conspicuously, Sancho) is not one character, but two. He is mad only on the subject of chivalry, and at all other times he is not only fully sane but exceptionally wise and knowledgeable. Don Quixote as a knight-errant can do nothing without bringing disaster upon himself, Sancho, other people, or everyone concerned. Even when he acts not because he has turned a windmill into a giant or an inn into a castle, but for excellent reasons—to spare a boy a whipping or to release prisoners—he is wrong since the boy received an even worse beating, and the prisoners were no sooner free than they set upon their liberator. For this to have happened Don Quixote must have upset a state of affairs having a more or less invisible fitness of its own (and indeed, the reader learns eventually that the boy no doubt "deserved" his thrashing and that one, at least, of the prisoners had resumed his mischievous existence). I have singled out these two adventures because they illustrate more clearly than any of the others what Lukács and Robert must mean when they argue that the fictional hero is a man engaged in the impossible task of introducing ethics into reality. But if we begin with the supremely reasonable hypothesis that the novel is going to contain what the class which produced and consumed it needed, then we cannot fail to see that if ethics cannot be forced upon reality it is because reality is already ethical, and all that is left to the hero is speculation about matters of detail.

Literary criticism has always been sturdily reluctant to recognize the soap opera content of the novel before Stendhal and Kafka (naturalism being simply black soap opera) because it represents the rational silliness of the class to which the critic belongs: the Luscinda-Cardenic-Fernando-Dorotea episode in *Don Quixote*, that of Camacho and Basilio, of Ana Felix and various others of less importance are examples of the commonsensical, pedestrian miraculousness of the great scheme, in contrast to the superstitious, nonsensical miracles to be found in the literature of the old order. The story within the story is a device found in almost all picaresque fiction and therefore cannot be simply ignored. As we have seen, novels of the first category are funny because the events they relate bring into contrast the immovable immensity of the cosmic order and the infinitesimal means being used to suspend it. But the question remains, and it will plague the entire history of the novel until Stendhal and Kafka, as to how exactly that order manifests itself in daily life; the picaresque novelist becomes momentarily serious in an attempt to answer this question through an "aside" taking the form of a brief tale inserted more or less artificially into the main body of the narrative. In *Don Quixote* almost all the emphasis falls upon providential encounters which resolve whatever difficulties or misunderstandings had brought about the separation of the people involved. As time goes on, however, not only do novels of the second category come into being, but more attention is given in those of the first to the moral qualities which enable a man to adjust himself to the order of things. The tale of the old man of the hill in *Tom Jones* is characteristic. It is, from a structural point of view, an anticipation of Dickens' *A Christmas Carol,* since in both stories the hero begins life as a thoroughly "good" person, takes on an appearance of "evil" and then reverts to his "true" identity. The old man of the hill is led into a life of dissipation by a rich fellow student at Oxford, and although here also coincidence plays a crucial rôle, it is assisted by the hero's study of the good book thanks to which he achieves harmony with the moral order and regains his original goodness. A similar effect may be produced by the use of a utopia as in *Gulliver's Travels* or *Candide*. If human life is nasty, brutish and short, it is not because there exists no universal order or because the translation of that order, or of the past, into useful ethical terms is problematic to the point of impossibility, but because most people are Yahoos and not Houyhnhnms; because most people refuse simply to refrain, simply not to intervene (the old man of the hill was a hermit) in what they do (Don Quixote) or in what they think (Pangloss, Thwackum and Square). In *Wilhelm Meister* there is the Confessions of a Fair Saint which takes up the whole of book six and which is an anticipation of the seeing-of-the-light-and-renunciation-of-society theme which would dominate Tolstoy's work. *Wilhelm Meister,* however, is a transitional novel in the sense that order is not asserted indirectly through humor and then confirmed by short stories within the novel; it tends to be embodied throughout in kinds of people, but people who, rather than being elaborately defined as individuals, as in the classical novel, exist, roughly, as two groups: the troupe of actors and the group which has its headquarters in Lothario's castle. These latter who, in mysterious ways, watch over Wilhelm Meister throughout the novel are instruments of the Lord, and it is thanks to them that Wilhelm Meister gradually learns (this being his "apprenticeship") that he did not belong with the troupe of actors, they being lesser kinds of people, but with the chosen. I do not know what Lukács means by Goethe's "light and ironic"[44] treatment of this weird band of omniscient, virtuous people (already Tolstoy's "company of gentlemen" he suggests as a solution for political problems in *War and Peace*), but there is an irresistible involuntary humor, especially in chapters one and two of book eight, where it turns out that the chief concern of our group of noble souls—and therefore that of God—is the protection of their property.

The second Don Quixote is a Houyhnhnm, Cervantes himself spreading the new gospel of sweetness, reason and light. This is the Don Quixote with whom the reader is expected to sympathize and who alone remains at the moment of death when he recognizes and regrets the madness of his "other self." The one episode in which Don Quixote's knight-errantry is not set in a comic light is the one in which he defends "reason": a girl should be free to marry the man she loves and not be forced to marry another simply because he is rich. After order has been rather preposterously reestablished Don Quixote protects the young couple against the wrath of the frustrated rich suitor and his partisans and then delivers a little homily "to induce Senor Basilio to give up the practice of his accomplishments (he is an exceptional athlete and swordsman) since even though they brought him fame they would bring in no money, and to devote his attention instead to the acquisition of a fortune by legitimate means and his own industry; for those who are prudent and persevering always find a way."[45] This last sentiment is so outrageous that Cervantes felt obliged to follow it immediately with: "The poor man who is a man of honour (if such a thing is possible) . . . ."

There is the whole dilemma of the Age of Reason in fiction: there exists necessarily and indubitably a benevolent order, but it is so completely concealed that to see evidence of it anywhere is to betray stupidity or a lack of experience of the world. The difficulty was to see real life honestly, since it was there that money, the very essence of the middle class way of life, was won or lost. But also, it was won or lost by individuals separately and sometimes competitively pursuing their own selfish ends, and if this were not to be profoundly shocking (we have now grown used to it, but for truly civilized—that is, primitive—peoples it is incomprehensible and abhorrent) then there had to exist a natural regulatory mechanism which was somehow coordinating all these individual efforts with a view to forwarding the common good. In addition to providential intervention (of which, clearly, only a limited use could be made) the difficulty was dealt with in one of two ways: in novels of the second category it was largely ignored, that is, reality became an unresisting function of identity; while in the first the author simultaneously shows reality and overlooks it by finding it funny. This is the indispensable, structural importance of humor in the picaresque. The two greatest novels of the genre—*Don Quixote* and *Tom Jones*—are also the two funniest, and that because the heroes' encounters with reality point up the absurdity of proposed solutions, those of the present as well as of the past. If such a state of affairs is not only not serious but comic, then it must be that things get sorted out in the great beyond. The relative inferiority of Lesage's *Gil Blas* in picaresque fiction may be explained by the total absence of proposed solutions which, in the very best picaresque, not only much improve the quality of the humor when events show them to fail pitiably short of their goals but also impress upon the reader the awesomeness of the universal plan which the minds of mere men cannot even begin to encompass. As the Protestants banned art from their churches on grounds it was a presumptuous sacrilege to attempt to picture divinity, so only in a degraded and impoverished universe could the Thwackums and Squares be right. Gil Blas wanders about in a society where it often seems that everyone is busy mercilessly preying upon everyone else; a moment's inattention and you can be stripped clean of all you own and find yourself in jail in the bargain. And yet, strangely, it doesn't matter. Gil Blas is soon back on the road, and we leave him at the conclusion of his interminable, monotonous adventures not only a happy, prosperous man, but one ennobled by the king. *Gil Blas* is therefore a success story, and we are a long way from the disillusionment required by the Lukács theory—a point if is fair to make because *Gil Blas* is by no means a negligible work in the history of picaresque fiction. Julien Sorel's reflections upon his society at the end of *Le Rouge et le noir* are not all that different from what one might gather from many passages of *Gil Blas*, but Julien's conclusions: "were such as to make one look forward to dying."[46] The difference, as we know, is that between a society governed in some mysterious but benevolent way by a transcendent order and one which is, in the last analysis, entirely man-made and for which, consequently, man himself is entirely responsible.

The problem for the pre-Revolutionary bourgeoisie was to assert an order which had not yet, thanks to feudal obscurantism, fully manifested itself. Novels of the first category therefore are necessarily humorous because only in such a way can the novelist simultaneously insist upon a transcendent and recognize chaos. So, while there is a problematic element in these novels it is not fundamental; for although we cannot see exactly how order performs its marvels this is simply because the human mind is too mean a thing, and/or because most men, at the moment at least, allow base passion to overrule reason and so act like Yahoos instead of Houyhnhnms. To put this differently, the notion that life is problematic in the Lukácsian sense always has been and still is absolutely indispensable to the middle class liberal manner of thinking: we are obliged to concern ourselves with the real (that being the domain of both business and science), but in the light of the universalism of scientific rationalism the reality of social and political life (which it is sufficient simply to show, as in Zola and Tolstoy) is unendurable. To explain why, nevertheless, that reality is happily endured by the well-to-do it must be made problematic, whereupon contemplative non-intervention becomes a whole way of life. The liberal intellectual plays a game which consists in transforming the self-evident into the problematic. But for this to be practicable there has to exist a transcendent; otherwise it becomes too clear that Western "civilization" since World War I has been struggling valiantly toward suicide.

We know that an indispensable preliminary to any act of scholarship is the fixing of one's position, since what is discovered will be visible only from there; it will be a function of that position; it will be what we have already decided we want to find. We are therefore obliged to consider whether alternative positions might not enable us to see more of the phenomenon under investigation. If this should result in our seeing what we would prefer not to see, then perhaps it is because what becomes visible from this new viewpoint shocks a particularism which, nevertheless, we know full well we should try to combat in the name of that universalism without which our culture falls immediately to unbelievable depths of barbarism.

In the case of *L'ancien et le nouveau* (and, of course, of practically all scholarly production) the position of Marthe Robert is that of a particular profession (peculiar to a given class) devoted to esthetic appreciation and problematic research, while no account is taken of a very different viewpoint—that of the vast majority of present-day students not yet professionally deformed—from which *Don Quixote* (and all the rest of our literary heritage) is simply unreadable (The relationship of the student to the university is therefore precisely that of a potentially revolutionary proletariat to the economic and political system. Workers who are told that their condition cannot be improved because economic "realities" are such as they are, know they are being victimized but do not know exactly how it is being done. The terrible boredom of the student confronted by our cultural heritage is the irrelevance of that past before the ever more pressing, self-evident demands of the universalism each of us carries within him. But nothing is more difficult to prove than the self-evident since it requires not proof but a different way of life; and since the present system is geared to preventing above all else the development of collective forms of existence which alone can make the universal real, the worker and student easily fall into the despair of listening to the specialists. There is no one to explain to them that, originally, the discoveries of all the specialists put together were to have led to the revelation of the great scheme. But since we know now that the rationalist-scientific order was a historical, cultural undertaking, and persists, in extreme forms, only in Stalinist and fascist imbecility, then the work of the specialists becomes an anachronistic particularism the main purpose of which is to blind us to the responsibilities universalism places upon all men of good faith.

The failure of scholarship (including much present-day structuralism, the function of which is to enable academic noninvolvement to continue to flourish apart from the brainless, empirical, fact research which has been the rule in the past) to situate historically both itself and its subject matter, that is, its failure to see both the past and itself as praxis, leads, in the case of *L'ancien et le nouveau* to precisely this error: first, the overlooking of the existence of two separate characters in *Don Quixote* (and Cervantes could not have made this much more clear), one ridiculous for seeking the answers in the past, the other a spokesman for the new order; and second, unquestioning adoption of the praxis of the scholar which converts the past into a given, into an area therefore in which it is natural (since we all come from there) to seek explanations. But, not surprisingly, the answers are such as to legitimatize the work of the scholar; first, the eternal validity of great art (whereas the entire novel before Stendhal and Kafka except for the explicit level of classical fiction is unreadable)[47] and then the problematic nature of what we learn from the past. That is, on no account must conclusions be drawn as a result of a reorganization (or possibly even an elimination) of the past in the light of a revolutionary determination to construct a future in which men, for the first time, will know themselves to be essentially attributors of meaning, making it intolerable that meaning come from groups within the collectivity (scholars, specialists) rather than from the collectivity itself.

Both Marthe Robert and the early Lukács, therefore, overlook, in *Don Quixote,* that implicit postulation of a benevolent—but, for a greater or lesser period, inscrutable—universal order which is as much the foundation of picaresque fiction as identity is of the classical novel. They furthermore attribute to Cervantes precisely that problematic view of things peculiar not to the novel (except in the limited sense we have discussed) but to intellectuals since the turn of the century and to intelligent novelists of secondary importance like Martin du Gard and Thomas Mann. It is these intellectuals and academics, the watchdogs of bourgeois culture as Nizan called them, who have been engaged in a quest for the absolute. Even though forced to acknowledge that the quest was without a real object (except for structuralist neo-positivism which has spotted a UFO of a somewhat different shape) the kind of person formed by centuries of objectivie waiting is one whose cultural and material interests forbid his dealing in the self-evident which requires the approach of a worker to his job and not that of an observer toward problems which do not really exist, since the position of the observer outside time and place does not exist.

It is from this mandarin's position that the immortality of *Don Quixote* rather than its unreadability comes into view; and in order to reconcile immortality with the dizzying social, political and economic change of the past century or so, Marthe Robert decided that change itself generates a constant: the difficulty of thinking the new with only the help of the old. No artist can be sure as to the exact significance of what he has put into his work; so it is possible *Don Quixote* expresses a nostalgia for the Aristotelian-Christian universe of the middle ages with its ceremonies and prescriptions for daily living and, simultaneously, an acute awareness of the hopeless obsolescence of everything medieval. This is possible but, surely, extremely improbable given what it compels us to overlook: the existence of two Don Quixotes and two Sanchos, and the comedy everywhere, except in the stories encapsulated, within the main narrative where its place is taken by the hand of providence. What is overlooked, furthermore, turns out to be the translation into fiction of exactly that metaphysics which would be of most use to those social groups which, unknowningly, had taken in hand the direction of Western culture, groups composed of autonomous individuals whose greatest need was freedom to pursue self-aggrandizement, whose greatest need, in other words, was nonintervention, from whatever quarter, in private affairs. But since those affairs involved the sacrifice of social to individual ends—the centuries-long conversion, all over the world, of the public (especially land) into the private—a process of which the Catholic and, in theory, the Protestant ethic disapproved, then necessarily the pillaging and exploiting that produced the primitive accumulation of capital had to be the expression of an undubitable order which, also, had to be, for a while at least, incomprehensible.

If it is a serious error to fail to see, in the interstices of *Don Quixote*, an all-embracing, reassuring order, Marthe Robert is perfectly right in finding no trace of a transcendent order, religious or secular, in *Das Schloss*. But then her thesis requires that the castle represent not only the past (which one can, in a way, accept) but a partially valid and even ideal past and one therefore which, when one measures it against the present, leads to the "problem" which, allegedly, it was the mission of Don Quixote to struggle with unsuccessfully. But how could the castle possibly represent a value of any nature whatsoever? One readily understands that the physicist's pursuit of ever more "concealed" atomic particles is essential; but in the study of man, the "concealed" is rendered essential to safeguard the position of the specialist. For what strikes the ordinary reader in the present case are the contrasts which could not be sharper: the whole tone of the narrative in one novel is unfailingly cheerful, and "problems" arise only to show that reasonable men easily reach agreement; while the atmosphere of *Das Schloss* is one of frustration, mistrust, apprehension and defeat. As for the two heroes, one is not only insane (since Lukács and Robert do not recognize the existence of the second Don Quixote) but is seen to be so by the author, by all the other characters of the novel and by many generations of readers, his insanity being invisible only to the specialist seeking to immortalize art in the teeth of ferocious opposition from students and the general public.

In *Das Schloss* the situation is precisely the opposite: it is the villagers, with the single exception of Amalia, who are insane (they suffer from the most dangerous of all insanities, blind conformism) while the reader finds himself at the hero's side sharing his wonder and dismay at what he finds. Don Quixote is a character offered to the reader's gaze, while K is the reader himself, a transparent medium, the purpose of which is to compel the reader to acknowledge what he already knows: that there exists a great divide (for which man himself is responsible) between what we know ought to be and what actually is. The only "problem" is the purely practical one of deciding what is to be done and how; as we shall see, it is the greatness of Malraux to be the only one to put this problem successfully into fiction. Kafka, of course, does not touch upon it; but does that mean, as it does for Marthe Robert, that K is engaged in a quest which cannot be concluded to his satisfaction, to be sure, but which nevertheless has a kind of validity in that the castle represents certain ineluctable conditions of human existence? "Does Kafka take the side of K against the castle, or is it the reverse? One will not find in the text itself a single word leading to anything more than conjecture; for the answers vary, or rather there are no answers."[48] This is like saying that, there is nothing to indicate clearly whether Picasso, in his painting Guernica, is on the side of the people of the town or of the fascist airmen doing the bombing! It is like saying there were no firm legal grounds for the prosecution of the Nazi war criminals, so that it would have been very difficult to know whose side to be on during the trials! The main responsibility for transforming the self-evident into the problematic falls of course upon our teachers; children must be taught at as early an age as possible that nothing is as it can be clearly seen to be. Thus, when K brings up the subject of the castle and of the count to the school teacher with his pupils, the teacher puts him off by saying—in French rather than German—"Please remember that there are innocent children present." In other words, the function of education is to avoid the essential (the castle) until children have been so conditioned that they will automatically transform the monstrous—the degrading absurdity of government by the castle—into the normal, until children have become the adult of Kafka's little tale *Vor dem Gesetz* in which a man is intimidated by a petty authority into waiting his life long before a door which, he learns at the point of death, had been placed there for his use.[49]

In a conversation with Olga, K has this to say: "Fear of the authorities is born in you here, and is further suggested to you all your lives in the most various ways and from every side, and you yourselves help to strengthen it as much as possible. Still, I have no fundamental objection to that. If an authority is good, why should it not be feared?'' And on the following page, K remarks that the villagers' reverence for the authorities is one that "dishonours its object.''[50] This conversation, and many others like it, is what Robert must mean when she argues that there is nothing in the text to indicate whether Kafka stands with K against the castle or the reverse. And yet to suggest that the authority of the castle might be "good" or that it could be "dishonored" is preposterous; if K nevertheless does so, it is because he had come to the village to take a wife and to life there, something he could hope to achieve only on condition of being able to communicate with the villagers and of learning as much as possible about the workings of the castle. In other words he had, to the limited degree practicable, to enter into the spirit of the place, but this does not alter in the slighest the fact that the villagers are "insane" and that the only power the castle has derives from the cowardly deference the villagers have for the "gentlemen" who work there. Amalia's completely justified insubordination is punished not by the castle by by her neighbors, and the mere presence of K at the *herrenhof* at an improper moment throws the castle gentlemen into a panic. The only precedent in fiction for the predicament in which K finds himself is not Don Quixote but Julien Sorel, whom Stendhal describes as being "an unhappy man at war with his whole society.''[51] With both these men it is a question of actual survival in a hostile environment, and K makes use of a feigned indulgence exactly as Julien Sorel uses hypocrisy.

For Robert, the castle represents not only the past, but "a natural joy . . . from which he [K] had excluded himself by the very excess of his efforts.'' She then quotes a passage from *Das Schloss* where Kafka describes the early morning awakening of the gentleman at their inn where there is created the joyous impression of "happy children preparing themselves for an excursion,'' with one of the gentlemen even imitating the crowing of a cock.[52] There are many passages in *L'ancien et le nouveau* where it is suggested that the castle and the villagers are simply life itself (with its inevitable weight of the past), and while K's quest is exemplary, he suffers nevertheless from an "inaptitude for life" which obliges the villagers to try to teach him, as they would a child, "how to live.[53]'' From our point of view, of course, this is absurd since a good part of the greatness of *Das Schloss* lies in the success Kafka has had in bringing home to us one of the most horrifying aspects of contemporary life: the coming into being of a robotized population (including the cultivated, objective intellectual) programmed in such a way that it will transform the monstrous into the normal. If the castle is to be seen as the normal conditions under which we all have to live, if these conditions are to be regarded as a given, then we lose all the advantages that accrue from our recognizing that the castle is not a transcendent. That is, we revive in one form or another and necessarily the question of the kind of individual we are dealing with. Given Robert's thesis—the continuity of the novel from Cervantes to Kafka—this is as it should be; but, once again, it compels us to overlook what cannot be overlooked, and it leaves us, as well, with no means of explaining Kafka's enormous influence in contemporary literature. What I mean is this:

There is an aspect of Kafka's novels, and a vital one, which no one can miss. He narrates and describes with painstaking accuracy, and yet the "real" which results is suffused with an irreality which is neither fantastic nor simply imaginary; so that it is impossible to say that the world of *Das Schloss* is real or unreal, objective or subjective. It is, at one and the same time, and inextricably, both.[54] It is therefore incomprehensible to me that Robert should write: "Entirely interiorized, shaken by personal conflicts for which the real of the collectivity offers, at the moment, no *normal* solution, K's search is purely subjective."[55] If this is true, then it is impossible to explain the paramount importance of Kafka's work and of *Das Schloss* in particular if we assume, as we must, that no genuinely great work of art can fail to give expression, in a manner peculiar to the genre concerned, to the fundamental cultural orientation of the time. No 15th century artist of any consequence could have worked without perspective; no important contemporary artist can work with it. In the same way, no present-day novelist who is worth reading will have anything to do with either of the three supports upon which the classical novel rests: a beyond, reality as given, and man as free-entity. Instead, the beyond is done away with entirely; thus man and reality, which it was one of the functions of the beyond to correlate, can no longer be envisaged separately. So the real as formerly conceived becomes the *pratico-inerte,* indistinguishably man (*pratico*) and thing (*inerte*); while the "self" of bourgeois culture becomes praxis, that is, a "movement-towards" (in the last analysis, the struggle against scarcity) which is fully intelligible only with reference to the real which that "movement" structures or, in other words, endows with meaning. This new reality which is, in a sense, simply man, and this new man who is, in a sense, simply the real, are nowhere more strikingly set forth than in *Das Schloss.* For K is "transparent"; his "subjective existence" *is* the "outside world" which, nevertheless, has an unmistakeable significance—its oppressive absurdity—which could have come only from K. But since we as readers see things as K does (there being no other point of view to adopt), and since, at the same time we are the villagers (otherwise there would have been no point in writing the novel), and since, finally, the castle, not being a transcendent, has no power of its own, so that men are not inevitably, as in Flaubert, victims, then an "appeal is being made to our freedom" to abolish a reality which is abhorrent to everyone, and self-evidently so. However, individuals cannot change reality but only, very occasionally, themselves; so that if there is an "appeal" it cannot be to men regarded as separate entities as in bourgeois rationalism, but to men defined as the future they envisage as a practical goal (as praxis, as "project," as non-substantive); so that there is no longer any ontological barrier to the formation (at least temporarily) of a group as "one man," a group as subject. Such a group is what Goldmann has called the collective hero of Malraux's *La Condition humaine.*

In *Pour une sociologie du roman,* Goldmann attempts to show that this novel can be satisfactorily accounted for on the basis of Lukács' theory of the problematic hero. For Goldmann, however, as we have seen, the transition from competitive to monopoly capital is reflected in contemporary fiction in the gradual disappearance of the hero as individual in the traditional sense; and the greatness of *La Condition humaine* according to Goldmann is that Malraux shows bourgeois individualism to be, in reality, a horrifying solitude for which the only cure is the absorption of the individual into the revolutionary group, into the collective hero.

The difficulty here is that, as in the case of *Das Schloss* interpreted by Robert, we must look beyond what the novel appears to be about in order to discover what it is really about. Almost any reader would assume that by man's estate Malraux means solitude. He comes back to it obsessively throughout the novel. One of the major characters, Gisors, who is in full sympathy with the revolutionaries, says, in so many words, that very few men can endure their lives (their *condition d'homme*) by which, given the context, he can only mean solitude. On the following page he explains that men spend their time trying to escape—and here he uses the title of the book—from man's estate and that these attempts are "chimerical," foredoomed to failure since they represent man's wish to be God.[56] Goldmann's answer to this would be that Gisors, sympathizer or not, does not belong to the group of revolutionaries who, toward the end of the novel, find themselves together as prisoners awaiting execution. Malraux makes of this scene an apotheosis of revolutionary solidarity; the lives of these men alone of all those in the novel find full meaning and justification. Revolutionary goals can be pursued only collectively, so that the pursuit of those goals and the suppression of solitude are one and the same thing. Goldmann maintains, consequently, that in this novel our lot as human beings is not solitude, but an "aspiration to dignity and meaning" or, again, a "revolutionary aspiration to dignity and to the making of history."[57]

No one would wish to deny that this is a crucial aspect of Malraux's novel, and yet to suggest that the moral of the story is that solitude can be eliminated from human existence will leave most readers with the sort of malaise Robert creates by arguing that the castle represents certain positive values. Death for the group which constitutes the collective hero "assures that solitude is once and for all overcome."[58] Yes, but what of the living? The execution of the militants takes place towards the end of the novel, but at the very end (and therefore as a conclusion?) we find one of those militants, May, tragically alone. It is worth noting also that nothing is more characteristic of revolutionary solidarity than joyful exhilaration, no trace of which can be found in *La Condition humaine* at any stage of the unfolding of the story. However, this matter cannot be settled conclusively until we examine Goldmann's reasons for holding that the collective hero is also, as in the past, a problematic one.

We have seen that it is not easy, using the Lukács-Goldmann theory, to decide how, if at all, the hidden god of bourgeois rationalism operates in the novel. We concluded it might be better to assume the theory requires that an absolute of some sort exist, although, of course, the hero never reaches it. In *La Comedie humaine,* however, there appears to be no question of that since Goldmann writes of the "dialectical relationship between the hero and the world that Lukács described so well and which makes possible the structure of the novel form."[59] A "dialectical relationship" is one in which the knower has made an essential contribution to the nature of the known; there is consequently no need for a trans-historical absolute guaranteeing the identity of the known, and its place is taken by the notion of a changing totality. So the "problem" becomes simply a disagreement over tactics between two factions of the revolutionary left. Goldmann sums it up in the following manner:

> There exists a hero which is *collective* and *problematic*; this latter characteristic, which makes of *La Condition humaine* a novel in the true sense, derives from the fact that the revolutionaries of Shanghai [the col-

lective hero] are torn by two loyalties at once essential and, in the world of
the novel, contradictory: on the one hand, the deepening and development
of the revolution, on the other, discipline towards the party and the International.

Now the party and the International, having adopted a purely defensive
policy, are absolutely opposed to any revolutionary action in the city; they
withdraw troops which are loyal to them and demand the surrender of arms
to Chiang Kai Shek even though it is clear to everyone that he is getting
ready to destroy the communist leaders and militants.

In such conditions, the Shanghai militants are inevitably headed straight
for defeat and masscre.[60]

This problem—the impossibility of deciding between party discipline
and the pursuit of the revolution—is an invented one, or, more accurately, it could only exist for a collective hero, certainly not for Kyo who is
the hero of the novel and every bit as much an individual one as is Julien
Sorel or K. It is perfectly conceivable that many of the Shanghai revolutionaries regarded the International as possessed of a kind of lay in-
fallibility which would have rendered unthinkable an act of indiscipline
despite what some of them might have seen with their own eyes: that the
International, for a greater or lesser period, and possibly even indefinite-
ly, was stifling the revolution. But, as we shall see in a moment, this is
certainly not the position of Kyo (who, incidentally, is as much Malraux
himself as Julien Sorel is Stendhal and K, Kafka). And, in addition, how
can the reader not see that the International is every bit as responsible for
the massacre, in unspeakable conditions, of the collective hero as is
Chiang Kai-Shek; and does this not risk overshadowing the alleged structural importance of the problematic? Goldmann admits that, since the
novel is written from the point of view of Kyo, May, Katow and their
comrades, "it implicitly puts the accent on the sabotage of their struggle
by the party leaders and on the responsibility of those leaders for the
defeat, massacre and torture of the militants."[61] Discipline could not
have weighed very heavily in such circumstances, and one would expect
Goldmann to insist upon its importance for the collective hero. Instead,
his assumption appears to be that the rôle of discipline would have to be
diminished, otherwise it would carry all before it, and the problem of
divided loyalties would vanish. He therefore argues that while Malraux's
position at the time of the writing of *La Condition humaine* was Stalinist
and therefore disciplinarian, his Stalinism in the novel is much more
"abstract and schematic than the rest of the narrative, and appears there,
up to a point, as a foreign body."[62] Goldmann is saying that this

Stalinism—artificial within the confines of the novel—makes it possible for the collective hero to be more attentive to the requirements of the Chinese revolution; but this serves merely to increase the perplexity of these men since discipline does not automatically impose itself. But what if, for Kyo, who is by far the most important of the militants, there is no perplexity at all, no question of discipline?

According to Goldmann one of the two passages in which Malraux expresses this extraneous Stalinism is the conversation between Kyo and Vologuine, the representative of the International, which takes place at Hankeow.[63] For Goldmann, one of the requisites of a great work of art is that it be non-conceptual; so that this passage, in which Malraux is said to be making a 'conceptualized' presentation of Stalinism, is necessarily of minor importance.[64] Yet it is as a result of this conversation that Kyo is confirmed in his opinion that the International is wrong. It is wrong because its orders are inspired not by a more thoroughgoing examination of the exigencies of the Chinese and world revolutions, but by reference to a transcendent. It is astonishing to me that Goldmann should see in this passage an expression of Stalinism, conceptual or otherwise. Malraux undoubtedly expects the reader to understand that Kyo is absolutely right.

The whole question is broached just before Kyo's journey up the river to Hankeow in a conversation he has with Katow who remarks: "The directions we have from the International are sound: spread the revolution and then deepen it. Lenin didn't say at once, 'Power to the Soviets.' " To which Kyo replies: "But he never said power to the Menchevicks. No situation could force us to surrender our weapons to the Kuomingtang. None whatsoever. Because then the revolution would be lost." A few moments later Kyo presses Katow to say whether he thinks they should give up their arms, and Katow answers: "I'm trying to understand . . . . What does the International want? First, use the Kuomingtang army to unify China. Then develop, by propaganda and the rest, the revolution which of itself will pass from a democratic to a socialist revolution." That "of itself" (d'elle-même) is the intervention of the beyond. We are back to that strange combination of determinism and freedom one finds everywhere in 19th century thought. Here, there are laws of history which cause nations to go through a period of democratic liberalism before proceeding to socialism. And yet, mysteriously, that law can be assisted by "propaganda and the rest."[65]

This exchange however is merely the prelude to the far more important one which immediately follows, this time between Kyo and Vologuine.

The same point is made at much greater length. Vologuine talks of discipline, the justification for which comes not from a keener analysis of the situation, but from an appeal to the tables of the law. He says, "The revolution will not last in its democratic form. By its very nature it will become socialist. We have to allow it to work itself out. We've got to assist with a birth, not bring about an abortion." To which Kyo replies, "there is in marxism a fatalism and the exalting of will power. Whenever the fatalism precedes the will power I'm sceptical."[66] And again, further along, Kyo says to Vologuine: "Don't you really think that its obsession with economic fatalism is keeping the Chinese Communist Party and perhaps Moscow from seeing the elementary necessity we have under our noses?"[67] The "necessity" was that of inventing (as did Mao-Tse-Tung shortly after the events related in *La Condition humaine*) a new form of revolutionary struggle in which the peasantry rather than the industrial proletariat would play the decisive role. All that, for Vologuine, of course, is "opportunism"[68] because it takes no heed of the law according to which: "The peasant always follows; . . . whether it be the worker or the bourgeois, he follows."[69]

So unless one absorbs Kyo into a collective hero there is no impossible choice in *La Condition humaine*. Immediately following Kyo's interview with Vologuine Malraux writes that, during Kyo's trip up the river to see Vologuine, "he had been constantly troubled by the meagerness of his information and by how difficult it would be for him to give his action a solid basis if he refused to purely and simply obey the instructions of the International. But the International was wrong."[70] So that Kyo's last doubts had been removed by his talk with Vologuine. One doesn't observe discipline when one's leaders cannot or do not wish to see "the elementary necessity they have under their noses." One might object that toward the end of the chapter in which this crucial conversation between Kyo and Vologuine takes place, Kyo thinks to himself: "all over China and westward across half of Europe men were hesitating as he was, torn between discipline and the slaughter of their own kind."[71] However this is immediately followed by the sentence which concludes the chapter: "But . . . how could one choose sacrifice here in this city sunk in impotence, starvation and hatred, and where the West was waiting for the fate of four hundred million men and perhaps its own, to be decided?"[72] Kyo, consequently, is trapped not in a tragic dilemma, but in a tragic situation (which was that of thousands between Stalin's accession to power and the events of May 1968 in Paris which revealed the revolutionary potential of the new left): the impossibility of accepting the tyrannical stupidity of the Stalinists and the equal impossibility of not working with them against what was even worse, fascism and imperialism.[73] The International was wrong, Kyo had no doubt about that; he also had no doubt that there was nowhere else to go (hence, May, at the end of the novel, is on her way to Moscow). Goldmann, therefore, to my mind, much diminishes the importance of *La Condition humaine* by placing at its center a problem involving tactics which the hero cannot possibly resolve satisfactorily. This is an aspect of the novel to be sure; but, in common with the best literature since Stendhal and Kafka, the real subject of *La Condition humaine* is the hero's rejection of a transcendent in favour of the self-evident; and that hero is neither collective nor an individual in the old sense, but a mediating third, a unique anyone.

There are remarkable similarities between Sartre's play *Les Mains sales* and *La Condition humaine*. No one would suggest presumably that the subject of this play is a disagreement among communists about tactics. The disagreement serves merely as a means of giving a practical illustration to the way in which men fall into the habit of allowing the beyond (in the play, principles derived from the "science of politics" which enables Louis "never to be wrong") to blind them to the "elementary necessities." But, in the play, as in the novel, there is no question of the hero (Hoederer) "going elsewhere"; he is, as a regulating third, a part of the only political movement not simply reformist that existed at that time. And yet what if the myth of materialism ends by destroying the revolution?[74] (In his novel *Les Conquérants*, which preceded *La Condition humaine*, Malraux clearly foretold that development.) What if the "Marxism" of the Stalinists, in other words, were an ideology, the invoking of a transcendent (since the "dialectical laws of history" is one of the forms in which 19th century scientism persists among us) as a cover beneath which a group or class might exercise political and economic power to selfish ends. This operation was called socialism in one country; and while that might appear a reasonable tactic, those who opposed it were said to be "objectively" wrong, which is to say that the party cannot be in error because it is permanently tuned in to the law.

We can now understand why the theme of solitude should have a structural importance in this novel, why it should be man's estate and why, at the same time, that solitude need not and must not be unremitting.

Our study of the novel has revealed that bourgeois rationalism rests upon two propositions of so fundamental an importance that if either is called into question that whole cultural structure enters into a period of crisis. First, there exist hidden transcendents (moral or scientific or both depending upon the writer or thinker concerned). Second, men are "things" (predestination, scientific determinism), but since the beyond is concealed, men can exist as individual things "freely" demonstrating their moral and/or intellectual quality by the ingenuity and conscientiousness they show in revealing unsuspected aspects (great intelligence) or exigencies (high moral achievement) of the beyond. In primitive societies where the transcendent reveals itself directly and unambiguously to the senses (and to the individual only as a chance representative of his group) solitude can have no particular value; while among us, from Montaigne through the Romantics to estheticism, solitude facilitates or is indispensable to a more perfect communion with, or more thorough investigation of, what remains inaccessible to all but the noble of soul, the gifted, the genial, the important. The five senses (the domain of the "elementary necessities") we share even with the important; but, luckily for the maintenance of order, the senses deceive, and the data we owe them must be carefully sifted by mighty minds (that of a de Gaulle or of a Kissinger perhaps, a Beria or a Franco) working solitarily and secretively so that the real may be successfully interpreted for the greater good of all men. The solitary work of the great,[75] insofar as it reveals "permanencies" (whether historical law, the immortality of art or the natural inferiority of women and of some races) shields us lesser individuals of Western society against the catastrophe of solitude, for our only form of communication with each other is by way of these concealed permanencies or principles invested in kinds of people. In these conditions the mediating third is one who insists that the principles are not the discoveries of great individuals but merely a choice of certain aspects of a real which lends itself only to historically subjective formulations as to its nature. In brief, men cannot be defined by eternal verities of their own invention. But then, incapable of knowing himself, existing only as a "transparent" awareness of what had been the explicit level of the classical novel, the hero as mediating third falls into a solitude which is not that of the meditating sage, but of a man overwhelmed by a self-evident reality which everyone else has carefully trained himself to look through in search of higher things; or, as a properly disciplined villager, to take for granted.

Kyo saw that the communists had to fall back upon discipline because their analyses were all corrupted by the use of a transcendent which, by the thirties, the well-educated (and the illiterate) could reject almost as easily as they could that upon which middle class morality had to rely. But no sooner does Kyo become finally convinced of this (in the passage from which I quoted a moment ago) than he feels himself overcome by "a great dependence . . . . by the agony of being only a man, only himself."[76] This is the solitude which, according to Malraux, is man's estate. It is *not* the solitude of the bourgeois individual of our day clinging desperately and in bad faith to the worm-eaten absolutes (the castle) upon which he depends to know who and why he is, but, on the contrary, the solitude of men who refuse to try to communicate by way of the palsied certitudes with which others struggle unsuccessfully (hence the incidence of psychosomatic illnesses) to shore up their increasingly insane existences. But this makes of the hero "a madman, a monster comparable to no other."[77] A "monster," however, not for what he is (otherwise, as we know, *La Condition humaine* could not be a great contemporary novel) but for what he does: he insists that the contradiction between what we all know to be right and what is allowed to happen has to be resolved before life can become genuinely worthwhile anywhere in the world. And this is not an opinion peculiar to the individual Kyo; it is the position occupied necessarily by the mediating third who is "the monstrous product of monstrous societies."[78] "Monstrous" not in himself, but because there is no place for him; he is outside everything acceptable and "normal." And yet if the reader has understood Stendhal, Kafka and Malraux, it can only be that he too is "freakish," since their novels make sense only on condition one see reality through the hero's eyes. Hence the solitude of the mediating third, unlike that of the self-monad of bourgeois rationalism, is not insurmountable since there is a universal accord (which we have already encountered on the explicit level of the classical novel) and, since that accord derives from the realization that man is now able to dominate the natural environment, that he could be successfully defined as praxis, in other words, then the mediating third can hope to find himself absolutely at one with that great majority (the world's poor) who can only benefit by destroying a reality which is purely and simply the domination of one group over others. Hence the theme of fraternity and revolutionary solidarity in *La Condition humaine* upon which, however, Goldmann errs in placing the entire emphasis.

Kyo and his comrades died for having given a meaning to their lives; and since "meaning," here, can signify only revolutionary project, and since for the Malraux who wrote *La Condition humaine* man is project and not substance," then men who share the same revolutionary future become, in a sense, the same being; so that the futile and self-destructive solitude of the modern individual is put behind them for good. But, as we have seen, this is not the solitude of Malraux's novel which is that of men who, no longer able to communicate through a transcendent in the light of which the real can be infallibly deciphered, may find themselves radically alone in insisting upon what everyone, in a sense, has to know but will not acknowledge; namely, that the contemporary real cannot possibly be accounted for in the old terms. In *La Condition humaine* the old terms are not only pre-revolutionary China, dismembered and exploited by the imperialist powers (the castle), but also the mentalities of those (the Stalinists) proposing to bring revolutionary changes while retaining a metaphysics which, since it involves a hidden transcendent, is purely and simply a survival of that bourgeois order which gives to the picaresque its unfailing cheerfulness and to the classical novel means of neutralizing the explicit level.[80]

It is true that the contemporary intellectual has few tasks more urgent than to insist that after one has removed from any individual what he derives from his group, what is left (intelligence quotient, "aggressivity," Freudian unconscious, etc.) has been placed there by the investigating group refusing to allow for the inevitable subjectivity, historical and social, of its questions. But what is to prevent that subjectivity from becoming what Sartre, in the third volume of his *l'Idiot de la famille*, calls an "objective neurosis" if not the existence of a tiny number of marginal beings, mediating thirds, alone and persecuted because they are sane? Sanity here being not an individual quality but simply the inability to live with the mad, simply the refusal to turn away from the self-evident.[81] For Goldmann, the great artist exists only insofar as he brings to more coherent expression what he takes from his group, so that the importance of *La Condition humaine* lies in Malraux's having contrived to create a group hero without destroying the novel since the problematic remains; the group hero, being part of a much larger group with which it disagrees, is faced by an insurmountable problem of divided loyalties. But if we refuse to allow the elimination of Kyo—entirely gratuitous apart from the requirements of Goldmann's demonstration—then the novel becomes a more important one because what it is saying is more important. Namely, while there is no life apart from revolutionary solidarity, there may be a need, through a perhaps indefinite future, for men so situated (and not so endowed) they can see that the new revolutionary group, in attempting to stabilize and reinforce its power, creates a *pratico-inerte* (the economy and all that exists to serve it of the bourgeois revolution, the bureaucracy of the Bolsheviks) in which men are once again becoming alienated, once again struggling to ignore the contradiction between universal self-evidence and particularist ideologies.[82]

CONCLUSION

Reason operates necessarily on the basis of certain cultural presuppositions which may or may not be historically relevant. The 18th century schoolmen reasoned just as effectively as did their adversaries, and they were wrong because their presuppositions were historically absurd. These presuppositions are the stuff with which not only the philosopher but the artist and novelist work as well. One has the impression, furthermore, that these latter are far more accurate than are the thinkers when it comes to determining what is historically relevant. Scholasticism persisted for several centuries after the disappearance of medieval art and, to take a contemporary example, the French "Marxist" Althusser is wrong for the simple reason that Kafka and Malraux are right. We know that the best contemporary fiction refuses the attempt to reach outside humanity with the result that the novel is entirely restructured; rather than a disembodied eye studying reality—including people—as a given, there has come into being a reality which is indistinguishably a "material" and the "shapes" men have impressed upon it. So man is redefined as that initiative, or praxis, responsible for a structured shape, or *pratico-inerte*, of this particular kind.

However, if man has no existence "in himself," then he risks being absorbed into a reality of his own making, like the villagers in *Das Schloss* or the Stalinists and imperialists of *La Condition humaine*. In these circumstances the role of the hero in fiction becomes that of denouncing the tragic discrepancy between the "shape" of reality and what, self-evidently, we all seek. This whole evolution of contemporary sensibility, of our presuppositions, remains a dead letter for a school of academic intellectuals who have succeeded, through structuralism, in reestablishing the illusion—which esthetical-scientism could no longer maintain—that something, after all, precedes man, that there is something outside man, and that, consequently, it is "natural" there be the teachers and the taught, special competencies, the bright and the stupid. The disagreement between Vologuine and Kyo was therefore reproduced in May 1968 in Paris with Althusser representing the scriptures and the students the elementary necessity we all have under our noses of destroying the system which is destroying us. Lyotard barely exaggerates in declaring that Althusser and his group represent a "resurgence of Stalinism."[1]

Apart from its crucial importance in linguistics, the status of structuralism is somewhat ambiguous. On the one hand it would appear to have removed once and for all the ethnocentric barriers of science and religion to an understanding on our part that Western culture is in no way better or more "advanced" than any other; it has simply structured reality in a different way as a function of a different practical challenge. But such a degree of relativism honestly accepted destroys the traditional, privileged position of the intellectual in our society; he is left with no alternative but to *labor* to resolve the contradiction between universal and particular, explicit and implicit we have seen to be indispensable to the best classical fiction.[2] Many intellectuals therefore prefer to argue that it is not praxis that creates structure, but the reverse: men do not speak, they "are spoken"; they do not think, but "are thought" by the cultural structure of which they are a part. It follows from this view that in order to undertake we must first know, and if it is impossible to understand why the process of knowing should not itself be regarded as an inevitably subjective undertaking, at least the function of the academic intellectual is safeguarded; at least we have succeeded in denying that anything much has changed since the classical novel. For if man is produced by the structure (formerly by scientific law) then he is "thing," yet a thing endowed miraculously in the case of certain exceptional individuals with the capacity of placing itself outside the structure (or outside scientific determinism) so as to view itself objectively from a non-position, that of the omniscient 19th century novelist. Structuralism as a science exists to keep alive the old illusion that there can be transcultural, trans-historical constants which it is the business of the academic to reveal and so bring about a compulsory enlightenment; those unwilling or unable to be so enlightened become—again as in the classical novel—defective things: stupid, perverse, insane, primitive, etc., rather than simply different people putting different questions because their positions are different.

Students throughout the sixties brought pandemonium to the university, and we scholars were not always able to get on with our work. As the economic situation worsens student militancy could well revive, so why should we not explain the nature and importance of what we are doing so that students will remain peacefully at their studies with the same sense of purpose which has always sustained their teachers through hard times?

I taught at the University College of Ghana during the reign of Nkrumah who, having sought to interfere with academic freedom, caused my colleagues (largely British and American) to issue a declaration of principles which was dated November 1960. I shall quote those passages which constitute an answer to the question every student has a right to put: what is the university for, why should we attend it?

> We the undersigned senior members of the University College of Ghana declare:
> That, to fulfill its true responsibilities, a university must:
> (1) function as a sanctuary for ideas, even if unpopular or unorthodox, promote freedom of intellectual expression, and stimulate research and the extension of the frontiers of knowledge,
> (2) train students in different disciplines and fields of knowledge,
> (3) promote a liberal outlook, which involves fostering such basic concepts as justice, freedom, equality, and human dignity, and
> (4) promote a rational and scientific attitude among its members, with an emphasis on truth as a supreme value.

A good majority of Western academics would subscribe to these statements (or, which comes to the same thing, they would have nothing else to offer). What ought to strike us first about them is that they should have been formulated in Africa, in one of the underdeveloped parts of the world; so we are left with the paradox of a Western institution, like parliamentary government and free enterprise, which nevertheless enjoys a universal validity. How could an institution having evolved under particular historical and geographic conditions be successfully transplanted to some distant part of the globe?

Many academics would deplore the anachronistic bigotry of those missionaries still intent upon replacing primitive religions with the debris of their own primitive religion. The university, in contrast, serves as a "sanctuary" not only for "ideas" but for whole religions and philosophies so that we can extend the "frontiers of knowledge" in respect to them. But such work will be successful only in proportion to our ability to foster "such basic concepts as justice, freedom, equality, and human dignity." Otherwise a "rational and scientific attitude" towards other peoples and institutions is not practicable. How could we have accurate knowledge of other mentalities, cultures and attitudes unless we respect their integrity, unless they remain as untouched as possible by our observing presence? We cannot successfully study (or have represented in parliament, if we are statesmen rather than scholars) another way of life if we are intolerant of it, if we do not allow it to be itself if we do not guarantee its freedom and equality. The university is profoundly "pluralistic."

Suppose now we confront a simple evidence: namely, that a "liberal outlook" and a "rational and scientific attitude" are the products of a particular time and place, that a scientific view is itself a specific view and therefore cannot "contain" other views, that the notion there can exist a "sanctuary for ideas" is itself an idea, and that we should be able to ignore this is a cultural trait which would be of great interest to men of other cultures were there any such men sufficiently coarse and presumptuous to treat us as objects of study and also so naive as to suppose themselves capable of not belonging to their own culture.

To say of a person or of a people that they lack a "rational and scientific attitude" is to say, purely and simply, that they are not like us. It is to situate them at some point within an area the center of which is occupied by *our* mind and gaze; it is to place them with their backs turned to us so that we will not have to acknowledge the existence of other centers. Such a relationship between peoples does not foster "justice, equality and human dignity," but it renders Western culture at the moment an immense service. For when, in the same breath, the professors, in their declaration, talk of "truth as a supreme value" and of the *"scientific* attitude," they refer to that conception of truth as single, concealed, and inalterably given we have found to be so important in the history of the novel. If such is truth, then of course in "pursuing knowledge" the university is concerned with—to quote our document—"the well-being of humanity as a whole." But while humanity as a whole has been waiting for the "frontiers of knowledge" to be pushed back to some decisive point events have, as we like to say, taken their course. History has been in the making, and we are researching into it in the hope of being able, before too long, to explain what really happened. But what if there exists a plurality of centers? What if, for instance, the New World were there before we discovered it, and Africa before we explored it? Peoples of other cultures have begun to "turn around," and we are obliged to consider how we may appear in *their* perspective. They know what "really happened," and as a result we appear in their light not essentially as people pursuing knowledge in the interests of justice, freedom, equality and human dignity, but as the great white destroyers. It is estimated that some 50 million Africans were taken across the Atlantic during the period of the West African slave trade.

This figure, of course, may well have been inflated by persons whose motives had little to do with objective scholarship—there may have been 40 or perhaps as little as 30 million. Room had been made for these Africans by the Spaniards who, in the space of some 50 years had cleared away about 15 million souls. (Montaigne spoke with one of these savages in Rouen and was asked why the poor and hungry of France did not rise up to take what they needed from those who obviously had too much—a question Europe did not entertain seriously until Marx). Shortly afterwards, the work of exterminating Indian, animal and vegetable life in North America was to get underway with whatever dispatch the technological equipment of the age allowed. Democratic individualism is the right to scramble to opulence over the prone bodies of our fellows, and when justification through economic law fails to convince, fascism arises and the slaughter once again becomes deliberate. Now, finally, atomic and biological weapons make possible the realization of that old dream of us white Christians—the obliteration of life on this planet. This, of course, is not what we intend, and above all not what we say; but from other "centers" our intentions are invisible, and only a fool would be impressed by what we say as opposed to what we do. Among many things actually seen from non-rational, primitive, viewpoints is the white Christian's unfitness for life in the very stiffness with which he walks, in his mania for privacy and cleanliness, in his need to establish a self (independence of others) which, to exist, must be acknowledged by others (absolute dependence), in his adolescent concentration of sensuality in sex which he then denies himself, and, perhaps to sum it up, his inability to live sensuousness as a state, tending as he does to make of it a deliberate and often self-conscious act.

But perhaps I am being too severe, for in the professors' declaration it is stated that "a university cannot and should not keep aloof from the society of which it forms a part, but should, on the contrary, actively seek to serve the needs of that society." The university, however, envisaged the needs of Ghanaian society in a rather strange way since it produced about twenty graduates in classics and divinity to one in agriculture, perhaps on grounds that men—including Ghanaians—do not live by bread alone. Nkrumah had sounder opinions (belatedly and ineffectually, however) as to the importance of bread, and his attempts to impress them upon university authorities was what induced the professors to issue their declaration. Any African leader concerned to preserve Africa from the clutches of Western capital, concerned to preserve Africa from the fate of South America, will find himself confronted by the extremely difficult problem of finding skilled government workers who have not been endowed by a missionary-university education with a mentality finding itself most at home in what the bankers call a favorable investment climate. In exchange for their free education graduates of the University of Ghana were bonded to teach school for five years, since the country desperately needed teachers. After a year or two most of then had taken jobs in business or industry where the rewards were more satisfying. And why not? There is nothing in "freedom of intellectual expression" or in a "rational and scientific attitude" which is in the least incompatible with the uniquely selfish pursuits of the free world. When "justice, freedom, equality and human dignity" are trodden upon by seekers of self-improvement, as they inevitably are, no one militantly determined to redress wrongs (increasing numbers of students, for example) can possibly adopt a rational and scientific attitude. Simone de Beauvoir puts it succinctly when she remarks somewhere that to observe someone getting his face stepped on is to accept that such a thing should happen. Any act not concerned solely with "extending the frontiers of knowledge" might easily remove us still further from that state of harmony which the academic presumably hopes to restore, or to which he hopes to discover some means of access by patiently pushing back the frontiers.

A diseased organ can be removed from the body which will continue to function. But whatever it is we refer to as "mind" cannot be removed, for the body is "imbued" with it. Similarly, the university is not just another organ in the body politic, it is the region to which we must look for remote and refined correlates of some nasty diseases. The university cannot dissociate itself from the crimes and stupidities of the body, for they are always psychosomatic. When, for instance, in the course of a television discussion on the war in Vietnam the interviewer pointed out to student protestors that since the beginning of the conflict the American government had changed several times while that of North Vietnam had remained the same, his stupidity was, in the final analysis, the responsibility of the professors. For just as they are unable to see that a "rational and scientific attitude" is in itself an attitude and not a universal container in which other attitudes can have assigned to them their place in the great scheme, so the interviewer could not see that his form of government relies for its stability, in part, upon fostering the illusion that it "contains" alternative forms of government, that it is not in itself a particular form of government. Almost any political opinion can of course be expressed, but its existence is something else. The culture of the

Brazilian Indians comes to expression, so to speak, in many university departments of anthropology, but these people are also being deliberately exterminated by successive Brazilian governments,[3] which could not exist without the support of those who govern the country of which the anthropologist is a citizen. Indians are peculiar in that they would rather exist than be understood. So would the world's young who watch with increasing revulsion a university content to trundle along in the baggage train of the great destroyer.

Some time ago I received from a university a document entitled, "A Brief to the Senate Committee on Undergraduate Education from the Ad Hoc Curriculum and Calendar Committee of the Faculty of Humanities, dated October 31, 1969." Let us look at this second document in the light of the reflections inspired by the first. Two paragraphs, which I shall quote in their entirety concern us. The first is headed Specific Aims of the Humanities and runs as follows:

1. To develop the skills and to impart the information necessary for the students' understanding and enjoyment of their cultural heritage in language and literature, history and philosophy, the visual arts, music, and religion.

2. To create an atmosphere where students may develop an active response to the perspectives and values of their heritage.

3. To encourage students to respect the best scholarly work in these fields.

4. To broaden the perspectives of students so as to enable them to attain a fuller understanding of the enduring qualities of human beings, and civilizations, and to discover the interrelationships between them.

5. To stimulate students to know themselves, to appraise themselves and their culture, and to enhance their capability for responsible and effective decisions and action.

The second paragraph, The Humanist Outlook states:

The Humanities have no quarrel with the sciences or with the scientific method which frequently plays a crucial role within each of the humanistic fields. The humanist views reality from a standpoint other than that of the scientist and the social scientist but with a full sense of the complementary nature of the three domains. The Humanities are concerned with man's inner consciousness of himself; they delight man's mind, heighten his awareness of what is within him and what surrounds him, clarify his responses to experience, and sharpen his insights. By their concern for the achievements and wisdom necessary for civilization, the Humanities, in matters both of individual personality and of public taste and policy, contribute to and affect enlightened choices and commitments.

The men who listed these aims of the humanities must have been greatly encouraged by the thought that growing numbers of students achieve them: (1) Students now understand their cultural heritage to be one of fantastically destructive wars, religious intolerance and bigotry, sexual repression, racism, colonialism, capitalist greed and selfishness, destruction or pollution of the natural environment and so on; (2) Their heritage excites a more and more creative response from students striving to tear the university down so a new one can be built; (3) Students ask nothing better than to respect the best scholarly work—that of Marx and Sartre for example, if it were taught to them—because it would greatly improve the effectiveness of their "active response"; (4) The "interrelationship" between the West and the underdeveloped world is one which allows the strong to plunder the weak with impunity. In exchange for raw materials upon which it depends the west reciprocates—as in the Congo and Nigeria some years ago—with war and starvation; and (5) Students "know themselves" as exploiters, and their attempts at "responsible and effective decision and action" must be a source of lively satisfaction to the academic community which has worked so hard to bring about this new self-awareness.

It is difficult not to be ironic also in commenting upon views (coming to the second paragraph) which still clearly reflect the 17th century's attempts to absorb the new science into a coherent philosophical system. The result—mind on the one hand, matter on the other, with no means of correlating them satisfactorily—which was at that time a necessary evil, has grown into something very different. Mind has become "our cultural heritage" and "man's inner consciousness of himself," while our rational and scientific attitude (here, the "scientific method") is now a disastrous ethnocentrism. Science once offered the inspiring prospect of a degree of control over nature which would insure far more security and well-being for men than they had ever known before. We know now that what was to have been man's control over nature has become a control exercized by a tiny minority to the detriment of the rest of us; but for as long as our attitude is rational and scientific there is nothing whatever that anyone can do about this except entertain widely approved sentiments concerning "public taste and policy" and "enlightened choices and commitments." It is true—unhappily—that the "scientific method . . . frequently plays a crucial rôle within each of the humanistic fields," but the scientific method certainly does not repay the compliment. Our "cultural heritage" is not an alternative or a corrective to our fundamental positivism; its function is to "delight the mind, and heighten the awareness," of people who, being individuals, are, by definition, unable to coalesce into a collectivity through which man could regain control of tools which will otherwise destroy him. Since full participation in truth envisaged as scientific requires long training in methods usually exceedingly difficult not only the masses but even the very well educated are excluded from any satisfying commerce with truth as our society defines it. And when one considers that the individual, educated or not, is also excluded from the public realm, the main function of our cultural heritage becomes clear: to give an appearance of substance to an entirely imaginary individual autonomy.

There can be no doubt then that the cultural presuppositions that made possible the classical novel are still exactly those of the contemporary academic intellectual. There is the explicit level with talk of "justice, freedom, equality, and human dignity" and, in the second document, even "choices and commitments," all of which makes up the domain of the pious wish and of sightless vision because the true endeavor (implicit level) of the university intellectual is to prove the existence of an individualism (an identity) capable of entering into communication with a concealed transcendent. If we date the coming into being of a progressive alternative from Stendhal and Marx, then for almost two centuries the university has existed as a class institution perpetuating privilege and falsehood.

INTRODUCTION

1. *Saint Genêt,* (Paris: Gallimard, 1952), p. 132.

2. Primitive societies which might appear to have achieved this security always occupied a limited territory (not the planet, as does contemporary man) and were therefore in danger of attack by less fortunate neighbors.

3. In Descartes' time the new method was deemed to be universally valid; and the same, of course, is true today. Dialectical reason (an aspect of which I have been describing) is considered to encompass the physical sciences as well as all other forms of inquiry since, as Husserl has shown, science reduced to its own resources is unable to account for the particular "initiative" it represents. It has, in consequence, led us into the impasse of contemporary absurdism.

4. For Sartre's opinion of Heidegger's attempt to retain an absolute, see his *Critique de la raison dialectique* (Paris: Gallimard, 1960), p. 248.

5. See Francis Jeanson, *Sartre dans sa vie* (Paris: Seuil, 1974), p. 278.

6. The best definition of a term is the way in which it is used; so I am going to allow all that follows to stand as a definition for these words, praxis and structure, at least to the extent that they are used to make sense of an art form.

7. Again our recurring difficulty: Granted our total historical subjectivity (which the liberal is compelled to reject, otherwise his objective abstentionism becomes unintelligible except in class terms), art ceases to be an epiphenomenal expression of certain gifted individuals and becomes, in our own time at least, the means by which the collectivity (Lukács, Goldmann) or the mediating third (Sartre) attempts to sense what may lie immediately beyond or "around" a given historically structured world view.

8. If the intellectual, especially the North American, wishes to ignore the existence of class divisions in his own society he can hardly do so on an international scale, since the unequal exchange which in the West enabled the city to exploit the countryside has now been reproduced globally between the rich and poor nations.

CHAPTER I

1. In the case of the manorial economy of medieval Europe a different division of labor (between warriors and serfs rather than between men and women as is the case with most primitive societies) produced a stratified as opposed to an "interrelated" group.

2. M.J. Field, *Search for Security* (London: Faber and Faber, 1960).

3. See Marie-Cécile and Edmond Ortigues, *Oedipe africain* (Paris: Plon, 1966), pp. 9, 10. Paul Parin, Fritz Morgenthaler and Goldy Parin-Matthey, in *Die Weissen Denken Zuviel* (Zurich: Atlantis Verlag, 1963) often use the expression "group self" in their psychoanalytic studies of the Dogan.

4. "Coming into contact with barbarian peoples you have nothing more to fear

than touching the left horn of a snail. The only things one should really be anxious about are the means of mastery of the waves of the seas—and, worst of all dangers, the minds of those avid for profit and greedy for gain." Chang Hsieh, as quoted in E.G.R. Taylor, *The Haven Finding Art* (London: Hollis and Carter, 1971), p. 278.

5. See François Châtelet, *Logos et praxis* (Paris: SEDES, 1962).

6. The coming into being of this individuality which, for a while, coexisted with the primitive conception of the noble as an institution, as the impersonal filling of a place without which an inconceivable gap would have been left in the hierarchical plenum of Aristotelean-Christian thought is what made Renaissance tragedy possible. Lear's abdication, which he decides upon for "individual" reasons, Macbeth's ambition, Hamlet's scruples, Othello's love, all enter into absolutely irreconcilable conflict with what was required of these men as institutions, as public beings with, ideally, no allegiance whatever to the self.

7. In medieval art, the more important the person the closer his position to that of God; in other words, the larger in size he would tend to be shown. With the introduction of perspective, of course, figures had to be reduced in size in proportion as they approached God (infinity).

8. The private individual can come into contact with the divine only indirectly, and shakily, through conscience; which is to say that religion falls to the level of morality, with its function as a cosmology being assumed by science.

9. Let me recall that, before the development in the 18th century of the labor theory of value, egalitarianism in the contemporary sense did not exist; so that the artist could in good conscience address himself to a "majority" which we would now consider an elite.

10. Even a painting of a forest absolutely untouched in any way by man would have no more "reality" in it than a primitive mask since the concept of nature as a separate entity existing as ·a spectacle or as "matter" is one peculiar to bourgeois rationalism.

11. Pierre Francastel, *La Figure et le lieu* (Paris: Gallimard, 1967), p. 40.

12. Collective authorship, *Structuralisme et marxisme* (Paris: Union Générale d'Edition, (10/18) 1970), p. 91.

13. The primitive accumulation of capital was made possible by usury, plunder, monopoly and unequal exchange. See Ernest Mandel's *Traité d'économie marxiste,* vol. 1, (Paris: Julliard, 1962), chapter 4; and Maurice Dobb's *Studies in the Development of Capitalism* (London: Routledge and Kegan Paul, 1963), chapters 3 and 4.·

CHAPTER II

1. Every primitive culture, to be sure, also possesses an explanation for the whole of the real but it is an explanation which has to be protected by a total incuriosity as to other cultures to be found sometimes only a few miles away. But the white man's curiosity is protected as well—by a dogmatism which is imper-

vious because derived from a scientific, that is, a "global" view of things. Our rationalism has produced one of the ugliest and most dangerous of all human types, the man who combines the utter assurance of a scientific outlook (to the point in some cases of being capable of carrying out lobotomies) with complete ignorance of science as simply "one form of emphasis," as A.N. Whitehead put it, after having remarked that "The self-confidence of learned people is the comic tragedy of civilization" (in *Essays in Science and Philosophy,* (New York: Philosophical Library, 1947), pp. 103, 95).

2. We will be returning to the pre-Balzacian novel in much greater detail later and with a better chance of being sure of our analyses since in the meantime we will have fixed the structure of a far more important form, that of the classical novel.

3. This individualism is "convertible" of course into that of the omniscient observer-narrator and, when we reach Joyce and Proust, into a subjectivity-domain.

4. *Le Père Goriot* (Paris: Livre de Poche, 1961), p. 153.

5. To appreciate the importance of this idea in economic thought (to take that example) one ought to look at Paul Baran's *The Political Economy of Growth* (New York: Modern Reader Paperbacks, 1968, pp. 234-35) where Baran refers to a number of economists who attribute the economic backwardness of the third world to the absence there of "entreprenurial talent." If this is one's view, then the novel can represent capitalism quite adequately in figures deploying "entreprenurial talent" like Balzac's Nucingen; we can then safely ignore Marx's *Capital* in which he insists that capitalism is a system (or structure, in contemporary language) "animated" by a particular group of individuals, but certainly not deriving from those individuals. But if this is the case then it follows, unpleasantly, that to bring about desirable changes we must change the system, especially since a part of our education consists in a study of the classical novel from which we learn that the system is its individuals rather than the reverse.

In a review of Ralph Miliband's book *The State in Capitalist Society,* which appeared in the *New Left Review,* number 58, Nicos Poulantzas is able to show that even authors of Marxist inspiration slip too easily into an overemphasis upon the activities of individuals in a structure which, to be sure, they "animate" and for which they are responsible, but which they did not create and which uses them as they use it.

6. George Eliot, *The Mill on the Floss,* book 3, chapter 8.

7. See Paul Lidsky's *Les Ecrivains contre la Commune* (Paris: Maspéro, 1970).

8. *La Rabouilleuse* (Paris: Livre de Poche, 1960), p. 207.

9. (*Le Père Goriot, op. cit.*), p. 415.

10. "These thoughts seemed to him [Prince Andrey] comforting. But they were only thoughts. Something was wanting in them; there was something one-sided and personal, something intellectual; they were not self-evident." *War and Peace* (New York: Modern Library, [n.d.] p. 925). The self-evidence of another life was to come to Prince Andrey, as to Ivan Ilyitch, at the point of death.

11. "Once admit that human life can be guided by reason, and all possibility of life is annihilated." *War and Peace*, (*op. cit.*, p. 1064).

12. See Henri Guillemin's *Napoléon tel quel* (Paris: Editions de Trevise, 1969).

13. This is the function of jails, of racism, of insane asylums, and it is all Western democracy has at the moment in the way of a political philosophy, the liberal being simply one who places less emphasis upon the elimination of the wicked and more upon voting the good into office. The fascist and the liberal are manifestations of the same economic and cultural system, and they both hate those young people who see more and more clearly that it is the *system* which must be changed.

14. *War and Peace, op. cit.*, p. 293.

15. The historical novel is a lesser form of fiction because its reality is no longer of sufficient concern to anyone to cause the novelist to develop the explicit in his work. Or, to put this differently, where the real is inaccurate, partial or unconvincing, where the novelist is a poor "spectator," as is the case with most fiction, especially, of course, the historical, there is necessarily too great a reliance upon the implicit. None of this applies to *War and Peace;* the Russia of Tolstoy's time was closer to the Napoleonic era than was Thackeray's England to the period of *Vanity Fair.*

16. Pierre Bezuhov and Nikolay Rostov (after the sort of conversion they both undergo) enjoy this inner, extra-rational guidance. (See *War and Peace, op. cit.*, pp. 1044, 1078). "But the older he [Levin] grew and the more intimately he came to know his brother, the oftener the thought occurred to him that the power of working for the general welfare—a power of which he felt himself entirely destitute—was not a virtue but rather a lack of something . . . many other social workers were not led to this love for the common good by their hearts, but because they had reasoned out in their minds that it was a good thing to do that kind of work . . . ." (*Anna Karenina* (New York: Norton Library, 1968), pp. 217-18). But why should not "heart" and reason be found occasionally in the same person?

17. *War and Peace, op. cit.*, p. 1101.

18. Only the "masses" are ignorant enough to suppose the matter is as simple as that. In the entertainment provided for them, therefore, the hero is almost always the man most successful at revealing and disposing of the villains.

19. The Russian novelists were not, to be sure, confronted by "middle class society." But this made their situation that much more dramatic and accounts, in part, for their extraordinary achievements. They were bringing the universalism of 1789 to bear upon a social order which had not had several centuries in which to make the necessary accomodations. The result was that the Russian aristocracy enjoyed both feudal and bourgeois privileges but without the responsibilities of either.

20. In *Anna Karenina* one finds an occasinal remark of this kind: ". . . this . . .spirit of evil and falsehood which had taken possession of her [Anna] . . . " (*op. cit.*, p. 135).

21. "These definite social functions are no outgrowths of human nature, but are the products of relations of exchange between men who produce their goods in the form of commodities. They are so far from being purely individual relations between buyer and seller that both enter the relation only to the extent that their individual labour is disregarded and is turned into money as labour of *no* individual. Just as it is, therefore, childish to consider these economic bourgeois rôles of buyer and seller as eternal social forms of human individuality, so it is on the other hand preposterous to lament in them the extinction of individuality. They are the necessary manifestation of individuality at a certain stage of the social system of production." Marx, *A Contribution to the Critique of Political Economy* (Chicago: Charles Kerr, 1904), pp. 119-20.

22. Or at least to fellow creatures who are recognizably such. Here is Levin, thoroughly good, and to a great extent Tolstoy himself: "The single fact that his wife, his Kitty, would be in the same room with a girl off the streets made him shudder with repulsion and horror" (*Anna Karenina, op. cit.,* p. 444).

23. On the other hand, far better the "resurrection" of an Ivan Ilyitch than the stony, definitive, death in life of the liberal intellectual unable to close the gap opened by scientific rationalism between his sentiments and what he imagines he knows.

24. As far as one can make out Levin's thesis is that not enough attention is given, in books on agriculture, to the nature of the agricultural laborer himself; so that, interestingly enough, Tolstoy is arguing that agriculture is largely determined by the laborer (it is a question, so to speak, of a "collective identity") rather than the laborer by agricultural conditions; this being, for the Marxist—and, one would hope, for most people by now—a question of plain common sense.

25. Ideally, of course, given the existence of other religions on this earth, the system of morality of which the novelist makes use should not be too narrowly Christian either. Tolstoy mentions this difficulty in *Anna Karenina* (p. 737) but then "resolves" it (p. 739) by an appeal to the self-evidence of religious truth, reason being simply one of the means by which society diverts itself from the inconvenient promptings of conscience.

26. Thackeray allows us to be amused occasionally by Becky Sharp, but there is nothing to keep us from condemning her without a qualm; and in fact she grows more loathsome as time goes on.

Apart from operating outside the structure of the classical novel, as does Stendhal, the only other possibility is to force the reader to mitigate his judgement by confronting him with a protagonist whose culture—and hence moral values—are not those of the reader. This is what Mérimée does in *Carmen,* and Emily Bronte's Heathcliff was mysteriously outlandish, possibly, like Carmen, a gypsy.

27. Tolstoy talks, to be sure, of the possibility of everyone coming together in faith (p. 724); but in reality fewer and fewer are anxious to share in anything belonging to us, our religion being as thoroughly discredited as our democracy and our humanism.

28. Individuals are regarded as determining the political destinies of their society. In *Les Employés* (Paris: Club de l'Honnête Homme, 1956), vol. 10 p. 64, for example, Balzac attributes the decline of great powers such as Rome and Venice to the increasing mediocrity of the men who ruled them. Balzac's view had little to do with the relative historical ignorance of his time since it is still that of the conservative-police mentality of our own day for which a social upheaval of any kind is never due to political and economic conditions but to the sinister activities of leftist agitators and other diseased elements of an essentially healthy system.

29. Reasoning of a very high order, incidentally, since Tolstoy anticipates Husserl's thesis in *Die Frage nach dem Ursprung der Geometrie* by pointing out (*Anna Karenina*, p. 739) that scientific calculation builds itself up on the basis of ordinary perception. The senses do not therefore "deceive"; they are the foundation upon which science rests.

30. See Lucien Goldmann's *Marxisme et Sciences Humaines* (Paris: Gallimard, 1970), p. 58.

CHAPTER III

1. Since the classical novel does not come unmistakeably to an end until Kafka there exists the problem of Stendhal's precocity. The answer, in part, may be that 1789 inaugurated a period of "permanent revolution" (hence the existence of the explicit level in the classical novel); so the reign of the bourgeoisie has always been threatened not only politically, from below, by the workers, but also culturally, from above, by a tiny number of men able to think or feel their way clear of a structure rendered intolerable by the gulf it allows to exist between what it professes and what it does.

2. Except that Zola sometimes uses alcoholism in the Rougon-Macquart series as a kind of pseudo-scientific concealed identity.

3. Sartre, *L'Idiot de la famille*, vol. 1 (Paris: Gallimard, 1971), p. 155.

4. The function of identity in the novel, to be sure, is to reveal differences in kind between men, but for the purpose of inviting a moral judgement. Here the issue is entirely different. It is that of deciding whether man is to be object or praxis.

5. *César Birotteau* (Paris: Livre de Poche, 1966), pp. 383-87.

6. It is true that after Kafka the novel loses the implicit level without ceasing to be fiction. The reason for this as we shall see, is that we are no longer able to separate the "subjective" from the "real."

7. This is not altogether accurate of course since for anyone to be able to choose—that is, prove—goodness, it must already exist as a given.

8. One can even find in Zola a combination of "science" and pure melodrama.

The hero of *Au Bonheur des dames* personalizes the "inevitable" and "benefi-cent" swallowing up of small businesses by larger ones; while on the implicit level the heroine rises from rags to riches by marrying the boss, and we are not far removed from either *Pamela* or an Horatio Alger novel.

9. In the final paragraph of Lucien Febvre's book *Un Destin, Martin Luther* (Paris: Presses Universitaires Françaises, 1968), p. 198 we read: "We are not judging Luther. Which Luther, in any case, and according to what criteria, his? ours? or those of contemporary Germany?" Febvre is in the happy position of practically all our historians, that of having no criteria; that is, of not living now, with the rest of us, for whom Luther's whole-hearted support of the princes against the peasantry is detestable. We cannot know the details of the punitive measures taken against the peasants without a feeling of moral outrage. We know that, in the historical past, people thought and felt in a manner strange to us now; so we cannot "be" those people. If we refuse to be ourselves (to feel moral outrage) then we are neither here nor there, we are objective scholars.

10. See Pierre Verstraeten's *Violence et éthique* (Paris: Gallimard, 1972), pp. 310-20.

11. The loathing one feels for fascist, Stalinist, and imperialist crimes the world over is universal. Except for the objective scholar, the uninformed and the senile we necessarily feel that loathing precisely because it is historically subjective.

12. They spring in their entirety from the simple fact that if means of produc-tion are to be used for the common good they must belong to the collectivity and not to individuals, whether owners or bureaucrats.

13. Even the physical scientist, as Bachelard has shown, must be prepared to put this question to himself.

14. Only the academic farceur would argue that our "cultural heritage," for the protection of which the wealthy make occasional contributions, has any func-tion other than that of adding a little credibility to the differences under dis-cussion.

15. Hence Sartre's use of the expression *la chose humaine* in the third volume of his work on Flaubert. See also his analysis of bourgeois distinction, and par-ticularly the passage in which he describes the bourgeois as being a combination of birth and merit (*Critique de la raison dialectique* (Paris: Gallimard, 1960), p. 719) or, in the language I have been using, he has an identity which must never-theless be proven.

16. Because the working class was illiterate and to become literate meant, in the vast majority of cases, to become middle class.

CHAPTER IV

1. Even forty years ago, to be sure, very few students coming to the university had read much; but their classmates looked upon these lettered few as being for-tunate, and this is what has changed.

2. See Sartre's "Plaidoyer pour les intellectuels," in *Situations VIII* (Paris: Gallimard, 1972).

3. *Portrait of a Lady* (Cambridge: Riverside Press, 1963), pp. 55-56.

4. Maggie Verver, for example, in *The Golden Bowl* has to undergo " . . . the horror of finding evil seated, all at its ease, where she had only dreamed of good; the horror of the thing hideously *behind,* behind so much trusted, so much pretended, nobleness, cleverness, tenderness." (London: Bodley Head, 1971), p. 507. The person referred to is Charlotte Stant, who had indulged in the ultimate evil, unauthorized fornication. Her husband, Mr. Verver, was one of the world's five or six wealthiest men and (one is tempted, with James, to say therefore) also one of its most perfect. It would be interesting to have James' views on the origins of great wealth; it certainly has nothing to do with: " . . . what's called Evil—with a very big E" (p. 318). Maggie's husband, Amerigo, without whose collaboration Charlotte could not very well have committed adultery is somehow the innocent victim of an intriguing woman; so James is not only conventional, he often sinks to convention's lowest levels.

5. How, otherwise, would we distinguish between Osmond and James himself? Of Osmond it is said that, "He has a great dread of vulgarity; that's his special line; he hasn't any other that I know of" (p. 210).

6. Or about how evil people create other evil people, as conceivably happened with Osmond and Madame Merle? It is hard to see what would be gained; for if political and social problems are to be reduced—as always in the classical novel—to questions of kinds of people (even though only by default, as in Zola) then our major concern would remain that of detecting evil people. I know of only one attempt on any scale to exploit the "evil by contagion" possibility, Musset's play (which ought to have been a novel) *Lorenzaccio.* However, Musset concludes that although his hero's original goodness had become heavily overlain with evil contracted from Lorenzo and his henchmen, it nevertheless survived.

7. Balzac's Pons is an art collector, but the question of his degree of esthetic refinement is totally irrelevant to the judgement the reader is invited to make of him.

8. Carl Sagan in his book *The Cosmic Connection* (New York: Doubleday, 1973) writes: "It has been suggested that the content of the initial message received [by us, from some other civilization in space] will contain instructions for avoiding our own self-destruction, a possibly common fate of societies shortly after they reach the technical phase." (p. 219). This would be funny were it not also what the pseudo-scientists (sociologists, political scientists and the like) are doing—waiting for a message, not from outer space perhaps but from their objective research the real purpose of which is to enable them to pretend we do not already know what must be done; we must, violently or peacefully, destroy a system which infallibly places things (profit) before men.

9. Lionel Trilling, *The Liberal Imagination* (London: Secker and Warburg, 1964), p. 83.

10. See Nicos Poulantzas, *Fascisme et dictature* (Paris: Maspéro, 1971), and Charles Bettelheim, *L'Economic allemande sous le nazisme* (Paris: Maspéro, 1971).

11. Trilling, *op. cit.*, pp. 90, 92.

12. Ibid., pp. 90-92.

13. Political opposition is the privilege of a few; countless others are reduced to the many different forms of unconscious opposition from sedatives to insanity.

14. See the collection of articles chosen and introduced by André Gorz entitled *Critique de la division du travail* (Paris: Seuil, 1973).

15. In the revolutionary group the self disappears before the urgency of what has to be done (abolition of class and special privileges, universal distribution of available food and services, etc.), while on the "superstructural" level, the fascist group exists precisely to *save* personal identity, to save the possibility of self-recognition by refusing to see that capitalism is threatened by its own contradictions rather than by the machinations of lesser races or evil individuals.

16. Husserl's use of this conception opened the way to the suppression of the self in the philosophies of Heidegger and Sartre, but Husserl himself did not go that far. See Sartre's *La Transcendance de l'ego* (Paris: Vrin, 1966).

17. The Catholic novelists (Greene, Bernanos, Mauriac) tried to reduce the cost by admitting that even in the case of the "criminal" (*Brighton Rock, Therese Desqueroux*) the responsibility of bourgeois society itself is overwhelming. But even though these authors reverse identity, with the respectable being seen for what they are (the manufacturers of evil) and the "evil" moving closer to God, the solution can come from nowhere except an individual experience, however obscure, of God. So, as in the classical novel, the more devastating the attack upon contemporary society (the opening pages of Bernanos' *Journal d'un curé de campagne* is one of the finest examples) the more outrageous that the answer to social problems should continue to be given in terms of individuals.

18. By the end of *A la Recherche du temps perdu* the Guermantes and their caste have been swallowed up by the Verdurins, and, in any case, except for the esthetical-historical lore of which they are the occasion they are almost as much figures of fun as are the Verdurins.

19. Joyce, with no hesitation, immerses the reader in the resuscitated, "lived" Dublin of the 16th of June 1904; while Proust, endlessly painstaking, has to seek out "lost time." He finds it, however, so this difference in approach need not concern us.

20. The explicit is by no means entirely absent to be sure; it is simply very weak when one thinks of men like Balzac, Tolstoy and Zola. In Joyce one could consider that it takes the form of revealing to a startled Western world the existence of the body, of toilets, of masturbation and the like. As for Proust—in his treatment of the Verdurin circle—he duplicates Tolstoy's feat of combining almost indistinguishably identity and the explicit, except that his intention is satirical. There are many passages in *A la Recherche du temps perdu* where Proust doubts that anything like what we have been calling identity can exist, yet in practise he

created the most extraordinary group of characters in the whole of fiction. Like Tintoretto he could paint in the style of any of the masters and improve upon it. The least member of the Verdurin circle is finer than anything in Dickens; Charlus or Saint-Loup superior to comparable figures in Balzac.

21. The only honest answer to the explicit in books like *Germinal* and *l'Assommoir* would have had to be that given by the Paris Commune.

22. James took from Flaubert not only the idea of fiction as an art object; he also introduced appreciation of such objects as a partial means of establishing identities. The importance of this is clear enough if we recall the case of Fleda Vetch who, in exercising her moral identity is grotesque, while as an esthete she is reasonably credible.

23. Michel Butor has hard words for the novelist who refuses to renew the form, for such a writer "has a quicker success, but he is also on the side of the deep malaise we all feel and of the darkness in which we are floundering. He makes the reflexes of our awareness even more automatic, he makes its awakening still more difficult, he contributes to stifling it so that, even where his intentions are of the most generous, his work, finally, is a kind of poison." *Essais sur le roman* (Paris: Gallimard, 1960), p. 11.

24. Valéry, *Oeuvres*, vol. 2 (Paris: Pléiade, 1957), p. 841.

25. Here is Valéry, for example, writing at the end of World War I: "And now, from an immense terrace of Elsinor, stretching from Basel to Cologne, from the sands of Nieuport to the marshes of the Somme, from the chalky lands of Champagne to the granite of Alsace, the European Hamlet contemplates the spirits of the dead in their millions" (Ibid., vol. 1, p. 993). The true spectator can always wring a little poetry out of the spectacle, however appalling.

26. "I want," said Joyce, "to give a picture of Dublin so complete that if the city one day suddenly disappeared from the earth it could be reconstructed out of my book." Quoted in Frank Budgen, *James Joyce and the Making of Ulysses* (London: Oxford University Press, 1972), p. 69.

27. Camus offers an excellent example of how indispensable it is to attack the system from both ends, since the existence of an inner and outer world is of its essence. *L'Etranger* and *La Chute* are effective criticisms of bourgeois inwardness in two of its forms; but then if our world is the place described in *Le Mythe de Sisyphe* and in *L'Homme revolté*, then clearly there is nothing more to be done than what Camus did to help the Algerians become an independent people—nothing at all. Then why not cultivate inwardness?

28. In his article on Husserl, in *Situations I* (Paris: Gallimard, 1947), p. 34.

29. See George Lukács, *La Théorie du roman* (Neuwied am Rhein: Gonthier, 1963), and the essay by Goldmann appended to it; and Lucien Goldmann, *Pour une Sociologie du roman* (Paris: NRF, 1964). The only attempt I know of to utilize this theory in a thorough study of a single important novelist is Goldmann's work on Malraux which takes up the greater part of the second of the two books just mentioned. I therefore prefer to leave a more detailed dis-

cussion of the theory until we come to the contemporary novel. In the meantime, this very brief description is all we need.

30. In politics, the good (as in Kafka's *Das Schloss*) are those who represent authority of whatever kind, those who represent order, without which (except in time of war, in time of *profitable* disorder) business and commerce suffer a decline. If the bourgeois order despite its crimes has proven so robust it is partially because those who hate it most are produced by it (the great majority of South American guerilleros are from petty bourgeois milieus), which means they vastly overestimate the effectiveness of individual competence or heroism. Given the weapons of which "order" disposes only a peoples' war can be successful, and the underlying rationale of the peoples' army is: "THE LIQUIDATION OF THE PRINCIPLE OF IDENTITY" (Régis Debray, *La Critique des armes* (Paris: Seuil, 1974), p. 262. (The capital letters are Debray's.) Thus far the only peoples' armies (China, North Vietnam, here and there in Africa) have been formed in cultures unaffected by the disease of bourgeois individualism.

31. *Romans, suivis de textes, contes, et nouvelles* (Paris: Pléiade, 1949), p. 346.

32. Victor Hugo in his play *Ruy Blas* would eventually spell this out clearly since Ruy Blas who, like Marianne, is of doubtful extraction, proves far more able than the king in the governing of Spain.

33. Laurence Sterne, *Tristan Shandy* (London: Penguin Books, 1967), pp. 141-55.

34. Robert Chasles, *Les Illustres Françaises* (Paris: Société d'édition "Les Belles Lettres," vol. 2, 1959), pp. 475-82.

35. There is a strikingly Balzacian passage in which Chasles reminds the reader that the bourgeoisie enriches itself by persecuting the poor (Ibid., pp. 283-84).

36. It is true that Richardson's Clarissa dies, but her death is a triumph over the real, virtue's refusal to be defeated.

37. (London: Oxford University Press, 1965), pp. 307-08.

38. For an account of the relationship between imperialism and starvation in the case of India, see Paul Baran's *The Political Economy of Growth* (New York: Monthly Review Press, 1968), chapter 5; and Charles Bettelheim, *l'Inde indépendante* (Paris: Maspéro, 1971).

39. *Captain Singleton* (London: Oxford University Press, 1969), p. 157.

40. (London: Oxford University Press, 1964), pp. 147-53.

41. *Colonel Jack, op. cit.,* pp. 128-50.

42. Ibid., p. 128.

43. Ibid., p. 142.

44. Had *Le Père Goriot,* for example, been simply a tale of how a man proved paternal devotion to be the essence of his character it would have been one of Balzac's lesser works. Its interest derives from the way in which Rastignac is put to the test through contact with the explicit (Vautrin). The results are conclusive; Rastignac's good and superior identity survives but, oddly enough, Balzac hints

that perhaps we ought not to be so sure since the novel concludes with Rastignac's famous: "à nous deux maintenant." One can appreciate from this point of view the vital importance of humor in Dickens since almost without exception his characters very easily become what they are; and, compared to continental fiction, the explicit in Dickens is very weak.

45. *Captain Singleton, op. cit.,* p. 263.

46. For instance, in *Moll Flanders,* (Boston: Riverside Press, 1959), pp. 112, 118.

47. Ibid., p. 239.

48. Ibid., p. 272. It could be objected, of course, that this is Moll's own view of the situation and therefore unreliable. I don't think so, but there is no proving it. This difficulty enables us to see clearly why, when the classical novel moved the investigation of character as a given-proven to the center of fiction it had, at the same time, to invent the God's-eye narrator, the omniscient spectator from whom no corner of the inner man can be concealed. Almost without exception the novels of our second category are in the first person (epistolary novels being a form of first person narrative) which gives rise to the problem just encountered with Moll Flanders or which can, in the interest of clarity, induce a character to concur wholeheartedly with the flattering opinion others have of him; Marianne does this repeatedly. On the other hand novelists practicing a more strictly picaresque form (our first category) are too "compromised" with their hero to enjoy the all-embracing view of society which is that of the 19th century novelist and which is as well the expression in fiction of the fact that the bourgeoisie had, at last, acceded to full political responsibility. The classical novelist therefore had to be omniscient not only so that there could be no doubt as to the identity of the protagonist but so that he could speak with full authority on the explicit level.

49. See especially pages 37 to 41 (*Roxana, op. cit.*).

50. Defoe's treatment of this question—whether or not survival is compatible with morality—differs in one very interesting respect from that of Balzac and Dostoevsky. Roxana considers that, in yielding to Amy, she would violate not only religious principles, but reason as well; whereas in the classical novel, as we have seen, reason becomes an instrument of the devil.

51. What would eventually become the explicit level of the classical novel intervenes here as it does from time to time in Defoe, the two most sustained examples being the feminism of Moll Flanders and Roxana. Crusoe, out of moral revulsion, makes preparations for killing as many of the cannibals as he can manage when it occurs to him that these people might, after all, be fully human, that many of our customs would legitimately appear to them as horrifying as theirs do to us (London: Oxford University Press, 1972), p. 171.

52. So ingrained is our racism that we attribute it to everyone, assuming, for instance, that when the ancient Greeks talked of "barbarians" they meant people of lesser *races,* whereas they meant people of lesser *cultures.* See Michel Leiris, *Cinq études d'ethnologie* (Paris: Gonthier, 1969), passim.

53. In Europe as well as in the colonies if we consider the peasantry, clinging

still, in Marx's youth, to the vestiges of their medieval rights, as the "original occupants." See Marx's article of 1842 in the Rhineland *Gazette* on the suppression of the age-old right of the poor to gather dead wood in the forests.

54. *Captain Singleton* and *Robinson Crusoe* are, like all novels of the second category, the classical novel and mass entertainment, novels about the testing of identities; but, given the period, they are also about what men can accomplish with ships and firearms.

55. "It was the sixth of November, in the sixth year of my reign, or my captivity, which you please . . . ." Such is Crusoe's conclusion after all the deliberation to be found on pages 96, 100, 128, etc. (Robinson Crusoe, *op. cit.* p. 137).

56. Hence, given his dates, Tolstoy could have worked only in a country at once European and underdeveloped.

57. "We must reserve a place in the rear of the shop entirely our own . . . where we can establish our true freedom, our main retreat and solitude" (Montaigne, *Essais,* book 1, chapter 39).

58. I doubt any novel could give me quite the pleasure of *A la Recherche du temps perdu,* but that would be a poor excuse for not seeing that both Kafka's *Das Schloss* and Malraux's *La Condition humaine* are greater books because they are so profoundly disturbing, because the inner refuge is gone. It is quite possible I would return from China to Hong Kong with a feeling of coming home: to the books, the leisure, the unpuritanical girls. But that would be a poor excuse for failing to see that Hong Kong's poor are in desperate need of Chinese communism.

59. The two World Wars appear as annoyances in the private life of Joyce the artist; while World War I comes into *A la Recherche du temps perdu* in the form of a colorful spectacle produced by one of the German bombardments of Paris.

CHAPTER V

1. Scientism is a class ideology because the 19th century bourgeoisie, at least after 1848, knew that its existence depended on maintaining working class poverty and oppression which, therefore, had to become an aspect of "scientific reality," of reality as a given. See Sartre's *L'Idiot de la famille,* vol. 3 (Paris: Gallimard, 1972), p. 243.

2. Sartre, "Conscience de soi et connaissance de soi," *Bulletin de la Société Française de Philosophie,* no. 3 (April-June, 1948), p. 82.

3. Husserl explains how this happens, especially in *Die Frage nach dem Ursprung der Geometrie* and *Die Krisis der europäischen wissenschaften.* One of the best ways to summarize Sartre's thought is to say that it makes it possible for us to understand how the pre-reflexive level of consciousness can be completely autonomous.

4. Stendhal, *Romans et nouvelles,* vol. 1 (Paris: Pléiade, 1952), p. 280.

5. Ibid., p. 557.

6. Ibid., p. 830.

7. What he has to say about the Church of the Madeleine in Paris and Saint Peter's in Rome is typical. (Ibid., p. 1216.)

8. Exactly as in Sartre's *La Transcendance de l'ego*.

9. *Oeuvres, vol. 1* (Paris: Pléiade, 1957), p. 577.

10. Ibid., p. 569.

11. Ibid., p. 565.

12. Ibid., p. 572.

13. *Romans et Nouvelles, op. cit.*, p. 495.

14. Valéry claims this to be one of Stendhal's great themes: be oneself and yet succeed. (*Ibid.*, p. 581).

15. Valéry, *op. cit.*, vol. 2, 1960, p. 20.

16. "To be really alone is not to be human" (Ibid., p. 532).

17. Ibid., vol. 1, pp. 579-80.

18. *Romans et Nouvelles, op. cit.*, vol. 2, p. 259. In *Le Rouge et le noir*, Stendhal warns of how deceptive physiognomy can be (Ibid., vol. 1, pp. 463-64).

19. Ibid., vol. 2, p. 259.

20. Ibid., vol. 1, p. 639. The emphasis is Stendhal's.

21. Julien Sorel remarks that since his crime (the wounding of Madame de Rênal) was not motivated by money it did not dishonor him. (Ibid., p. 665).

22. *Le Père Goriot* (Paris: Livre de Poche, 1961), p. 175.

23. Ibid., p. 141.

24. I know of only one exception which occurs at the beginning of *Le Rouge et le noir* (chapter five). Julien happens to find on a bench in the church, where he will eventually wound Madame de Rênal with a pistol shot, a newspaper account of the execution of a certain Jenrel at Besançon; he also imagines he sees a blood stain on the floor. Julien's fate is thus spelled out in advance. However we need only compare *Le Rouge et le noir* to another novel, *Madame Bovary*, also inspired by a *fait divers* and ending also with a kind of execution-suicide of the hero, to see that this incident is out of place in Stendhal's novel.

25. There is not a single reference in all of *L'ancient et le nouveau* to Lukács or Goldmann; and yet it is impossible not to think of their theory throughout Robert's book. Her most recent work (*Roman des origines et origines du roman* (Paris: Grasset, 1972) abandons the Lukácsian for a much more Freudian approach to fiction, with disastrous results. It is almost as though Marthe Robert were trying to demonstrate Goldmann's often repeated principle according to which a great work of art is far more the product of a collectivity than of an individual; hence the striking inadequacies of any purely Freudian analysis.

26. "Sociologie du roman," *Cahiers Internationaux de Sociologie* vol. 32 (1962) p. 64. The importance of this issue may be judged by the fact that in the paragraph I quote from Goldmann refers to Julien Sorel, and yet, as we have seen, the whole importance of Stendhal lies in his having suppressed the beyond in whatever form.

27. Ibid., p. 70.

28. Lucien Goldmann, *Pour une sociologie du roman* (Paris: Gallimard, 1964), p. 195.

29. *Recherches dialectiques* (Paris: Gallimard, 1959), pp. 74-75. It is interesting that we should have here already the definition of man peculiar to Protestant scientific rationalism: he is controlled or determined by the beyond and is therefore a thing (here, he is totally unaware that, in everything he does, he conforms to the Great Plan), and yet this is so only on condition the age is not "corrupt" (man must therefore be free in some sense). In his book on Jean Genêt, Sartre says that "in this magical concept nature and freedom are one and the same: in chains since he cannot change himself, the thief is free since he has been condemned. One thinks of Calvinist predestination which makes the wicked entirely responsible for their evil, while depriving them of all possibility of doing good" (*Saint Genêt* (Paris: Gallimard, 1952), p. 25).

30. He also deals at some length with Flaubert's *L'Education sentimentale*; but talk of "hope" in connection with this novel or with anything Flaubert ever wrote is so aberrant that we can safely ignore this section. See *The Theory of the Novel,* (Cambridge, Mass.: M.I.T. Press, 1971), p. 126.

31. Ibid., p. 132.

32. For example: ". . . the mood of the epilogue to *War and Peace,* with its nursery atmosphere where all passion has been spent and all seeking ended, is more profoundly disconsolate than the endings of the most problematic novels of disillusionment. Nothing is left of what was there before; as the sand of the desert covers the pyramids, so every spiritual thing has been swamped, annihilated, by animal nature." Ibid., pp. 148-49.

33. See "Sociologie du Roman," *op. cit.,* p. 61; *Pour une sociologie du roman, op. cit.,* p. 36; and Goldmann's essay appended to the French translation of Lukács' *La Théorie du Roman,* (Neuwied am Rhein: Gonthier, 1963), p. 178.

34. See *Pour une sociologie du roman, op. cit.,* pp. 49-50.

35. *Le Rouge et le noir*, vol. 1 (Paris: Pléiade, 1966), p. 690. Stendhal's emphasis.

36. The error of Robert and Goldmann, as we shall see, is to have looked for that discussion in *Das Schloss* and in *La Condition humaine.*

37. *Situations IV* (Paris: Gallimard, 1964), p. 79.

38. One finds traces of this even in pre-revolutionary literature; there is the case not only of Defoe but of Diderot, capable of a masterpiece like *Le Neveu de Rameau* and of contributing at the same time to the lamentable *drame bourgeois.*

39. There are innumerable passages in Stendhal where he mocks not only the absurdity of restauration government but the bourgeois alternative which, for him, was not an alternative at all.

40. *L'ancien et le nouveau* (Paris: Grasset, 1963), pp. 160-61.

41. Ibid., p. 48.

42. It does happen, however: "He was warned—doubly warned; but those strange accidents, through which a higher intelligence seems to be speaking to us,

his passion was not able to interpret." Goethe, *Die Wahlverwandtschaften*, end of chapter 13, part 1.

43. I am making use here of Sartre's definition of the comic to be found in volume 1 of *L'Idiot de la famille, op. cit.,* pp. 811-24.

44. *The Theory of the Novel, op. cit.,* p. 142.

45. All this will be found at the very end of chapter 21 and the beginning of chapter 22 of part 2. To appreciate the extent to which the second Don Quixote, far from being oppositional, is a spokesman for the growing middle class one has to read his remarks to Sancho who is about to leave to take up his governorship of the "island": "Not all those that govern come from the race of kings." "The number of persons of lowly birth who have gone up to the highest pontifical and imperial posts is beyond counting." ". . . blood is inherited but virtue is acquired, and virtue by itself alone has a worth that blood does not have." (chapter 42 of part 2). Sancho acquits himself with great wisdom and so justifies Don Quixote's observations. However, it was not safe to suggest that absolutely anyone might be fit to rule (rationalist universalism), and it is easy to see therefore that first category novels had to be supplemented by novels of the second—whose domain is moral quality (that is, bourgeois particularism)—until means could be found to combine the two (Balzac).

46. *Le Rouge et le noir, op. cit.,* p. 690.

47. There is, of course, always the interest of the artist and writer in what his predecessors have done, but that does not concern us here. Otherwise one reads, as in my own case, to explain why, as all students know, there is no longer any point to reading the literature of the past; just as every worker knows he is being exploited without that making Marx's "proof" of that exploitation any the less necessary.

48. *L'ancien et le nouveau, op. cit.,* pp. 31-32.

49. Max Brod tells of Kafka saying to him: "How undemanding these people [the poor] are, they come to submit petitions. Instead of storming the place and destroying it, they submit petitions!" (Quoted by Marthe Robert in *Kafka* (Paris: Gallimard, 1960), p. 25).

50. *The Castle,* trans. by *Willa and Edwin Muir* (New York: Alfred A. Knopf, 1968), pp. 239, 241.

51. *Romans et Nouvelles* (Paris: Pléiade, 1952), p. 526.

52. *L'ancien et le nouveau, op. cit.,* p. 274.

53. Ibid., pp. 249, 293.

54. Again the only precedent is Stendhal, who is the most consistently and unrepentantly subjective of the 19th century novelists and who, for that very reason, since his was not a "romantic subjectivity," has left us a more accurate account—in the true sense of the "feel" of a period—of the life of his time than anyone else.

55. *L'ancien et le nouveau, op. cit.,* p. 307. Robert's emphasis.

56. *La Condition humaine* (Paris: Pléiade, 1947), pp. 348, 349.

57. *Pour une sociologie du roman, op. cit.,* pp. 247, 271.

58. Ibid., p. 187.
59. Ibid., p. 160 (note).
60. Ibid., p. 160.
61. Ibid., p. 161.
62. Ibid., p. 192.
63. Ibid.
64. See Ibid., p. 161 (note).
65. This conversation is to be found on pages 272 and 273 of *La Condition humaine* (Paris: Pléiade, 1947).
66. Ibid., p. 281.
67. Ibid., p. 285.
68. Ibid., p. 286.
69. Ibid., p. 281.
70. Ibid., p. 287.
71. Ibid., p. 296.
72. Ibid.
73. Such was the situation in which Sartre found himself for many years. Simone de Beauvoir comes back to this repeatedly in *Les Mandarins*.
74. This being the question with which Sartre concluded his article, written in 1946, "Matérialisme et révolution." (*Situations III* (Paris: Gallimard, 1949), p. 225).
75. Which, let me recall, was legitimate until the beginning of the crisis of bourgeois rationalism with Hegel, Marx and Stendhal.
76. *La Condition humaine, op. cit.,* p. 287.
77. Ibid., p. 218.
78. Sartre, "Plaidoyer pour les intellectuels," in *Situations VIII* (Paris: Gallimard, 1972), p. 401.
79. It is true that if one reads a little further in the passage from *La Condition humaine* quoted a moment ago (p. 287) Malraux seems to be saying that what May loves in Kyo is himself and not "what I did or will do." But this remark has little weight when one considers that Malraux, in delineating his characters, always puts the question of what, more or less consciously, they may be trying to do. The conversation between Kyo and Gisors about Clappique is a good example (pp. 208-09); Clappique is the man he is because he tries to keep in being an imaginary existence as a shield against an intolerable reality. Ferral, the representative of Western imperialism in China, is one of those most responsible for that reality, so that his life becomes, in all its aspects, the expression of contempt for others. Insofar as these various "praxes" can be unified, men seek the "full possession of themselves" (to be God, as Gisors puts it)—Tchen through terrorism (p. 316), Ferral, eroticism (p. 352), Clappique at the gaming table (p. 361). It is man's inevitably futile endeavor (and this is exactly the analysis Sartre carries out in *L'être et le néant*) to be at once entity and a consciousness which, however, can give that entity its meaning only on condition that it (consciousness) be not

a thing; but rather a praxis in the light of which things receive their "contours" and their mutual "adjustments."

80. Which does not mean that Stalinism—at least in the underdeveloped world—is not preferable to the old order. But it means also the revival of anti-Semitism in Poland and the USSR; so that a Soviet bureaucrat—like the one in Solzhenitsyn's *Cancer Ward*—can be a fascist quite as easily as members of the Harvard University faculty called to high government posts in the United States.

81. The psychiatry of Ronald Laing and his associates is based on the assumption that a society capable of deliberately starving millions of people (American and European imperialism could not function otherwise) and of poisoning its own food, air and water will, by the intermediary of the nuclear family, drive some of its best members out of their minds. Furthermore, this "insanity" is recognized as a protest, since those guilty of it are locked in institutions and punished with drugs and electroshocks.

82. See Sartre, "Masses, Spontanéité, Parti," in *Situations VIII* (Paris: Gallimard, 1972).

CONCLUSION

1. *Dérive à partir de Marx et Freud* (Paris: Union Générale d'édition, (10/18), 1973), p. 11.

2. There is the utter nihilism of a Beckett, but that is no more visible to most of us than is Althusser's "science of history."

3. See Jacques Meunier and A. M. Savarin, *Le Chant du Silbaco* (Paris: Editions Spéciales, 1969).

LIST OF FOREIGN WORKS CITED IN THIS TEXT
AND CORRESPONDING ENGLISH TRANSLATIONS

A la Recherche du temps perdu, Marcel Proust
In Remembrance of Things Past

l'Ancien et le nouveau, Marthe Robert
The Old and the New

Anna Karenina, Leo Tolstoy

l'Argent, Emile Zola
Money

l'Assommoir, Emile Zola
The Drunkard, The Gin Palace, The Dram-Shop

Au Bonheur des dames, Emile Zola
The Ladies' Paradise, Ladies Delight

The Brothers Karamazov, Fyodor Dostoevsky

Candide, Voltaire

Les Caves du Vatican, André Gide
Vatican Cellars

César Birotteau, Honoré de Balzac

Le Chant du Silbaco, Jacques Meunier and A.M. Savarin

La Chartreuse de Parme, Stendhal (Henri Beyle)
Charterhouse of Parma

La Chute, Albert Camus
The Fall

Cinq études d'Ethnologie, Michel Leiris

Un Coeur simple, Gustave Flaubert
A Simple Heart

Colonel Chabert, Honoré de Balzac

La Comédie Humaine, Honoré de Balzac
The Comedy of Human Life, The Human Comedy

La Condition Humaine, André Malraux
Man's Estate

Les Conquérants, André Malraux
The Conquerors

"Conscience de Soi et Connaissance de Soi," Jean-Paul Sartre

Crime and Punishment, Fyodor Dostoevsky

Critique de la division du travail, André Gorz

Critique de la raison dialectique, Jean-Paul Sartre
The Critique of Dialectical Reason

Critique des Armes, Régis Debray

Critique of Political Economy, Karl Marx

La Curée, Emile Zola
The Kill

The Death of Ivan Ilyitch, Leo Tolstoy

Dérive à partir de Marx et Freud, Jean François Lyotard

Un Destin, Martin Luther, Lucien Fèbvre

Le Diable Boiteux, Alain-René Le Sage
The devil upon two sticks

Discours de la Méthode, René Descartes
Discourse on Method

Don Quixote, Miguel de Cervantes Saavedra

L'Economie Allemande sous le Nazisme, Charles Bettelheim

Les Ecrivains contre la Commune, Paul Lidsky

L'Education sentimentale, Gustave Flaubert
Sentimental Education

Les Employés, Honoré de Balzac
The Civil Service, Bureaucracy

Essais sur le Roman, Michel Butor

l'Etranger, Albert Camus
The Outsider

l'Etre et le Néant, Jean-Paul Sartre
Being and Nothingness

Fascisme et Dictature, Nicos Poulantzas

La Figure et le Lieu, Pierre Francastel

Die Frage Nach dem Ursprung der Geometrie, Edmond Husserl
The Origins of Geometry

Germinal, Emile Zola

Geschichte und Klasserbewusstsein, George Lukács
History and Class Consciousness

Gil Blas, Alain-René Le Sage

l'Homme Revolté, Albert Camus
The Rebel

The Idiot, Fyodor Dostoievsky

l'Idiot de la famille, Jean-Paul Sartre

l'Inde indépendante, Charles Bettelheim

Jacques le Fataliste, Denis Diderot
Jacques the Fatalist

Jean Barois, Roger Martin du Gard

Journal d'un Curé de Campagne, Georges Bernanos
The Diary of a Country Priest

Die Krisis der Europäischen Wissenschaften, Edmond Husserl
The Crisis of European Science

Les Illusions perdues, Honoré de Balzac
Lost Illusions

Les Illustres Françaises, Robert Chasles
The Illustrious French Lovers

Les Liaisons dangereuses, Pierre Choderlos de Laclos
Dangerous Acquaintances

Logos et Praxis, François Châtelet

Lucien Leuwen, Stendhal (Henri Beyle)

Madame Bovary, Gustave Flaubert

Les Mains sales, Jean-Paul Sartre
Crime passionel, Dirty Hands

Les Mandarins, Simone de Beauvoir
Mandarins

Marxisme et Sciences Humaines, Lucien Goldmann

"Masses, Spontanéité, Parti", Jean-Paul Sartre

"Matérialisme et Révolution", Jean-Paul Sartre

Les Misérables, Victor Hugo

Le Mythe de Sisyphe, Albert Camus
The Myth of Sisyphus

Napoléon Tel Quel, Henri Guillemin

Le Neveu de Rameau, Denis Diderot
Rameau's Nephew

La Nouvelle Héloïse, Jean-Jacques Rousseau
The New Eloïse

Oedipe Africain, Marie-Cécile and Edmond Ortigues

Les Paysans, Honoré de Balzac
The Peasants, The Peasantry

Le Père Goriot, Honoré de Balzac
Old Goriot, Pere Goriot

"Plaidoyer pour les intellectuels", Jean-Paul Sartre

Pour une sociologie du roman, Lucien Goldmann
Towards a Sociology of the Novel

I Promessi Sposi, Alessandro Manzoni
The Bethrothed

Qu'est-ce que la littérature? Jean-Paul Sartre
What is literature?

La Rabouilleuse, Honoré de Balzac
The Black Sheep

Recherches dialectiques, Lucien Goldmann

Resurrection, Leo Tolstoy

Roman des origines et origines du roman, Marthe Robert

Le Roman expérimental, Emile Zola
Experimental Novel

Le Rouge et le Noir, Stendhal (Henri Beyle)
The Red and the Black, Red and Black, Scarlet and Black

Les Rougon-Macquart
The Rougon-Macquart series

Ruy Blas, Victor Hugo

Saint Genêt, Jean-Paul Sartre
Saint Genet

Sartre dans sa vie, Francis Jeanson

Das Schloss, Franz Kafka
The Castle

Les Séquestrés d'Altona, Jean-Paul Sartre
The Condemned of Altona, Loser Wins

Sodome et Gomorrhe, Marcel Proust
Cities of the Plain

Structuralisme et Marxisme, collective authorship
Structuralism and Marxism

La Théorie du roman, George Lukács
Die Theorie des Romans
The Theory of the Novel

Thérèse Desqueroux, François Mauriac

Les Thibault, Roger Martin du Gard
The Thibaults

Traité d'économie marxiste, Ernest Mandel

La Transcendance de l'ego, Jean-Paul Sartre
The Transcendence of the Ego

Le Ventre de Paris, Emile Zola
Savage Paris

La Vie de Marianne, Pierre de Marivaux
The Life of Marianne

Vor dem Gesetz, Franc Kafka
Before the Law

Voyage au bout de la nuit, Céline (Louis-Ferdinand Destouches)
Journey to the End of the Night

Die Wahlverwandtschaften, Wolfgang Goethe
Elective Affinities

War and Peace, Leo Tolstoy

Die Weissen Denken Zuviel, Paul Parin, Fritz Morgenthaler and
    Goldy Parin-Matthey
Les Blancs pensent trop
Whites think too much

Wilhelm Meister, Wolfgang Goethe

Der Zauberberg, Thomas Mann
The Magic Mountain